Aldham Rob

Liverpool John

WITHDRAWN

POLITICAL UNIONS, POPULAR POLITICS AND THE GREAT REFORM ACT OF 1832

Studies in Modern History
General Editor: J. C. D. Clark, *Joyce and Elizabeth Hall Distinguished Professor of British History, University of Kansas*

Published titles include:

Conal Condren
THE LANGUAGE OF POLITICS IN SEVENTEENTH-CENTURY ENGLAND

Bernard Cottret (*editor*)
BOLINGBROKE'S POLITICAL WRITINGS: The Conservative Enlightenment

Philip Hicks
NEO-CLASSICAL HISTORY AND ENGLISH CULTURE: From Clarendon to Hume

William M. Kuhn
DEMOCRATIC ROYALISM: The Transformation of the British Monarchy, 1861–1914

Nancy D. LoPatin
POLITICAL UNIONS, POPULAR POLITICS AND THE GREAT REFORM ACT OF 1832

W. D. Rubinstein and Hilary Rubinstein
PHILOSEMITISM: Admiration and Support for Jews in the English-Speaking World, 1840–1939

Jim Smyth
THE MEN OF NO PROPERTY: Irish Radicals and Popular Politics in the Late Eighteenth Century

Lynne Taylor
BETWEEN RESISTANCE AND COLLABORATION: Popular Protest in Northern France, 1940–45

Political Unions, Popular Politics and the Great Reform Act of 1832

Nancy D. LoPatin
Associate Professor of History
University of Wisconsin-Stevens Point
USA

First published in Great Britain 1999 by
MACMILLAN PRESS LTD
Houndmills, Basingstoke, Hampshire RG21 6XS and London
Companies and representatives throughout the world

A catalogue record for this book is available from the British Library.

ISBN 0–333–73637–0

First published in the United States of America 1999 by
ST. MARTIN'S PRESS, INC.,
Scholarly and Reference Division,
175 Fifth Avenue, New York, N.Y. 10010

ISBN 0–312–21564–9

Library of Congress Cataloging-in-Publication Data
LoPatin, Nancy D.
Political unions, popular politics, and the great Reform Act of
1832 / Nancy D. LoPatin.
p. cm. — (Studies in modern history)
Includes bibliographical references and index.
ISBN 0–312–21564–9 (cloth)
1. Great Britain. Parliament—Reform—History—19th century.
2. Great Britain—Politics and government—1800–1837. I. Title.
II. Series: Studies in modern history (St. Martin's Press)
JN543.L66 1998
328.41'0704—dc21 98–20136
CIP

© Nancy D. LoPatin 1999

All rights reserved. No reproduction, copy or transmission of this publication may be made without written permission.

No paragraph of this publication may be reproduced, copied or transmitted save with written permission or in accordance with the provisions of the Copyright, Designs and Patents Act 1988, or under the terms of any licence permitting limited copying issued by the Copyright Licensing Agency, 90 Tottenham Court Road, London W1P 9HE.

Any person who does any unauthorised act in relation to this publication may be liable to criminal prosecution and civil claims for damages.

The author has asserted her right to be identified as the author of this work in accordance with the Copyright, Designs and Patents Act 1988.

This book is printed on paper suitable for recycling and made from fully managed and sustained forest sources.

10 9 8 7 6 5 4 3 2 1
08 07 06 05 04 03 02 01 00 99

Printed and bound in Great Britain by
Antony Rowe Ltd, Chippenham, Wiltshire

For Chris

Contents

Acknowledgements

This work has been a long time in the making and there are many people to thank for their assistance, guidance and encouragement. I wish to thank the librarians and archivists at the BL, BL Newspaper Repository at Colindale, the Public Record Office, and the many university and County and Town Record Offices I visited. My work was funded by the generosity of Washington University's Dissertation Fellowship, the National Endowment for the Humanities, the American Philosophical Society and the University of Wisconsin-Stevens Point University Professional Development Fund. I am also grateful to Dartmouth College's Department of History for its appointment as a Visiting Scholar during my sabbatical year, which enabled me to do much of the writing.

I would like to thank John C. Moore and George Jackson at Hofstra University for their excellent training as an undergraduate. Little did they know that I would spend so many years researching a topic I stumbled upon while writing a senior honours thesis. Derek Hirst and Gregory Claeys provided great training and advice at Washington University and the camaraderie and support of Rose Feurer, Donna Fulkerson, Lynn Johnson and Denys Leighton during the graduate school and dissertation years made my time in St. Louis particularly memorable. Thanks also to my colleague at Stevens Point, Eric Yonke. As the other 'modern western European historian' in my department, he has read more about 1832 than any German historian should be asked to and I thank him for his help and friendship over the years.

For their encouragement I wish to thank Marc Baer, James Epstein, Harvey Kaye, James Sack and Reba Soffer. I am particularly indebted to Peter Mandler for his interest in this work and the tremendous generosity he has shown in helping me complete it. I cannot thank him enough for the consideration he has shown in its publication. Many thanks as well to Joseph Hamburger and Frank O'Gorman who graciously read and commented on early drafts of this book as well as numerous others who read sections of the whole, including the late and much missed John A. Phillips. My gratitude to Philip Harling and Miles Taylor for their perceptive suggestions as readers of the manuscript. I am deeply indebted to Jonathan

Clark for all his efforts and assistance as editor of this series and this book. Aruna Vasudevan and Ruth Willats of Macmillan have been invaluable in answering many queries and guiding me through the publication and editing process. Jan Swinford of the History Department at UWSP graciously assisted me in preparing the final typescript.

My greatest debt is to my dissertation supervisor, adviser, editor and friend, Richard W. Davis. I cannot adequately express my admiration and my gratitude for all he has done for me over the years. A superb historian and teacher, I have learned – as have all his students – that he is that rare blend of scholar, teacher and gentleman. Whatever I have learned about being an historian, it is the result of following his example. I am deeply grateful for his guidance, encouragement and unfaltering faith in me, particularly when I needed it most. I am so very proud to call him my friend as well as my mentor. Thank you to my parents, Arnold and Gloria Lo Patin for their encouragement over the years and instilling in me my love for history.

Finally, I wish to thank my husband, Christopher Lummis. Though he gratefully acknowledges he came into my life late in the development of this project, he also knows how integral he was in its completion. Without his encouragement, humour and honesty, this project, and many others – both academic and non-academic – would not have been possible. With love and thanks, I dedicate this book to him.

List of Abbreviations

BL	British Library
PRO	Public Record Office, Kew
BCL	Birmingham Central Library
BRO	Bristol Record Office
BaRL	Bath Reference Library
BrCL	Bristol Central Library
LRO	Leicester Record Office
NCL	Norfolk County Library
NRO	Norfolk Record Office
NoRO	Northumberland Record Office
NtRO	Notthinghamshire Record Office
SRO	Staffordshire Record Office
ScRO	Scottish Record Office
TWRO	Tyne and Wear Record Office
UNMD	University of Nottingham Manuscript Department
WRO	Worcester Record Office

The Political Union was founded on 25 January 1830; the public mind was asleep; within two short years the public mind was aroused, the people put forth the majesty of their strength, and on the 7th day of June 1832, the Reform Bill became the law of the land! No blood was shed; no crime committed; the people spoke, and the will of the people was law.

Manifesto of the Nottingham Political Union,
Nottingham Review, 8 November 1833

Introduction

> Union is the watchword of the day.[1]

> It was not only political enthusiasms but political union, which enabled the people to achieve their political regeneration. It mattered not for the comparative freedom of the press, and the general education of the people – upon which political power should depend – if the people had not united themselves to counteract the combinations, wealth, and influence of the aristocracy, which, if unopposed by Political Unions, would have proved more than a match for the whole people of England, but which, when imposed by those institutions must ever succumb to the power and wealth of the country.[2]

When the Reform Act became law on 7 June 1832, more than 100 Political Unions celebrated the success of the Whig government and their own vigilance in peacefully securing the first parliamentary reform legislation in England. The Unions rejoiced for two reasons. First, the measure provided significant reform in the electoral franchise and the distribution of parliamentary representation throughout Great Britain. Second, the Political Unions believed they had been critical in its enactment. For more than two years, Political Unions had focused public opinion and the political activities of the English people in support of the government's bill. Many Unionists believed this had prevented Lord Grey from backing away from the parliamentary battle required for its passage. In short, Political Unions celebrated the acquisition of political power by the people – at least to some degree – between 1830 and 1832.

Lord Grey's concerns over popular reaction to the government's failure to secure the measure were real. He feared ignoring public opinion on this matter might prompt a revolution.[3] He also knew the people would not rest until the measure became law. How did Grey know that the people felt so strongly about parliamentary reform? Political Unions. These extra-parliamentary organizations had demanded parliamentary reform before the Whigs came to office. Their numbers and their intensity had only increased when Grey's government published the Reform Bill. The Home Office had informants throughout the country monitoring Political Unions' activities and the provincial press reported in detail what occurred at Union meetings. The government and the King received numerous petitions from Political Unions endorsing the government's measure and expressing both gratitude and support. Members of the government even kept in correspondence with, and hosted delegations from, provincial Political Unions. The Unions' organized extra-parliamentary political campaign – even their very existence – tells us a great deal about what motivated the government during the difficult two years of significant political resistance. Lord Grey was constantly aware that his hopes for reform rested, in part, with the support of popular opinion and the Unions. He and his ministers recognized the potential power of the people, at least in the form of the Political Unions.

POLITICAL UNIONS AND THE WHIG REFORM BILL OF 1832

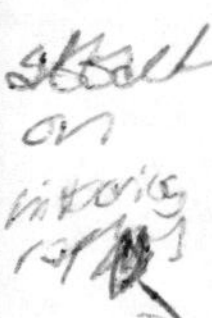

Political Unions did affect national politics in 1830–2. Yet, amazingly, nowhere in the vast historiography of 1832 is there a study of them or even of popular agitation more generally for the Reform Bill. Historians' failure to discern that the Political Unions were a phenomenon unto themselves has severely compromised our understanding of 1832. Political Unions have received some mention in studies of the Reform Act by Michael Brock and Joseph Hamburger, but only in the context that extra-parliamentary organizations frightened the King, worried the government and vindicated the fears of anti-reformers by their aggressive rhetoric and behaviour.[4] Derek Fraser argued that the Unions of 1832 grew out of both the County Associations of the 1780s and the agitation against the Orders in Council of 1812, but dealt far more with the consistency of popular pressure tactics through the decades than with any effect the Union campaign had on the fate of the Bill,[5] and L.G. Mitchell demonstrated how the Tories used the Unions to discredit the entire reform process.[6] Generally, however, Political Unions have not figured prominently in the historiography of the 1832 Reform Act.

In contrast, the intentions behind, and results of, the Reform Act have long been debated. The idea that the Reform Act was a great leap forward for democracy held until a few decades ago. Then Norman Gash tentatively and D.C. Moore quite boldly proclaimed that the Reform Act had changed nothing. Both argued that politics was still concerned with attaining and distributing the spoils of high office, and that 1832, far from weakening, served to underpin deference, and assured the continuation of the aristocratic oligarchy.[7]

Responding as to a red flag to a bull, Richard W. Davis, followed by other historians, seized the challenge and began to test such claims, rejecting them one by one.[8] Detailed work on the Bill and what its proponents intended it to be produced a body of work demonstrating that 1832 did not maintain politics as usual in Britain. John Cannon and Peter Mandler both view 1832 as a compromise which would extend the vote to the wealthier middle classes, thereby uniting the landlords of commercial property of the aristocracy with manufacturing interests in a new 'liberal' political faction among the Whigs.[9] Jonathan Parry described it as a 'bold means to respond to social tensions, unrest, and grievances . . . [so as to] secure popular confidence in more active, disciplinary rule' and presumably less arbitrary and corruptible rule at that.[10] The new biography of Lord Grey by E.A. Smith reminds us that while Grey is perhaps best known as the champion of parliamentary reform, he was 'the most aristocratic of men, by temperament and by conviction, and a firm believer in the aristocratic principle of government'.[11] Grey's Reform Bill was a clear attempt to eliminate the most outrageous problems with electoral representation in order to bring round detractors to the support of upper-class political rule.

Other recent literature on 1832 tests whether or not the reform measure significantly changed anything in English electoral politics. Focusing on the [re-]emergence of party and popular political participation among the electorate, John A. Phillips and Frank O'Gorman have done more for the study of electoral behaviour through statistical and rhetorical analysis than probably even they ever imagined possible.[12] Numerical testing of polling samples and voting behaviour, however, still portrays the importance of the Bill to a distinct minority in England – the voters. In this significant way, both historians look at politics from the 'bottom up', but both do so from the perspective of electoral behaviour and political culture. They look at electoral practices and 'outdoor' agitation orchestrated and controlled by established politicians and parties. Political Unions do not figure in Phillips' or O'Gorman's accounts of reform, no doubt because only some Political Unionists were electors (both before and after enactment of the Reform Bill). The Unions were *extra-parliamentary* and, therefore, not part of quantifiable and accountable political studies which require registered voters, polling numbers and identification with the traditional political rituals of the 'long eighteenth century'. Again, Political Unions could more fully round out the picture, but are missing from the discussion of 1832 and parliamentary reform.

The only Political Union to receive critical and detailed study during the Reform Bill agitation is the Birmingham Political Union.[13] The primary work on the BPU itself, Carlos Flick's *The Birmingham Political Union and the Movements for Reform in Britain, 1830–39*, is a local study in extra-parliamentary action. While acknowledging the existence of other Political Unions during the Reform Bill agitation, Flick dismisses them as insignificant satellites of the BPU, most of which were within geographical proximity to the parent organization.[14] Joseph Hamburger, in his study of Political Unions and their connection to James Mill's use of 'threat' in the reform campaign, proposed a similar argument, claiming that about a half-dozen Political Unions existed between 1830 and 1832, but concluding that it was 'difficult to determine how large and viable these organizations were', being in the shadow of the BPU.[15]

Flick is right to argue that historians have given too much credit to the BPU for organization of popular agitation for the Reform Bill;[16] but he is wrong to suggest that all Political Unions were branches of the BPU, just as Hamburger is wrong to suggest that all other Unions were eclipsed by Attwood's organization. To argue that the BPU was the only significant Political Union during the Reform Bill agitation – an assumption made in nearly every work discussing 1832 – is to misrepresent the advanced state of popular political organization in the mid-nineteenth century and dismiss the possibility that early historiographical interpretations of 1832 were accurate. Large numbers of provincial Political Unions did form independently of the Birmingham organization.[17] Local studies have noted individual Unions and their contributions by placing them in the context of their connection to past radical activities and future campaigns such as Chartism, trade unionism and the Anti-Corn Law League. Still, there is no study of Political Unions as part of any national popular political movement during the Reform Bill agitation.

POLITICAL UNIONS IN THE CONTEXT OF POLITICS OF 'THE PEOPLE'

In addition to what a study of Political Unions will tell us about other facets of the Reform Bill agitation, such an exploration will also help scholars further define that confusing and far-reaching range of activities known in the late eighteenth and early nineteenth centuries as 'popular politics'.[18] The Reform Act of 1832, it has been argued, was the defining event for a number of studies on popular politics and emerging class consciousness in England.[19] James Vernon's political examination of popular politics has categorized 1832 as part of an emerging middle-class dominance in society. He has argued that 1832 was so clearly a 'middle-class' measure that it really served as 'a brake, or at least a restraining force, upon the largely expanding and dynamic unreformed electorate ...' or, in other words, somehow a limitation on the 'the people'.[20] In short, the 1832 reform campaign and the Political Unions which led it were somehow a hindrance to the development of truly 'popular' political action.

In fact, nothing could be further from the truth. Political Unions were at the end of an evolutionary line of popular constitutionalism and extra-parliamentary agitation beginning with John Wilkes and the American Revolution.[21] The French revolution – or at least the English reaction to it – also affected the popular organization.[22] Extra-parliamentary organizations, such as the Society for Constitutional Information and Corresponding Societies, demanded extensive and fundamental reform and excited fears of revolution in the people if parliamentary reform were not achieved. These associations or clubs, thanks to the numerous parliamentary petitions their members forwarded to Westminister, received attention from a series of ministries that otherwise might have ignored accusations of governmental corruption and demands for the restoration and protection of rights and liberties according to the English 'constitution'. The Foxite faction of the Whigs, especially Charles Grey, who formed the Society of the Friends of the People in April 1792, gave extra-parliamentary reform organization a more reputable presence.[23] These organizations sought reforms proposed by Major Cartwright in his *Take Your Choice*, of 1776. These points (later to be the core of *The People's Charter*), included universal manhood suffrage, annual parliaments, the ballot, equal constituencies, the abolition of property qualifications for MPs and salaries for MPs.

The link between Political Unions and the Corresponding Societies of the 1790s is unmistakable. The Unions focused their demand for reform on the same key criticisms of the existing system, borough-mongering, sinecures, monopolies and other complaints against government corruption know as 'Old Corruption'.[24] Cartwright's legacy to the Political Unions was of primary importance. The Unions adopted three of the points – universal manhood suffrage, annual parliaments and the ballot – as their primary objectives, but dropped those goals upon the introduction of the Reform Bill as imperative in order to secure a fair representation of the English people and end aristocratic privilege.

But this was not the only tradition the Unions drew on. The publication of Thomas Paine's republican proposal, *The Rights of Man*, combining reformism and economic and social equality for English citizens, seemed to launch a second direction for radicals and reformers, towards the expropriation of property.[25] One response to this fear was that advocates of reform from within, such as Grey, suspended their political efforts at parliamentary reform, and concentrated their attack on government corruption and Anglican exclusiveness.[26] Grey believed that the consensus against reform, or perhaps more importantly a lack of sufficient interest in it, would prevent success: 'I have now no hope of seeing a moderate and useful reform effected during my life,' he wrote to Christopher Wyvill, 'and we have to thank Major John Cartwright, Mr. Cobbett and Co. principally for it.'[27] Grey and the Political Unions cooperated because they shared a reform tradition handed down by Cartwright.

Those who argued that England's corrupt political system needed to be overhauled if its ancient constitution and rights of Englishmen were to survive continued their reform activities in the early nineteenth century.[28] One such reform figure was Henry Hunt, landowner-turned-radical populist. Hunt's formulation of a platform for the masses – a slightly revised version of Cartwright's six proposals – while revolutionary in its references to the working and labouring classes, had the potential to link the traditions in the form of extra-parliamentary political action.[29] Hunt asserted a no-compromise commitment to the masses and built a reform campaign from the bottom up, thereby giving a more revolutionary feel to Cartwright's proposals while maintaining their original goals, as he spread them through all levels of English society. He laid the basis for popular acceptance of such a political solution, one that included all adult men regardless of property qualifications, adding numbers to the Unions' adherents and giving legitimacy to their claims that they represented the goals of the 'people' of England.

Hunt's work enabled another new popular political voice to emerge in the 1820s: the campaign that linked religion and politics, and again evoked the need to clean away political corruption which violated Englishmen's right of religious freedom. Indeed, the most direct connection between the Political Unions and the reform efforts of the 1820s was that of Daniel O'Connell's Catholic Association. In fact, the *Birmingham Argus* described the Catholic Association and the Birmingham Political Union as 'a noble pair of twins spun from the same parents – Disenchantment and the Love of Self-Aggrandisement'.[30] O'Connell specifically designed this extra-parliamentary organization, created in 1823, to bring public opinion to bear on the issue of Catholic emancipation by threatening to boycot the payment of tithes and taxes until political disabilities against Catholics were removed. The association united Irish people of every conceivable background, occupation and socio-economic standing, and its formidable size and power were not lost on Tory ministers. When Wellington introduced and successfully carried legislation through Parliament, English reformers learned an important lesson: a political organization that could peacefully unite a whole nation could be a powerful lever for change. If the Irish could present a united will for Catholic emancipation, then, reformers concluded, advocates of electoral reform, the almost universally recognized first step in long-term political and socio-economic reform, could certainly do the same among the English. If people from urban and rural areas, Anglicans and Non-conformists, professionals and labourers, manufacturers and artisans, could somehow find common ground and cooperate, then 'the people' could persuade politicians to carry parliamentary reform legislation, if necessary by using the same fiscal threats to shut down the government. William Biggs of Leicester, a former framework-knitter turned cloth manufacturer and Unitarian radical reformer – and one of the founders of the town's Political Union – neatly summed up the influence of the Catholic Association's example on English reformers as 'a lesson to us. We see what O'Connell has effected in Ireland by co-operation and union. He was enabled to bring to bear the whole public opinion of Ireland . . . until he . . . was enabled to overpower the bigotry and despotism of this government by the united voices of millions.'[31]

Political Unions were the culmination of the two strands – the radical programme of Cartwrightian democracy and the more respectable and moderate objectives of the commercial and educated 'middle class' represented by the Parliamentary Radicals. They also reflected the mass popular radicalism of Hunt. As organizations with their own constitutions, regulations, criteria for membership, code of behaviour and very specific and well-defined objectives, Political Unions were illustrations of popular political behaviour in the context of institutions and concrete action. There are clearly important ties and distinctions which need to be made in placing Political Unions in the context of popular or 'the people's' political organization during the long eighteenth century. At the heart of the movement was the relentless desire to abolish political corruption, abuses of power, and a number of perceived violations of the rights and liberties of the English people which they believed to be guaranteed by the English constitution, specifically the freedoms of speech, assembly and the press.

Political Unions do not fit in the new interpretation and redefinition of the popular politics offered in James Vernon's 'new' political history of England in the nineteenth century. Vernon distinguishes popular politics from orthodox politics (such as parliamentary elections) by focusing on the neglected cultural components that took the form of the 'imagined' – 'ballads, banners, cartoons, handbills, statues, architecture, the use of time and space, and the rich vein of ceremonial and iconographic forms.'[32] But the popular political campaign in support of the Reform Bill was not simply filled with identities and perceptions; it was one of organizations, personnel and agendas. Political Unions, working locally, focused their energies on national politics and did campaign for 'collective claims'. They crossed class and geographical boundaries, and utilized the 'standard' methods of agitation: public meetings and parliamentary petitions. By Vernon's own definition, they would clearly fit in his category of traditional politics.

Political Unions would also fit in Charles Tilly's category of English popular politics: 'collective interaction'. His 'decoding' of this political activity in his recent study of the long eighteenth century reveals 'how the concentration of capital and the expansion of the state pushed popular struggles from local arena and from a significant reliance on patronage toward autonomous claim-making in national arenas.'[33] Tilly's study is compelling, demonstrating the transformation of popular politics, which he traces from the mid-eighteenth century to the conclusion of the Reform Act agitation. 'Short of revolution,' he argues,

> the successive popular mobilizations and parliamentary actions of 1828–1834 deeply altered British politics. Popular politics nationalized as the role of Parliament became even more salient. Although workers continued to battle for the right to act in concert against their employers, for the other purposes the public meeting, the demonstration, the petition drive, the formation of specialized associations, and related forms of social-movement politics became the standard means for pressing popular collective claims.... Mass popular politics had arrived on a national scale.[34]

A study of the Political Union movement and the Reform Bill agitation is, I would argue, compelling evidence that mass politics reached a new, more sophisticated and effective level by 1832. Not fitting neatly into any single reform tradition, completely middle-class or working-class, Political Unions were a hybrid of popular politics. Nonetheless, their existence and role in the Reform Bill agitation certainly suggests an alternative to Jonathan Clark's contention that ordinary people could affect national politics in the early nineteenth century only by the 'presence or absence of revolution'.[35]

THE FIRST POLITICAL UNION

When Thomas Attwood founded the first Political Union in Birmingham, he argued that 'the general distress which now [1830] afflicts the country, and which has been so severely felt at several periods during the last fifteen years, is entirely to be ascribed to the gross mismanagement of public affairs.'[36] Only one solution remained: 'an effectual reform in the Commons' House of Parliament'.[37] The Political Union was not meant to be a 'middle-' or 'working'-class organization; quite the opposite. It was meant to represent the 'industrious' class or classes – a construct that included both the middle and working classes.

The term 'industrious classes' grew out of 'Old Corruption' arguments and socio-economic changes as a result of early nineteenth-century industrialism. The term 'industrious classes', according to David Nicholls, was designed to be inclusive and 'classless' in that it only distinguished between just two socio-economic groups: aristocratic landlords, receiving their income from others' productivity, and those industrious creators of wealth – labourers, craftsmen, agricultural labourers, small, independent farmers, bankers, manufacturers or anyone whose income resulted from his or her own physical or mental productivity. The landed classes were certain to stand against any change that might threaten their political power and thus their control of both economic policy and the industrious classes. Whether employer or employee, master or labourer, political and economic interests were in jeopardy unless reform was introduced.[38]

For Attwood, Political Unions represented a particular kind of popular politics:

> Their [the Unions'] principle is this: that Union can either mitigate or remove a certain number of acknowledged grievances, which are felt by that immense class in the community who are invited to enter into political combination . . . these species of associations differ from all former Unions in that in these inept particulars; that it lays down a plain rule of proceedings, which, concurring with public opinion, has in view of amelioration of every individual members of which it is a mass, all the grievances which are diffused amongst different classes of the community.[39]

Political Unions were a tool, not part of an ideological tradition. Attwood simply saw the economic problems of the day – paper money and excessively high taxes – as solvable with an extension of the franchise.[40] Though not precisely what Birmingham's working class reformers envisaged for a popular political organization, many saw the merit in the logic of seeing their middle-class brothers represented in Parliament as opposed to complete domination by the aristocracy. The Political Union would prevent the 'divide and conquer' policy of what some Radicals felt was an effort by the aristocracy to 'split the community into hostile sections'.[41]

THE POPULAR APPEAL OF POLITICAL 'UNION'

Attwood insisted that sophisticated reformers would come to understood **'THE SECRET OF UNION** . . . and find that while they [the borough-mongers and aristocracy] keep us so disunited they are themselves as firmly banded together as a gang of brigands . . . let us for once take a lesson from our oppressors and teach them honesty and industry.'[42] Keeping the industrious classes together and singular in their purpose was the key to reform. Many provincial reformers embraced Attwood's logic that parliamentary and other reforms were attainable 'by union, by organization, by general contribution, by patriotic exertion, and by discretion [and] keeping always within the law and the constitution. These are the elements of reform.'[33]

The Birmingham Political Union represented an English attempt to replicate the success of the single-issue campaign of the late 1820s which offered popular organization a successful model to follow. Until the passage of the Reform Bill, England witnessed the successful single-cause campaign for parliamentary reform (regardless of varying definitions and objectives of what that might entail) led by associations of the 'industrious' classes, fighting for the protection of their rights against the mutual enemy – the abuse of political power and the domination of economic policy among the landed classes. As Attwood put it, Union would end government in its present state which was 'too far removed in habits, wealth and station, from the wants and interests of the lower and middle classes of the people . . .'[44] Though the name 'Union' prompted a number of assumptions about the working-class composition and agenda of Political Unions – for example, the Home Office under Sir Robert Peel received information that the organizations were not political at all, but merely trade unions disguised – substantial evidence supports the uniqueness as well as the continuity of the radical tradition in the organizations.[45] The middle class used rhetoric and organization and focused their identification, as a group, on political ideology rather than on themselves as individuals or as a group. Forging an association of both the working and the middle classes, the latter reconceptualized themselves as 'the English people' at the same time they asserted more and more power over their own lives, and those of the working classes, dependent upon them for leadership, respectability and publicity.

The idea of 'Union' had enormous linguistic and even visual appeal. As George Ashworth, a Unionist from Todmorden, explained, 'as each [Unionist] brings a small thread, then entwined together by mutual interest and affection, this would unite all classes for their mutual benefits, and bring all our energies to a focus.'[46] Or, as the Council of the Bridgwater Political Union described it, Union 'will be like a mighty stream, it will burst every barrier and roll triumphantly . . . [or] like the Israelites of old in the desert, when the trumpet sounded and the walls of Jericho fell down.'[47]

POLITICAL UNION: THE MOVEMENT

What exactly were these Unions which reveal more about the 1832 agitation and the evolution of British popular politics and parliamentary reform agitation? Where did they come from? Who joined them? What did they want to achieve? How did they go about pushing the government towards securing a fairly extensive reform measure? Exactly what kind of relationship did they have with the Whigs, and how much influence?

Political Unions were extra-parliamentary organizations, largely composed of radicals, which sought parliamentary reform. They specifically hoped to return reformers, as well as the new manufacturers and business interests, to the House of Commons through an extended franchise and redistribution of parliamentary representation. They also provided a forum for the English to voice their political, economic and social concerns, and thus emerge as an important arena for a wide array of popular interests. Political Unions were widespread, found in almost every English county, but with the greatest concentration in the industrial north and midlands. Between 1830 and 1832, dues-paying members numbered between 15,000 and 18,000.[48] Attendance at Political Union rallies or public events during the same period attracted well over 200,000 nationwide.[49] They ultimately endorsed the reform objectives of aristocratic politicians in the Whig ministry.

But who exactly was 'united' in the cause of reform by these political organizations? Political Unionists were an eclectic mix of individuals from a wide variety of occupations, philosophical and religious backgrounds, and socio-economic groups. Their numbers included MPs, provincial town mayors, newspaper publishers, aldermen, JPs, bankers, lawyers, manufacturers, landowners, artisans, small shopkeepers and industrial workers. Electors and the unenfranchised joined in relatively equal number.[50] Such diversity – with sizable numbers of members giving representation to almost all levels of wealth, education and standing in the local community – enabled Union leaders to argue that their organizations truly represented public opinion and to claim that through them 'the people' sought a peaceful and legal way to achieve parliamentary reform.[51] More importantly, at least as far as many contemporaries were concerned, Political Unions met a common contemporary test for 'public opinion' – 'a proportionate middle class . . . [as] requisites for public opinion.'[52] As a result, the unenfranchised from both the middle and working classes took seriously the only political role open to them – that of 'public opinion' and the unity as 'the industrious classes'.

A significant number of Political Unions began their popular campaign with a programme of radical political and economic reforms that went far beyond the Whigs' Reform Bill. Most Political Unions formed prior to the introduction of the Reform Bill embraced a platform based on Major John Cartwright's six points of radical reform. Support for the government's measure pushed more radical demands out of the Unions' rhetoric and those members who would not endorse the Reform Bill were isolated by the Union Councils, eventually breaking with the organization and forming their own popular campaign for more radical reform.

A few Unions, such as those in Nottingham and Dudley, though supporting the Whig Reform Bill continued to demand the ballot, until the Bill ran into serious trouble in October 1831. All the Unions, in the end, supported the Reform Bill, believing it to be the best first step towards a variety of additional reforms and in no way forced Grey's hand when he took office by inciting revolutionary activity.[53] Their discussions on forming militias, boycotting taxes and staging a run on the banks to force the resignation of the Duke of Wellington during the May Days crisis made it essential that Grey and the Whigs carry the Bill with all speed. The Unionists themselves did not seriously plan to carry out any of the plans, but the presence of Political Unions made an impact. Grey argued that if he failed to secure reform, the Unions could turn on the government as easily as they had supported its reform efforts. William IV did not need much convincing, and had serious reservations about the loyalties of Political Unions from the outset.[54]

THIS STUDY AND ITS SOURCES

My study is the first of the creation, development and influence of Political Unions. This work gives concrete detail to the hazy historical image of the 'people' and their activities during the two and a half years it took for the Whig government to fulfil its promise of reform. Further, this study should provide significant weight to the view that the people forced the issue of reform in 1832 and the government responded to a potentially dangerous public with the Reform Bill. While it might be seen as 'revisionism' revised, this work is an attempt to fill a void in the historiography of 1832. The lack of scholarly research in the area of popular politics has allowed historians of high politics and electoral behaviour to assert and defend positions that they presume are borne out by the evidence. Interestingly, few historians seem to question that the Reform Act of 1832 was, regardless of motivation, an aristocratic offering designed to protect that class's own political and economic interests. It is as if the revisionist view is gospel and older interpretations of reform are hardly worth the trouble to test by examining new evidence. Of course, the possibility of such extant evidence should have motivated historians to investigate it a long time ago. They would have concluded, as I have, that the role played 'the people' in securing reform in 1832 cannot be dismissed as insignificant or too limited in size or scope to merit study. Political Unions and the force of public opinion played a vital role in seeing the Reform Bill through Parliament and setting England on the path of peaceful, legislative reform. Political Unions were significant in stiffening government and parliamentary support for the Bill, serving as a powerful reminder of the dangers of ignoring public opinion and demonstrating the moral and political determination of the people to eliminate corruption and privilege in British politics.

Yet, as I make a case for the historical importance of Political Unions based on their widespread popular appeal throughout England and the perception of authority they enjoyed with politicians, I also recognize that, despite the prevalence of the Unions, concrete information concerning local Political Union membership and activities is uneven at best. While provincial newspapers provide a wealth of information when Unions held public meetings or invited speakers to address their members on the issue of reform, few Political Union records remain. The story of the creation and activities of the majority of local Unions in this study comes from printed sources: newspapers, handbills, broadsheets, and so forth.

Because virtually no records or membership lists have survived, it was very difficult to piece together a picture of Political Union memberships. In attempting to find out exactly who joined Political Unions, I have traced memberships by reading the provincial newspaper accounts of local Political Union activity. Union speeches frequently appeared verbatim in newspaper reports of Union meetings. This source enabled me to accumulate the names of the most active and visible Political Union members.[55] From there, I tracked as many names as possible through town directories and poll books, trying to ascertain the occupation and electoral status of Political Unionists. The results reveal that Attwood's goal to create a Union of both the middle and lower classes was, by and large, successful throughout the Reform Bill agitation. Political Union composition embraced a wide socio-economic spectrum. Members of the military, local officials, professionals, the commercial and banking community, artisans, industrial workers and a few progressive gentry joined the Unions in their quest for reform.

While the middle class dominated the leadership roles in the Unions, there was more representation of working-class members on Union Councils. Those who founded the organization generally led it; and since the more wealthy citizens of a town could most easily place announcements in the local press, and print and distribute handbills, as well as secure the magistrates' cooperation in public meetings, they tended to dominate proceedings.

In about a dozen instances, thanks to more detailed primary sources, I have been able to piece together a fuller story of local Political Union activity. A few of the Political Union officers or local newspaper editors active in the Union left records and letters relating to Union activity, and in a few instances, the Home Office informants' letters add information about internal Union decision-making. I found additional printed materials for a number of other Political Unions.[56] Such numbers, I recognize, though hardly a statistically sound sampling of Political Unions throughout the kingdom, do demonstrate that Unions formed among industrial northern towns and market towns of the south and midlands, wool and cotton manufacturing areas, shoe and ribbon centres, ports and mining regions, and in existing parliamentary boroughs as well as unenfranchised urban areas. Because sampling reflects the diversity and something of the breadth of the Political Unions even this small sampling is significant. For example, it reveals much about the national consensus on the issues of parliamentary reform, public support for the Reform Bill and the Whigs, and the commitment to the peaceful, orderly demonstration of public opinion.

This study naturally includes, but does not give detailed attention to, the better-known Birmingham Political Union and the London-based Metropolitan and National Political Unions. Though this study includes a chapter on the creation of the BPU, it is meant to introduce the reader to the organizational 'model' of Political Unions (which nearly all Unions utilized in one degree of another). As well, this background explains why some of the public, as well as the King, his government and loyal opposition, all believed the BPU to be the leader in a nationally organized political movement. The Metropolitan Union went bankrupt very early on in the Reform Bill campaign, partly because of members' reluctance to put their dues in the hands of the treasurer, Henry Hunt. The National Political Union was established by the Radical leader Francis Place quite late in the campaign, at the same time as numerous other Unions. One can easily conclude that the formation of the NPU was part of a national response to the state of the Reform Bill, and the organization itself was hardly a leader in the Reform Bill agitation.

Somewhat problematic is the issue of 'ephemeral' Political Unions. Upon the foundation of these organizations, leaders consciously chose the name 'Political Union' and perceived themselves to be political part of a Union movement. The organizations, however, then disappeared without a trace. In the two years of the reform campaign, approximately 30 such Unions existed.[57] While critics may argue that these were Union meetings rather than Union organizations, it is significant that these extra-parliamentary organizations called themselves Political Unions – particularly after the publicity (not all complimentary) following the Bristol riots and the very public role the local Union played during that crisis. However brief the life of some ephemeral or inactive Unions, their existence reminded contemporaries that there was a popular reform movement in England. The 'people' intended to make themselves heard on the matter of reform and should no longer be dismissed by historians on the basis of 'thin' evidence.

Political Unions were an important part of both the Reform Act's passage and the later development of popular political action in the nineteenth century. They connected the ideological premises behind and the tactics pursued to achieve radical and constitutional reform with a view to reforming rule by an aristocratic oligarchy into a system which required a much broader base. Their emphasis on representing the 'industrious' classes and the difficulties that posed also linked Political Unions to the emerging debates – political and socio-economic – in later Victorian Britain. Political Unions are an important key to understanding the nineteenth century and the evolution of their understanding of participatory democracy.

1 The Birmingham Political Union and the Origins of the Union Campaign

> Mr. Attwood had long had the project in contemplation, and we must admit that the prudence with which he has ever directed the Union, was guaranteed to us by that sagacity which enabled him to select the exact time for the formation of that Union.[1]

> All the other Unions look to the Birmingham one and that looks to its half dozen leaders, who consequently act under the most intense consciousness of moral respectability.[2]

Contemporaries, particularly reformers, felt that the BPU, and its founder Thomas Attwood, were essential to, perhaps mainly responsible for, the passage of the Great Reform Act of 1832. BPU members believed wholeheartedly that their mass meetings, processions and petitions convinced the government and anti-reformers alike that they would not stop their campaign until the Reform Bill was law, thereby helping ensure its passage. New Union medals and beer mugs fashioned in his image and scarves and garters bearing his speeches or the phrase 'Attwood Forever' were sold throughout the city.[3] Daniel O'Connell proclaimed, 'It was not Grey and Althorp who carried it, but the brave and determined men of Birmingham.'[4] Lord Durham concurred, remarking that 'the country owed Reform to Birmingham, and its salvation from revolution.'[5] Grey himself thanked Attwood for his efforts 'to maintain popular support for the measure outside the House of Commons.'[6] Following the Reform Bill's passage, the Northern Political Union in Newcastle, an organization with numerous ideological differences with those of the BPU, toasted 'to the health . . . of Mr. Attwood of Birmingham, the Father of Political Unions'.[7]

There was little to make reformers doubt the potency of the organization. Members of the government communicated with Attwood during the Reform Bill debates, particularly in November following the Bristol riots and again during the May Days crisis.[8] The King and his ministers usually referred to the BPU when they talked of public opinion and Wellington directly attacked the BPU for inflaming the masses with visions of democratic reform. [9] Newspapers constantly printed the addresses of Attwood and news of the BPU's meetings and rallies. Politicians referred to the potential strength of the Union in their parliamentary speeches.[10] There was a widely held perception that the BPU was the leading force behind a nationally orchestrated campaign on behalf of parliamentary reform.

Historians furthered that perception. Asa Briggs began the modern historical investigation into the BPU, calling it the first extraparliamentary political organization to unite reformers from 'both the middle and lower orders', and arguing that its founder, Thomas Attwood, orchestrated the entire popular campaign behind the Reform Bill, continuing that campaign into the Chartist movement of the 1840s.[11] The BPU has, until now, been *the* Political Union of the reform agitation. Certainly his assertion that 'Attwood's ideas were dominant, and his organization supreme' set the tone for assessing the importance of the BPU and dismissing the effectiveness of any other extraparliamentary reform efforts.[12]

Joseph Hamburger's fascinating study of James Mill work carried further Briggs' emphasis on the BPU as the national leader in popular politics during the Reform Act agitation and publicized by the press releases of Joseph Parkes, or directed by the BPU clone, Francis Place's London-based National Political Union.[13] Although he acknowledged the existence of other Unions in the provinces, Hamburger relegated them to insignificance by observing how 'difficult [it was] to determine how large and viable these organizations were.'[14] The recent biography of Attwood by David Moss furthered this interpretation.[15] Moss argued that Attwood and the BPU 'set the ground rules for future extraparliamentary action.'[16] It even provided the basic organizational and tactical model for future generations: 'rarely in the years which followed was there a popular movement which did not use the Birmingham model as its guide.'[17]

Carlos Flick was the first to challenge such interpretations. In his *The Birmingham Political Union and the Movements for Reform, 1830–39*, he argued that the Union was nothing more than a local organization with limited goals and limited appeal, and lacked the political savvy to assume the directing role in a national campaign. For the leaders of the BPU, 'theirs was a local triumph . . . which through the peculiar lens of provincial conditions got magnified into national pretensions.'[18] The Union's efforts had little direc-

tion 'and involved almost no coordination of activity with reformers in other places.'[19] From currency reform to Chartism, the BPU was able to transcend ideological positions to accommodate the ambitions of Birmingham reformers, but in the context of 1832, Flick argued its scope and appeal was an illusion.

This chapter is an introduction to the broader study of Political Unions in England and challenges the contemporary historiographical presumptions concerning the BPU. Its size and self-promotion did dwarf other provincial Political Unions. Yet, as later chapters will demonstrate, dozens of neighbouring midland Political Unions flourished independently of Attwood's directives. Contrary to the assumption that the BPU ran satellite or branch Unions, those based in the midlands – even in neighbouring towns such as Coventry and Wolverhampton, or in smaller places (Walsall, Dudley and West Bromwich) – were independently created and locally led by individuals from the towns themselves.[20] In addition, the goals of other Unions differed from those of the BPU. As Charles Larkin of the Northern Political Union (ironically a Union founded by Attwood's younger brother, Charles) would later point out, 'he gladly acknowledged the very active part that Birmingham took the cause of reform in 1832, yet to the town of Newcastle belonged the honour of having secured the 10 pound franchise. . . . Birmingham [was] willing at the time, to accept a 20 pound franchise.'[21] This chapter reexamines the Birmingham Political Union model and the campaign for political reform around 1830–2. It is only then that we can determine in what ways the BPU was a model for other Political Unions and critically examine its exalted reputation in the Political Union and Reform Bill campaign. In reviewing the ideological commitments of Thomas Attwood and the origins of his Political Union – the rhetoric of currency reform and the unification of the industrious classes against aristocratic interests, the specifics of the BPU reform platform, and its organization and tactics – there emerges a clear model, both ideologically and organizationally, with which to compare the BPU to other Political Unions' activities and objectives.

I

Attwood's reform campaign began in earnest in 1829. The conditions of that spring were dismal in Birmingham and throughout

the midlands and the north. Poor harvests resulted in riots in Manchester and Macclesfield; authorities called out the militia to maintain the peace on more than one occasion. Severe depressions existed in both commercial trade and agricultural markets. Attwood, a banker, determined that the crisis, and indeed all the economic woes following the Napoleonic Wars, resulted from gross government mismanagement and politicians' refusal to recognize that the gold system strained the pockets of farmers by inflating their debts and deflating agricultural prices. By spending more on agricultural products, Englishmen of all economic classes had less money to spend on non-staples. Tariffs and taxes only added to the woes of tradesmen and shopkeepers.

The solution to this imbalance and the corresponding doldrums of local trade, Attwood decided, was the adoption of paper money.[22] But this would be impossible, Attwood lamented, thanks to the composition of Parliament. Not only were manufacturing cities such as Birmingham and Manchester lacking any parliamentary representation, but those towns that did send MPs to Westminster did not reflect the interests of the middle class and the commercial society. This existing political system responded to the interests of the landed classes and great financial interests of London bankers only, and thus would only guarantee a continuation of economic hardship throughout the country.[23]

Certain of this causal relationship between parliamentary membership and economic distress, Attwood held a public meeting at Beardsworth's Repository in May to discuss the need for parliamentary reform. It was there that the foundation for a parliamentary reform campaign began. Attwood lectured to a crowd of businessmen and artisans as to the 'class' divisions in England. The country really consisted of two distinct economic groups with separate and competing interests: the landed classes and industrious classes: the parasites and producers. While the aristocracy and London financiers, neither of whom created wealth, lived off the profits created by other people's industry, they dominated politics. Those whose ideas, investments and labour created products and additional wealth – namely bankers, manufacturers, shopowners, craftsmen and labourers – were politically powerless to change the situation.

The hardship, Attwood believed, resulted from the government policies of monopolies, taxes and tariff-restricted trade opportunities, all measures designed to protect the landed classes' economic interests: the parasites. The landed and London banking establishment, he argued, controlled the economy and trade only because they controlled politics. Attwood argued:

> The manufacturers, the traders, the mechanics, the labourers ... are obliged to sell their labour, and the products of their labour, for about one half of the money which they ought to obtain ... and the interests of the country are thus starving for the want of money [while] at the very moment that half the circulation [of money] of the kingdom is in stagnant masses in what is called the money market, in order to gorge monied interest![24]

Such arguments fell within what the populist and radical William Cobbett had called 'Old Corruption' and stemmed back to the eighteenth-century 'country' ideology. The selfish oligarchy which controlled England's Parliament monopolized all the good things for itself and prevented any chance for the people to receive adequate representation of their interests in the House of Commons. Attwood chose his rhetoric carefully, intending to arouse indignation. 'I have no fault to find with the House of Lords,' claimed Attwood.

> Nor have I any fault to find with the House of Commons (whom I would call a House of Little Lords) as far as the rights and interests of the aristocracy are concerned, or even so far as the interests of the upper class of tradesmen are concerned. The House of Commons represents these rights and interests. But it does not properly represent the rights and interests of the working classes, and of what may be called the inferior classes of tradesmen.[25]

He also revealed his visions of parliamentary reform.

> First, repeal the Septennial Act, and then to abolish or buy up about one hundred of the rotten boroughs, and to introduce in their place, in the House of Commons, about two hundred representatives of the working classes, chosen by some kind of universal suffrage from among the people.[26]

Attwood's desire to abolish rotten boroughs was not unique. The press and many politicians had long discussed the inequities of parliamentary representation – Penryn being the example closest to Birmingham's heart. In May 1826, Lord John Russell had moved in the Commons disenfranchisement of Penryn and East Retford, following charges of electoral corruption. Penryn's seats were to go to Manchester, but the proposal was amended to transfer the East Retford's seats to Birmingham. Birmingham staged a large public meeting at Beardsworth's Repository with Attwood delivering the main speech and introducing a petition endorsing the enfranchisement of the town's commercial and manufacturing classes.[27] The *Birmingham Argus and Public Censor* endorsed the notion:

> With a population of ONE HUNDRED AND FORTY THOUSAND INHABITANTS: with a manufacture equal in importance and extent to that of any other town in the Kingdom; and contributing immensely to the support of the government under the present system of taxation, we ask, is it fair, is it equitable?[28]

But nothing came of the proposal as the Whigs withdrew from the government coalition following George Canning's death, but the popular campaign for the enfranchisement of Birmingham and continued right through the creation of the BPU.

Attwood's use of the term universal suffrage in his speech was, however, unusual for reform talk in Birmingham, particularly coming from a staunch Tory, though his qualifier 'some' in proposing universal suffrage suggests that Attwood had in mind something other than democracy. He never elaborated on what qualifications he envisaged for those receiving suffrage. 'The interest of the employer and employed are both one,' he had contended. Therefore, universal suffrage was desirable in order to secure the interests of the industrious classes.[29]

Attwood's audience appeared interested in extra-parliamentary agitation led by an organization that would represent the political interests of the 'people' as a whole, not just the landowning classes and wealthy businessmen (which no one could have denied). Operating on this assumption, he borrowed O'Connell's concept of 'unity', which had been so effective in forming the Catholic Association. Attwood even incorporated the word 'union' in his extra-parliamentary organization's name, directly referring to the Association in his speech announcing plans for a 'Union – such as the Irish exhibited'.[30] He believed that parliamentary reform was possible, as Catholic emancipation had been, if reformers launched a popular campaign and demonstrated the widespread public opinion favoring reform legislation.[31]

On 22 December, Attwood and fellow currency reform advocates called another public meeting at the Globe Tavern to discuss the continuing economic crisis and 'Old Corruption'. He urged the middle and working classes to join him in a currency reform campaign because every one would benefit. 'If the masters prosper, the men are sure to prosper equally,' he assured his audience. 'The masters, therefore, ought not to say to the workmen, 'Give us your wages', but take their workmen by the hand, and knock at the gates of the Government and demand the redress of their common grievances.'[32] Attwood offered his leadership to form a popular campaign: 'If my fellow townsmen declare it, I am ready to cooperate with them with heart and hand in every just, legal and constitutional exertion to obtain a radical reform in their Commons House of Parliament.'[33] The result of the meeting was an agreement to plan an organization or a 'Union' and to petition the Tory government and campaign for a parliamentary reform measure. Attwood told his listeners that though their campaign would be legal and peaceful, things might turn ugly if their demand for reform was ignored by the King and his government. 'If there is to be no peace for the cottage,' he hinted, 'there can be no safety for the palace long . . .'[34] Beyond the promise of an organization, Attwood offered few other details as to the role of the Union, let alone reform legislation. Other than the abolition of paper money, he did not address additional economic reform such as repeal of the Corn Laws or reduction in taxes and the Civil List. He did not call for annual parliaments, nor did he discuss his views on how the redistribution of parliamentary representation would be transferred to unrepresented towns such as Birmingham.

But Attwood had laid an important foundation for the next step – the creation of an extra-parliamentary association. First, he had portrayed the existing political world as aristocratic, London-based and corrupt. Then he had idealized hard-working provincials who remained unenfranchised, such as the Birmingham community. By creating an 'us' and 'them' attitude between corrupt politicians in the metropolis and honest, industrious classes in the provinces, he tried to eliminate the possible divisiveness of economic issues among the classes in his own community and to focus all blame for distress on the aristocratic oligarchy. Who would wish to argue against his economic principles when he pronounced, 'every honest labourer in England has as good a right to a reasonable maintenance for his family in exchange for his labour as the King had to a crown on his head'?[35] Attwood could parlay this acceptance of his rhetoric into support for parliamentary reform through the establishment of an organization which would bring the middle and working classes together 'in harmony and union, and mutual cooperation' against the aristocratic abusers of power.[36]

A 'union' would produce the maximum display of public enthusiasm for parliamentary reform. Reform would benefit both the middle and working classes, and if the two groups worked together to attain it, that fact would underline the seriousness of public opinion on the issue. Together, without any cause for the middle-class employer and working-class employee to 'criminate and injure each other', the industrious classes would take on their common enemies: the aristocracy and London banking establishment.[37] Such a union, Attwood believed, eliminated any danger that the campaign would be violent or revolutionary, as men of means and education would lead it. It also eliminated, or so he hoped, any prospect of economic conflict over wages or job security during a parliamentary reform campaign in which both employers and employees were members of the same reform organization, fighting a common enemy. He did not seem to consider that work and political issues might become separate, or that even a successful reform measure which might not be broad enough to satisfy all the members of the new Union. The Birmingham Political Union would be an association of 'the Lower and Middle Classes of People' or 'the Industrious Classes', united and strong in their public demand for reform, not such as to realize the theory in practice, but rather simply to 'enable that great and influential body of men, the middle class of the populacy [*sic*] of the United Kingdoms, conscientiously and patriotically . . . to rally around the Government'; that is, it meant to enfranchise them, not the lower classes.[38] For those listening carefully, Attwood was stating his position clearly: 'union' was a way to demonstrate equal support for reform among the working and middle classes, but the benefits of electoral change were not, despite lip service to the concept of universal manhood suffrage, to be distributed equally.

II

The task before Attwood was daunting. In order to achieve that, it would be necessary to galvanize 'public opinion [so that] instead of being scattered and diffused throughout the country, and concealed within the breasts of individuals, will be collected and concentrated in influential masses . . . and directed into wholesome and legal operations upon the legislature of the country.'[39] Attwood's plan to use extra-parliamentary agitation for enfranchising Birmingham is not known, nor how he intended to revise it to create a national movement. No doubt he believed that other commercial and manufacturing centres would accept his arguments concerning provincial England's economic plight and embrace his solution of currency reform.

Attwood began the process of creating this movement by enlisting the cooperation of other currency reformers in Birmingham to form the core that would create the Birmingham Union.[40] Most considered themselves Ultra-Tories. Only Joshua Scholefield was a Whig, and perhaps for this reason Attwood selected him as his Vice-Chair. Attwood sought a broader range of leadership to include a wider range of interests that required parliamentary reform as a beginning. In the spirit of unity, and to attract as much support as possible, Attwood sought cooperation with the Birmingham Radicals and Dissenters, who, he believed, would support the Union's campaign, at least for parliamentary if not currency reform. Birmingham's Radicals distrusted local Whigs and thus drew them together with the Tories as political outcasts in the town. Joining forces with Attwood would not be out of the question if the two could agree on the nature of political reform proposed. Radicals such as George Edmonds, a legal clerk and son of a Baptist minister, who had led the Birmingham reform agitation in 1816–19, did accept Attwood's invitation to serve on the Union's organizing committee.[41] A proven organizer who had formed a local Hampden Club in 1816–17 and successfully hosted a speech by Major John Cartwright spoke at Newhall Hill in 1819, Edmonds was, Attwood believed, the key to attracting Dissenters and Radicals to join the organization. An enviable speaker besides, he would be a great asset at public rallies.[42] Edmonds too felt that the Union was a good way to examine the possibility of reform from the Tories. He complimented 'the conduct of the Tories [and criticized] the insincere dirty conduct of the Whigs.'[43] William Pare and Joseph Russell completed the organization team. Pare, a tobacconist and secretary of the Birmingham Mechanics Institute, ran the Owenite Co-operative in Birmingham. He would bring Owenites and working men to the organization. Russell, a printer and Radical, would be important in publicizing the organization. An additional eight men were sought out to join the Council prior to the public meeting in January.[44]

In particular, Attwood sought out Joseph Parkes, Birmingham's self-proclaimed Utilitarian and part of the Benthamite circle known as Philosophic Radicals. Parkes, unenthusiastic about the currency reform proposal, but a strong advocate of parliamentary reform, was not at all certain about the motives of the new people's champion. He agreed to advise Attwood on the formation of a Union, but Parkes refused Attwood's invitation, primarily out of a sense a loyalty to the Whigs and Lord Grey, whom his father worshipped. Parkes was an integral party of the Union's campaign and its strongest link to the Whig ministers. He never, however, joined the BPU.[45]

The coalition of Birmingham Tories and Radicals drafted 'Union for the Protection of Public Rights' and formed the first 28-man Political Union Council.[46] This Council, the ruling body, possessed unlimited power to act and speak for the general Union membership between the organization's general meetings, which would be held at least once a year. It would usually meet on a weekly basis and be responsible for all financial arrangements, all publicity (primarily the placing of advertisements in local newspapers as well as the distribution of handbills and broadsides), the retention of solicitors and legal advisers as required, as well as produce the Union books for inspection of the general membership at the annual meeting.[47] Council members were also responsible for watching the proceedings of Parliament, presenting petitions and remonstrances to the King and Parliament, and organizing and inviting leading reformers outside Birmingham to their Union's parades, meetings and public dinners.[48] The Union president and chair, secretaries, deputy chair, 'collectors of contributions' all sat on the Council, as well as others who would be elected annually.[49] There were no guidelines for election to that elite body, at least not written in the Union's official papers. Council members would be selected at the July general meeting, but other than Union membership, there were no further guidelines for election to that elite body. The Council had the right to add to its numbers at any time.

The Council's approval was essential for any Union activity, or so its members claimed. George Ashworth, a Council member of the Todmorden Political Union which had adopted the BPU's Rules and Regulations almost to the letter, described the Council as the fulcrum to the general Union's lever. Only when the Council initiated action 'can the union accomplish an efficient reform'.[50] The Union was clearly no democracy and its leaders were able to keep a tight hold over the general membership and the way in which the organization would agitate for reform. The Council justified the concentration of such power in its hands by arguing that only a central authority, not a collaborative effort, could handle such responsibilities. Unity was possible, Attwood evidently believed, only when there was strict order, discipline and the leadership of respectable men with a history of public service.

Individual membership in the BPU required payment of one shilling a quarter (a steep rate for an organization hoping to attract workers) and a willingness 'to obey strictly all the just and legal directions of the Political Council', as well as 'be a good, faithful, and loyal subject of the King'.[51] Members were expected to 'obey the law of the land' and to 'protect the rights, liberties, and interest of the community, and to get them changed by just, legal, constitutional, and peaceful means ONLY.'[52] Failure to adhere to the Council's decisions was a violation of Union rules and resulted in loss of membership.

The BPU's agenda and tactics proved a great deal more difficult for the organizers than the structure of the organization. Tension between the currency reformers and the Radicals mounted in early union discussions. The Radicals, led by Russell, Pare and Edmonds, brought arguments of ancient rights and natural law into the debate, to the annoyance of Attwood. While he had used the term universal suffrage in May, Attwood was retreating, to the relief of the Tories and the distress of the Radicals. Now that Attwood's vision was turning into a reality, he did not want to commit himself too much. His vision of reform attacked rotten boroughs and corrupt politicians while offering paper money as the solution to economic problems.

The BPU borrowed the general tactics of earlier extra-parliamentary organizations: meetings, speeches, newspaper publicity and their most salient feature, parliamentary petitions.[53] The BPU regularly sponsored large public events where Attwood and others would stir the crowd with speeches and union hymns. But as peaceful as the meetings were, the sheer numbers gathered at Newhall Hill or Beardsworth's Repository gave the impression that the Union was more an army waiting to muster than a simple congregation of people.

A publication launched in 1830 to promote Political Unions defined Union tactics in terms of 'congregating physical power' and implied that a major tactic of the Unions was physical force – and only confirmed that fear for many.[54] But that impression was false. Attwood emphasized that strength of the BPU would derive from '*peace, order, unity* and [the] legality of our proceedings'.[55] He denounced those who 'in any way, invite[d] or promote[d] violence, discord, or divisions, or any illegal or doubtful measures'.[56] Violence, apart from unsubstantiated rumours that the Union was buying arms, did not enter the BPU's reform campaign.[57]

To facilitate good will with local and national government, the unions avoided any and all private or secret proceedings which would give any impression of 'concealment of any view of the union'.[58] They would legally prosecute anyone, 'in whatever station, who may be found to have acted from criminal or corrupt motives' in their participation in Union activities.[59] These were not new tactics, but they were very effective.

Joseph Parkes provided another tactic: generating 'steam'.[60] He argued that Unions could best achieve reform 'by means of public meetings, petitions, and a use of the Press, and by extending everywhere the means of public education.'[61] That the newspaper should be used 'expressly for the collecting and concentrating of the public opinion on this highly important question . . .'. This was a common refrain of newspaper editors and individual reformers.[62] The councils 'prepare[d] petitions, addresses, and remonstrances to the Crown and both or either House of Parliament, respecting the preservation and restoration of public rights, and respecting the repeal of laws, and the enactment of a wise and comprehensive code of good laws.'[63] Unions utilized their unquestioned right to petition Parliament. They also drafted hundreds of addresses to their representatives, the House of Commons, and Lord Grey and the government. Accordingly, the King and government would determine that the will of the people, so eloquently demonstrated by the Union's obvious popularity in the public forum, could not be ignored.

III

Attwood's opportunity to convince the average Brummie of the wisdom of parliamentary reform for currency reform's sake took place at the inaugural meeting of the BPU in January 1830. The high bailiff, William Chance, refused to announce the event, claiming it was not his 'duty to call a meeting of the inhabitants of the town for a purpose of this kind'.[64] Attwood decided to call the meeting without the sanction of the legal authorities. After much debate, the council agreed upon Beardworth's Repository as the site of the meeting where a Union would form in order to 'remedy the current state of political corruption by an effectual reform in the Commons' House of Parliament . . .'[65]

The organizers distributed handbills in enormous quantities announcing the first meeting of the new reform organization for 25 January 1830 which read:

> We, the undersigned, being of opinion that the GENERAL DISTRESS which NOW AFFLICT [*sic*] THE COUNTRY and which has been so severely felt at several periods during the last fifteen years, is entirely to be ascribed to the GROSS MISMANAGEMENT OF PUBLIC AFFAIRS, and that such mismanagement can only be effectually and permanently remedied by an EFFECTUAL REFORM IN THE COMMONS HOUSE OF PARLIAMENT; and being also of opinion that, for the legal accomplishment of this GREAT OBJECT, and for the further REDRESS OF PUBLIC WRONGS AND GRIEVANCES, it is expedient to FORM A GENERAL POLITICAL UNION BETWEEN THE LOWER AND MIDDLE CLASSES OF THE PEOPLE.[66]

The advertisement achieved the desired effect. It did not alienate anyone by talking about currency reform or universal manhood suffrage (although Edmonds had insisted that it should talk about the latter) and approximately 10,000 attended the meeting.[67] Attwood once again talked about the need for the industrious classes to seek parliamentary reform in order to bring the provincial manufacturing and trade interests into Parliament. He then presented the *Rules and Regulations* of the Birmingham Political Union as well as a set of objectives and methods to achieve them. The main objective was parliamentary reform, though defined only in the most general terms. Leaders did not commit themselves as to whether 'an effectual reform' in the Commons meant universal manhood or household suffrage, or simply gaining parliamentary representation for Birmingham with a restricted franchise. No specific proposals were made for abolishing rotten boroughs and shifting those parliamentary seats to industrial cities, and no one discussed the frequency of elections to parliament or the ballot.

The specific reform goals in the document presented in January focused on economic concerns. The Union sought the adoption of paper currency and repeal of particular taxes, such as the beer and stamp duties. This prompted Joseph Parkes to accuse Attwood of

using parliamentary reform merely to entice thousands to join a campaign that had no real objective but to push a scheme for paper money through Parliament.[68] Attwood protested, claiming he only wanted to unite, 'two millions of people to think speak and act as one man'.[69] The crowd decidedly rejected Parkes's accusations and endorsed the whole Union agenda. Despite his heated accusations, Joseph Parkes agreed to help Attwood in the drafting of newspaper accounts and handbills, taking care that there should be strict conformity to the law and safeguarding the Union from any accusation of treacherous language.[70] All that the people assembled were interested in was that the BPU offered the hope that 'the rights and interests of the industrious classes in the community be represented in Parliament . . . and the cause of the distress be ascertained, and the proper remedy be applied without delay.'[71]

The London newspapers lost no time in reacting. They openly speculated about the new BPU which represented an alliance of the middle and working classes. Some hinted at revolution and urged the Duke of Wellington to, 'look at Birmingham . . . and see what public spirit can do when driven to extremities.'[72] *The Morning Advertiser* remarked on 'one of the most extraordinary and remarkable meetings which has ever been held in the kingdom'.[73] In Manchester, *The Courier* warned that 'if they [political unions] were to become general, and were to obtain their influence over the proceedings of the legislature which their promoters seem to anticipate, the independence of the Parliament would be lost.'[74] Thomas Barnes, editor of the *The Times*, was the only one from the major dailies which dismissed the organization, calling it 'nonsense' and assuring readers that it would soon, 'die away quietly'.[75] England waited and watched the BPU for signs that its reform campaign had begun.

But the BPU was relatively inactive after the initial January meeting. Subscriptions for membership were coming, but slowly. Some Council members expressed concern that only 2,200 names were listed on the Union's roll. Attwood himself was worried that those who had joined the BPU were almost exclusively workers or small shopkeepers, brought to the organization by Russell, Pares or Edmonds. Manufacturers and professionals were not joining.[76] Determined to attract greater numbers (and in some cases, more selects members) to their cause, 13 members of the Council opened their businesses to collect dues, now changed to one penny per week, and distribute union rules and regulations. A union office opened at No. 1 Paradise Street.

But the Wellington ministry showed no indication of any interest in either parliamentary or currency reform, and the BPU leaders had few ideas as to how to continue with a campaign. William Cobbett, a reluctant supporter of the BPU, openly questioned whether the organization would really be able to bring itself to do anything concrete for parliamentary reform. 'The Political Union founded by Mr. Attwood, is very laudable in itself; but it will produce, I am convinced, no effect whatever.'[77] He criticized its regulations and its lofty aims, but he printed the BPU Rules and Regulations in his *Weekly Political Register* on 6 February. He proclaimed that it was the borough-mongers who had united the classes for the purpose of reform: 'At last the middle class begins to perceive that it must be totally sacrificed unless it makes a stand, and a stand it cannot make without the support of the lower classes.'[78]

Cobbett was particularly antagonized when the BPU invited Sir Francis Burdett to be its guest of honour and main speaker at the first annual meeting in July.[79] 'Reform', Burdett had written, 'must be something more than a bit of paper, it must, to be productive of harmony, cause something to be done to better the state of the people; and, in order to do this, it must produce a change in the management of the affairs of the country . . . a very great change.'[80] Attwood hoped to have a man with Burdett's Radical credentials join his organization, suggesting to him that 'the best proof you could give the House [of Commons] of your approving it [the union] would probably be to say you had felt it your duty to join it.'[81]

Attwood left for London in order to persuade Burdett to support the union. Though Burdett never did, he did help to bring Attwood into Radical political circles by introducing him to Edward Davenport, Tory MP for Stafford, but part of the Westminster reform group, with whom he shared an interest in, and correspondence concerning, currency reform. On his way, Attwood met Daniel O'Connell to seek his opinion on the legality of the Union and its constitution. The two met at Coventry on O'Connell's way to London to take his seat in Parliament.[82]

IV

May became the decisive month in the formation of the BPU, both in securing members and in committing it to a set of objectives, thereby orienting the organization ideologically as well. The event which precipitated this latter development was the Marquis of Blandford's presentation in February of a plan to transfer seats from close boroughs to large towns and to reform suffrage qualifications. Blandford contended that boroughs found in a 'state of decay' should lose their parliamentary seat in favour of the unrepresented northern towns. Electoral qualification in these large towns would be scot and lot. In addition, the franchise was to be given to all copy- and freeholders, which would have extended the electorate beyond that proposed in the Reform Bill.[83]

Here was the proposal Attwood needed. Blandford was already connected to the Union, becoming an honorary member on 29 January.[84] Such a distribution of representation as he proposed would enfranchise manufacturing and commercial interests Attwood was certain would endorse currency reform, and at the same time, keep the lower classes happy and supportive of the Union. The BPU Council adopted Blanford's reform proposal as their own.[85] Of course, Edmonds and the other Radicals hoped for it all: universal suffrage, annual parliaments and the ballot. But Attwood persuaded Edmonds and his followers that if the BPU endorsed Blandford's proposal, the fears expressed in the newspapers as to the organization's revolutionary composition and intent would be alleviated, and bad publicity would be replaced with good.

This position became the centre of discussion during the first annual general BPU meeting, held on 27 May. The streets surrounding Beardsworth's were densely crowded. Bands played and the Council members paraded through the crowds with marshals surrounding them for protection.[86] On-the-spot Union membership soared, as did the sale of official Union badges, sold on the streets and worn by hundreds in the crowd.[87]

Attwood announced the Council's decision to adopt the Marquis's reform proposal as their own. Only a mechanic named Bibb, who was newly elected to the Council, challenged this decision.[88] The Council denied him the right to speak, a decision supported even by Edmonds. Speeches were made by Council members as to the soundness of the proposal and the wisdom of adopting scot and lot rather than universal manhood suffrage, as the Union's chief goal. Attwood's son Bosco presented his lyrics for 'the Union hymn'.[89] The meeting ended with cheers for Attwood and the Marquis, and membership in the following days continued to rise.

With heightened confidence, Attwood returned to London in June. He met Radicals Francis Burdett, J.C. Hobhouse, his old friend

Davenport and Lord John Russell. They discussed the idea of 'Union' and he impressed upon them that the BPU was composed of respectable men and not wild revolutionaries. Although Attwood was not the centre of attention at their meeting, he did try to present the BPU in a good light, asserting its usefulness if the Whigs, as rumoured, were going to pick up the issue of reform now that the Blandford proposal had failed.

On the basis of the rumours Attwood heard in London, the BPU Council authorized public celebrations when, on George IV's death, the new king issued a proclamation calling for a general election. The Union Council adopted and distributed a new set of resolutions, all calling for a reform bill.[90] But in spite of the parades and the guest speaker Sir Francis Burdett, attendance at the 26 July meeting was lighter than the previous one.[91] Attwood, however, believed it was just a matter of time before the Tories were forced out of office and the Whigs came to power and produced a reform measure. He himself was also beginning to display delusions of grandeur and demagoguery. At a Political Union dinner held in October, Attwood played upon the emotions of the 3,700 community members in attendance by asking, 'Where is the man among you who would not follow me to the death in a righteous cause? [Cheers and cries of, 'all, all'] I see gentlemen your hearts are mine, and mine is yours.'[92] The *Argus* praised the Union's position on reform and urged reformers to 'go as far as he does, AND NO FURTHER,' Attwood seemed, at least to the newspaper's editor, to be 'a wise and prudent leader'.[93]

V

Things were not so clear when, instead of espousing the proposals of a rejected scheme, the prospect of a government-sponsored parliamentary reform measure appeared. When Wellington resigned in November 1830 and Lord Grey led the Whigs into office, parliamentary reform was no longer a dream. But the Blandford proposal was not a likely proposal either. Clearly, the Whig government, publicly committed to a reform measure, agreed with the BPU's criticisms of 'Old Corruption'. What was the BPU to do?

Attwood seized upon the opportunity for the BPU to connect itself with the new government. He intended to support whatever the government proposed, but bolstered support among union ranks with rhetoric which heightened members' commitment to reform and to him personally. 'Grey would do his duty,' Attwood promised, 'the BPU would do all it could to make certain of that.'[94] Of course, Attwood's promise did not include any plan for how the Union might do so. By January 1831, Attwood claimed that the union had 9,000 members, represented '150,000 souls, and that nearly equal influence which they exercise over the inhabitants of the populous manufacturing towns and districts around them, containing from 200,000 to 300,00 inhabitants more . . . was far too great to be disregarded.'[95] Francis Place referred to him as 'the most influential man in England'.[96] Still, there is no indication that 'the most influential man' was in the least aware of the discussions going on between Grey and members of the committee drafting the Reform Bill.

Nor was he clearly directly associated with (or perhaps even aware of) the 23 other Political Unions that existed by the end of 1830.[97] While a few of the new provincial Unions made specific reference to the BPU in their own initial meetings, and some wrote to the secretary of the BPU requesting a copy of the Rules and Regulations of the BPU, Attwood and the union Council made no effort to establish ties with these unions, even those in neighbouring Worcester, Coventry and West Bromwich. The organization never pursued reformers to join the Union movement.[98] It seems by its relative inactivity that the BPU decided to wait until the Whigs' Reform Bill was made public before it committed itself to anything. It acted just as the government hoped it would: peacefully, quietly, and patiently.

VI

When the Whig plan for reform was made public on 1 March 1831 with Lord John Russell's introduction of the measure in the House of Commons, Attwood was happy to readjust the Union's position on reform. With great praise for the government, the BPU, which once advocated the bolder (at least in terms of the franchise) Blandford scheme, enthusiastically endorsed the government's proposal of a ten pound householder qualification in the boroughs, the elimination of rotten and closed boroughs, and the enfranchisement of industrial cities including Birmingham. For the BPU, there was reason to support the measure, except for that nagging problem of maintaining the unity of the middle and working classes, the latter still to be excluded from politics even if the Reform Bill become law.

For Attwood, this dilemma was an easy one. He simply passed the responsibility to the Whigs. The government proposal should be supported at all costs. If pledged reformers were unwilling to support them, then anti-reformers would have no trouble defeating the measure and there would be no gain at all. If the BPU, with its significant numbers and widespread publicity, stood behind the government, there would be far less chance that enemies of reform could silence the will of the people. The Union was quite willing to advise its working-class members that the government measure would inevitably help them attain the vote – one day in the future – and it was largely successful in persuading them to maintain their membership and support of an organization, and a Bill whose performance was not up to their expectations, and would leave them in the first instance excluded from the franchise. Attwood could shift the responsibility for not adopting the rhetoric of universal manhood suffrage from his shoulders and onto those of the ministry. The BPU could be quite effective, Attwood assured union members, keeping the Whigs up to scratch.

The first activity of the BPU in the new situation was a meeting on 7 March to approve a petition of support for the government, attended by over 15,000 people. But as the government was a Whig government, the local Whigs naturally were anxious to join in activities related to the Bill. Attwood, who had reached out to the Radicals and other reformers in Birmingham, now attached the BPU to the local Whigs and extended his network of reformers even further. At the Warwickshire county reform meeting on 4 April, the Union was there in force. As Samuel Tertius Glaton, one-time chairman of the Pitt Club, observed, 'The flags of the Political Union look beautiful ... but it was much regretted that the members of the Political Union took a prominent part in the business and thereby prevented the representatives of ancient country families from moving the principal resolutions.'[99] Following the meeting, the BPU sent an 'Address to the King' on the 9th and a petition to the House of Lords on 10 March. Attwood fretted over rumours that the Bill would not even get in to committee, and in spite of his protestations, the Council began talking about a general election and reform candidates. The BPU's agenda was to see the Whigs' Reform Bill became law and currency reformers returned in the new Parliament.

No further attention to the working-class union members, or more radical reform seemed desirable or necessary. The working-class Union members raised no objections, accepting that their support was necessary to help secure a bill that would extend no political benefit to them.

VII

Asa Briggs has written that the language of the BPU was not one that talked of abstract rights and liberties or indulged in the traditional Whig discussion of reform politics. The language of Attwood and the BPU instead stressed 'local interests and practical objectives, and capitalized on local hardship and distress'.[100] The BPU was an organization steeped in local concerns, particularly economic ones. Attwood's success in bringing reformers of various ideological persuasions into the leadership relied upon his ability to relate the distress of the economy to the 'Old Corruption' arguments, hardly an original idea, but one done to the satisfaction of Birmingham's industrious classes. This, as well as the ability to paint a plausible (if rather new and different) picture of a divided society – the unrepresented industrious classes versus the corrupt landed classes – enabled him to create the organization he did.

But also heard within the BPU were frank discussions of universal manhood suffrage, household suffrage and 'Old Corruption'. Certainly the rhetoric of taxation, monopolies, tariffs, length of Parliament and paper money were all targeting Brummagen wallets as a means of drawing people to the Union. While Edmonds and the more Radical members of the Union Council knew that Attwood sought currency reform alone as the panacea for the distress, they ignored his arguments and focused on securing electoral reform. Even Cobbett was both supportive and critical of the Union, uncertain as to the wisdom in denigrating the only reform organization of its kind because of a pragmatism which shunned ideological purity.

The BPU, in short, was an extra-parliamentary organization which made economic concerns its focus and parliamentary reform a means to an end, not the great principled goal of other reformers. It did not matter what *type* of parliamentary reform measure passed, provided it allowed for the representation of manufacturing and business interests and led to a currency reform measure. The BPU was also a tightly organized and led hierarchy in spite of its claim to be a popular political organization. While it linked the middle and working classes of Birmingham, the Union Council, dominated by wealthy businessmen and respectable Radicals, controlled all union activity and communication.

Attwood's charisma and emotionally charged speeches gave the Union its reputation and appeal, but Asa Briggs was wrong when he claimed that Attwood's 'philosophies provided the guiding principles of the Political Union'.[101] The majority of the Union did not embrace his ideas on currency and, as we have seen, it would be difficult to say what his 'philosophies' were on parliamentary reform: they changed with circumstances. Even close associates in the BPU's campaign like Joseph Parkes did not entirely trust Attwood to focus squarely on what was best in terms of political reform. It is perhaps for both these characteristics that the BPU failed to link up with the emerging Political Unions elsewhere. Attwood, the BPU and Political Unions everywhere were flexible in their campaigns for parliamentary reform.

It is, therefore, a fair question whether or not the BPU was the influence that it claimed to be among reformers. Was it, indeed, the model for the Political Unions which were popping up through the provinces from March 1830 and with greater frequency after the general election and the Whigs' taking office? *The Morning Chronicle* once commented that Attwood and the BPU claimed to lead a movement, but merely took credit for the work done independently by local reformers. 'The leaders [of the BPU] could have all the merit of their offers without any of the hazards' of going out into the country and organizing a political movement, running the risk of a legal response by the government.[102]

The following three chapters trace the creation and activities of the provincial political unions and test whether the *Morning Chronicle* was right. In looking at the Unions in three stages of the Reform Bill campaign, it should be possible to determine whether or not there was a national Political Union movement, and if so, whether the BPU was its dominating force and Attwood its leader, or merely an organization and individual who contributed enormously to the reform movement, but whose historical reputation has been slightly exaggerated.

LIVERPOOL
JOHN MOORES UNIVERSITY
AVRIL ROBARTS LRC
TITHEBARN STREET
LIVERPOOL L2 2ER
TEL. 0151 231 4022

2 The Creation of a Movement: Political Unions, March 1830–February 1831

Thomas Attwood may have created the first Political Union, but others immediately followed suit. Contrary to contemporary and historiographical assumptions, a number of towns and boroughs established extra-parliamentary reform organizations in order to petition the Tory government to draft a parliamentary reform measure. Economic distress and the long-standing criticisms of 'Old Corruption' affected more than Birmingham manufacturers and labourers. This chapter will look at those Political Unions that formed following the foundation of the BPU, but prior to the Whig government's introduction of a specific piece of reform legislation. It examines Political Unions unrestricted in their goals by the fears that excessive radicalism would jeopardize the success of government-sponsored reform legislation. Pragmatism and politicking were not yet a concern and thus these early Political Unions, founded before 1 March 1831, perhaps give the best indication of what reformers in England really believed was necessary in order to end 'Old Corruption', restore English political rights and liberties, and alleviate economic distress. If the BPU was indeed the 'dominant' and 'supreme' Political Union, as most contemporaries and historians have assumed, then logically one would also assume that provincial Political Unions would have modelled themselves after Attwood's Union, not only organizationally but also in the reform platform espoused by the BPU. This chapter will examine the new wave of Political Unions chronologically, in order of their creation, and compare the following characteristics with the BPU: rules for membership; style and structure of the organization in terms of leadership, participation, and the means of operation; and objectives – specifically whether or not parliamentary reform was the means to an end such as currency reform, as it was in Birmingham.

THE METROPOLITAN POLITICAL UNION

Although this study is primarily concerned with Political Unions in the English provinces, one of the first Political Unions to follow the BPU – and an important influence in the future of the Unions' extraparliamentary campaign – was not provincial but in London. In early March 1830, Henry Hunt, Daniel O'Connell and other Radicals called a public meeting at the Eagle Tavern in London, for the public to 'discuss the general [general] distress . . . [and the possibility of] obtaining an Effectual and Radical Reform in the Commons' House of Parliament' and to form 'a general Political Union between the middling and labouring classes of people of the metropolis'.[1] Hunt, discouraged by the failure of his Radical Reform Association to excite the public into doing anything about political reform, initially welcomed the creation of the BPU as a useful model for London. 'The reformers of Birmingham have cast the die,' he wrote to members of the Reform Association. 'They have set in motion this great, national, practical, political engine. . . . Let our exertions be to promote and to concentrate Union; let no consideration induce us to endanger Union, by departing one iota from the Birmingham plan, either in theory or practices.'[2] The MPU was to prove very different from the BPU in both the organizers' chief motivations for creating the organization and in the objectives sought. The MPU and Hunt would also offer very different reasons (and reasoning) for a campaign for parliamentary reform, one that relied less on economic rationales and more on the constitutional principles ingrained in the Anglo-Saxon and English tradition.

At the outset, Hunt's proposed Metropolitan Political Union declared its intention to 'campaign [for a reform bill] by petitions, addresses, and remonstrances to the Crown, and both or either of the Houses of Parliament, respecting *preservation* and *restoration* [*sic*] of public rights, and the principles of the free constitution of this realm which have been lost and which a real reform in Parliament would restore,' much like the plans announced by the BPU.[3] Hunt announced the first public meeting of the MPU for 8 March. Some 20,000 gathered in the grounds of the Eagle Tavern to hear Hunt describe this new organization that would fight for radical reform through 'constitutional and peaceful resistance'.[4] The MPU replicated the organization structure of the BPU with a 36-member Council and its criteria and rules for general and Council membership, but its objectives remained distinctly more radical than those of the midland Union.[5]

But Hunt and O'Connell founded their organization for the ultimate purpose of restoring Cartwright's ancient constitution and eliminating 'Old Corruption' rather than attaining currency reform. Reform was an end in itself for the organizers of the MPU, unlike their Birmingham counterparts. While Hunt's speeches gave much attention to economic inequities and the plight of many working people, he ignored the allegedly dire economic straits of manufacturers and bankers. Hunt attacked the entire political system as corrupt and a violation of the principles of the old constitution that supposedly had secured the rights and liberties of all Englishmen – and assumed, without being very specific, that reform would promote all legitimate economic interests.

Consequently, the MPU's objectives departed from those of the BPU. The MPU called for universal manhood suffrage, annual parliaments and the ballot, as the best means to clean up government corruption. These, of course, were three of the proposals in Major Cartwright's *Take Your Choice*. The justification for reform came from long-standing ideological beliefs. Attwood had also used 'Old Corruption' arguments to persuade Brummies of the need to join his Union, but his primary concern was fiscal reform and the BPU leaders (as well as their Birmingham critics) never lost sight of that.

Though initially quite popular with the London radical and reform communities, Hunt's appointment as treasurer of the organization was responsible for its almost immediate failure.[6] The MPU lost its membership of 'merchants, manufacturers, tradesmen, mechanics and artisans' almost as quickly as people had signed their names to the Unions rolls. Additionally, the MPU never drew the support of Radicals such as Francis Place and Francis Burdett, necessary supporters for any Radical organization in 1830. Though the Union Council met weekly at the Globe Tavern, it was, for the most part, invisible until the BPU publicly endorsed Blandford's reform proposal.[7] The MPU then denounced the Birmingham organization and tried to set itself up as the real Union of the people. New objectives and resolutions were drawn up and Hunt promoted the MPU heavily in the north.[8] Hunt's recruiting took him to the north, but the MPU in London, by then, was hardly functioning. In the provinces it was a different story.

ORGANIZATION IN THE PROVINCES DURING THE WELLINGTON GOVERNMENT

Reformers in Nottingham formed their Political Union in March 1830, approximately the same time as Hunt established the MPU.[9] The local press announced a public meeting to discuss the creation of a reform organization: 'a Political Union of middling and labouring classes for the protection of the public rights and prevent encroachments upon the rights of all classes by achieving an effective reform in Parliament'.[10] The Nottingham Political Union was the work of George Gill, a local lace agent and Robert Goodacre, the founder of the Standard Hill Academy (the most prestigious of the private schools in Nottingham), and it soon became a centre of radical politics and opposition to the powerful and close Whig Corporation. Though the Corporation would support the Grey ministry's reform measure, at the time of the Union's formation its founders viewed the Corporation as anything but open to political reform.

Richard Sutton, the editor of the *Nottingham Review*, was perhaps the most influential member of the Union Council and he used the paper to promote the Union and its proposals. He publicized the Union as a thoughtful attempt 'to rescue our common country out of its imminent periods, of almost inevitable ruin and desolation, and preserve us equally from the relentless fangs of despotism, on the one hand, and from the indiscriminate violence, the frantic horrors of anarchy, on the other.'[11] To do this, the Council offered the reforms of universal suffrage, the ballot and annual parliaments, which Sutton promoted as the best means for 'reformers, from all classes of society, [to] unite against the oppression of the people's rights . . . [and] enable ourselves to combine and concentrate our power and to give our final determination on pending topics an adequate impetus, an effective momentum.'[12] The Union also called for a significant reduction in the National Debt and all 'oppressive and intolerable taxation, the growing burden of the poors' rate'.[13] The abolition of pensions, monopolies, corn and game laws, and currency reform were also discussed at the meeting by perspective Union members.[14]

The Union's *Rules and Regulations* reflected the influence of the BPU in a way that its objectives did not. For one shilling per quarter, anyone could join the Nottingham Political Union, although the price of membership severely limited the number of workers who would be able to join. Apparently the founders did not find this problematic and later discussions of Union activity suggest that workers did join the Union. The annual meeting (to be held on the first Monday of July) would elect a Council of 36 who would manage the organization at weekly meetings. The Council would control all financial, legal and public activities of the Union between annual general membership meetings.[15]

Economic and 'Old Corruption' arguments were both clear in the Nottingham Union's proposal. The founders borrowed the structure of the BPU organization, the platform and justification for reform based on constitutional guarantees cited by the MPU and added local concerns – namely the Duke of Newcastle's electoral influence and the Whig Corporation's restrictions on economic development – to form a reform platform. Its members felt that these objectives, far from excessive, were 'strictly conservatory, [and] are calculated to restore the just rights and interests of the industrious classes . . .'[16] The Union platform indicated a particular commitment to one specific electoral reform, at least from the frequency of the discussions and the petitions drafted – the ballot.[17]

The Political Union Council consisted of the most powerful (and most ardent anti-Corporation) manufacturers in Nottingham. Some of the town's largest manufacturers joined the Union, including the hosier T.P. Sewell and Benjamin Boothby, the ironworks magnate. Parliamentary reform for them was a means to achieve Corporation reform and make local government more responsive to the changes in the new industrial society emerging in Nottingham. They took on the role of leaders of the Political Union.[18] Other Political Union members from the industrial community included William Taylor and Edmund Hart, both hosiers.[19] The Council estimated initial membership at 700.[20]

Not all opponents of the Corporation joined the Union. Radical Thomas Bailey, an opposition borough candidate in the 1830 election, did not join, fearing democratic tendencies. The longtime Radical John Blackner does not appear to have been an active member either, although there is no explanation for his absence. As demonstrated by Sutton's reports in the *Review,* however, this unwillingness among a few well-known reformers did not dissuade a new generation of political outsiders from giving it strong support.[21] But that group, and the Union's membership was still small as of July. The Council reported that,

> some are influenced by a fear that danger may result to them personally from thus associating together; others are withheld

from joining because those whom they have been in habit of regarding as their political pastors, are not taking an interest in the Union; while others are kept back [afraid] it [the Union] should have its influence in controlling the spirit of elections [resulting in] mere names prevailing to the great disadvantage of real political principles.[22]

In an attempt to attract more members, particularly among the working classes of Nottingham, the Council adopted a more radical position. It would put the Political Union in the position of advocating a greater political role for the industrious classes by pointing to municipal government, industrial concerns, and poor relief as the next stages of reform, but offering no specifics as to the nature of these reforms.[23] This strategy gave the Council, not the Corporation, more credibility with Nottingham labourers as advocates of radical political reform. William Shoults, later to become Secretary of the Union, encouraged framework-knitters to break with their custom of supporting *official* reform activities organized by the Corporation and to attend Political Union meetings instead, increasing the numbers within the Union.[24] Apparently there was no corresponding increase in members; failing to lower the membership dues might explain this. The *Nottingham Review* harangued those manufacturers and shopkeepers who had not registered at the newspaper's office for eschewing their natural leadership role in the Political Union.[25] Evidently, the middle and manufacturing classes believed there was more to be gained from an association with the Whig Corporation's reform agenda than the extra-parliamentary campaign of the Political Union. Both reforming camps, however, concurred that the first step was Wellington's resignation and a Whig ministry that would propose a Reform Bill.

The Union also adopted a test for future parliamentary representatives of the borough. The questions included whether the candidate would vote for a reform measure; would advocate 'a free trade in corn and exert [efforts] for the abolition of the East India Company monopoly'; and would support every motion for cutting 'profligate expenditure of public money'.[26] Though convinced that it would play an active role once a reform measure was adopted, the Nottingham Political Union inexplicably would remain quiet through the election of 1831 – until the local riots following the Reform Bill's defeat in the House of Lords the following October. Perhaps the Council believed that a low profile would antagonize the Corporation less than an active presence, and since they both sought the same thing, there was no reason to create any ill-will.

In April 1830, reformers in the unrepresented northern manufacturing town of Bolton organized a Political Union.[27] Master weavers William Naisby and John O'Brien founded the Union 'upon the same principles as the Birmingham Union, in order to render it palatable to all parties, and . . . not on the broad basis of annual parliaments, universal suffrage and vote by ballot.'[28] The need for some parliamentary representation in this growing textile town was obvious, as Naisby pointed out to growing numbers of middle class reformers and potential Union members:

> We have nothing to expect from Parliament as it is at present constituted, for the men who compose it are useless, except for the purpose of voting money out of the pockets of the people.[29]

John Asten, leader of the weavers' trade combination, explained that he had

> Used his utmost endeavours to prevail upon his fellow weavers to join the Union at its commencement. As ignorant as the Boltonmoor weavers are, little as they know of politics, they could see through the juggle. When the lower classes some years since had asked for reform they were cut down by the middle men, it was not likely they would join any plan of reform which would only be of benefit to those who had butchered them.[30]

Asten identified the first problem of 'unity' within the Union campaign. While the leaders of the Bolton Union tried to draw middle-class reformers into an organization whose goals would not seem threatening to their economic and social status, but rather compatible with their own need to seek parliamentary representation, the rejection of a radical reform platform alienated the weavers and working class of the town. The latter remembered only too well the reaction to earlier attempts at reform in the 1810s and were not at all eager to relive the government response.

Naisby and O'Brien offered a revised reform platform in the spring of 1830 in which they asked their fellow weavers to join them as 'we ask the King for Annual Parliaments, Universal Suffrage and Vote by Ballot'.[31] The Union soon afterwards adopted the proposal from the spring and, according to Naisby, 'its prospects are now of the most flattering nature.'[32] They criticized the BPU members for not standing firm on real reform, accusing many of its members of 'sign[ing] and voting away their privileges in anticipation of a reform measure which will serve twenty pound renters and householders.'[33] But in appealing to the weavers, the Bolton Political Union alienated moderate middle-class reformers. O'Brien invited them not just to join the Union, but to take on the role of director: 'I shall say unto them, do not for God's sake place us [the workers] in the front of the battle . . . [but if they lead the Union] they shall have all the assistance from us they may require.'[34] No evidence exists that O'Brien's plans met with success.

Little other information concerned the Bolton Political Union.[35] The local newspapers announced meetings of the Council, indicating that it did not disband, but did not publish any details of public meetings or debates. What is clear is that Bolton reformers had originally used the BPU's objectives as their own, but soon discovered that they needed to broaden the goals of the organization in order to attract workers. The Bolton Political Union, though attempting to create unity around the issue of parliamentary reform, was unable to succeed and instead, focused on creating a base of support from the town's artisans and workers. It adopted the radical platform of the MPU and seemingly abandoned attempts to bring middle-class moderates into their campaign.[36]

In contrast to the troubled attempt to create a Union in Bolton, April also saw the creation of smaller, but more successful Unions. The Keighley Political Union formed, described at the time as 'a branch of the BPU', although there is no evidence that there was any contact between local leaders and the BPU Council, or that Keighley had fiscal reform in mind along with electoral reform.[37] A Political Union also formed in Almondbury, 'respectfully requesting [Henry Hunt] to become leader and adviser', but beyond one petition to the King, no evidence exists that the organization lasted beyond the autumn of 1830.[38] Though Union leaders here also saw the BPU as their model, they adopted the MPU's platform of universal manhood suffrage, annual parliaments and the ballot.

During the last months of the reign of George IV, only a handful of Political Unions existed throughout the country. The BPU might be expected to receive attention, but the Union received hardly any notice, either from Wellington's Tory government or from the ageing monarch. There is no mention of Political Unions in Home Office reports or in any memoranda between the King and the Duke of Wellington. Undoubtedly, the government felt that these few Unions were not threatening, particularly as there was no chance that the Tories would propose a reform measure.[39] Indeed, Wellington's information was that Attwood was a 'crank' solely concerned with currency reform who 'thinks it unattainable except by means of reform in Parliament.'[40] The reports that the BPU's 'chief doings have been to interfere in local politics and to interrupt the more respectable part of the town in effecting measures for the good of the town', no doubt alleviated any fears Wellington might have had as to the Union's power to do real mischief.[41]

The Unions themselves displayed little suspicious or threatening behaviour. Even the Bolton Political Union – one of the most radical in their goals and their tone – displayed, if not preferred loyalty, at least a lack of republicanism in its rhetoric when it claimed as its objective, to ask 'the King for Annual Parliaments, Universal Suffrage and Vote by Ballot'.[42] Other acknowledgements of the King's power and authority were present in the Keighley Political Union's petition to the King.[43] When, in a parliamentary speech on the Marquis of Blandford's reform motion, Sir Francis Burdett referred to the BPU, declaring that the rejection of any reform would 'unite the whole country with the people of Birmingham in demanding fair and full reform', the government did not react with alarm, publicly or privately.[44]

There was a short lull in the creation of provincial Political Unions in the spring of 1830. In June, George IV died. William IV was unique among Hanoverian monarchs in judging political reform as an effective tool in maintaining peace and order in his kingdom. His concern that reform should not be interpreted as a weakening of the Crown was understandable and made this a criterion for any reform measure his new government might present in Parliament. Now, the Tories faced an election at time of increasing public support for parliamentary reform and a more amenable monarch.

The Whigs played to reform interests as Grey and other leaders met a deputation from the BPU in London in early July, just before the elections.[45] Though the meeting seemed to focus on legislation in the Lords concerning the Governors of the free grammar schools, the connection was an important one for the future of parliamentary reform and extra-parliamentary agitation. The Whigs made clear to the public and King that they were the party of reform.

Though the Whigs did not win the election, they were returned in greater number to the House of Commons. No Political Unions formed during the election to promote or encourage reformers in their campaign efforts, but certainly the growing interest in these reform organizations and Grey's meeting with BPU leaders reflected the improving prospects of turning out an anti-reform government and replacing it with a Whig ministry, reform legislation and, many hoped, a working alliance with Political Unions.

With the changing political winds, more Political Unions formed. Between the summer and autumn of 1830, 12 new Political Unions emerged. Thomas Leadbetter formed the first of these Unions in Kirkheaton. This small Political Union, like those in Nottingham and Bolton, embraced Radical reform on the model of the MPU. Its *Objectives* called for universal suffrage and other Radical reforms.[46] At this time, reports circulated that Salford had formed a Political Union, rumours that historians have accepted as fact,[47] but for which no evidence exists. October saw the formation of two new Political Unions. The Chorley Political Union's goal was the restoration of 'the civil rights of the people and [the] promotion . . . [of] a Radical reform in the House of Commons, upon the principles of short parliaments, vote by ballot and universal suffrage'.[48] Union members tried to link it to 'Hunt's Great Northern Union' – a circle of northern cities that were sites of a regular speech-making itinerary for the Radical orator, but were not an organization. Though he assisted local reformers in drafting an address to the King, there is no further evidence of Hunt's connection to the organization.[49]

The other northern Union was formed in Stockport.[50] There, Political Unionists, under the leadership of George B. Cheetham, voted for a reform platform of universal suffrage, triennial parliaments and vote by ballot.[51] Some referred to the Stockport Political Union as 'a gentlemen's union' as its organization grew from a suggestion made by the MP for Stafford, Edward Davenport. Davenport served as an honorary chair of the Union, although he never actually joined it.[52] After the initial meetings, the Stockport Political Union remained inactive until the general election of 1831. Then, with the workers of the Manchester Political Union, its working-class members severed ties with Davenport and formed a new Radical reform organization.[53] It is not clear whether middle-class members continued to meet after the split. As was the case in Bolton, cooperation between middle- and working-class reformers in some industrial towns proved too difficult, particularly after the announcement of the Whig Reform Bill. Even the helpful hand of a seasoned politician failed to keep reformers in Stockport focused on the value of reform for reform's sake.

Plans had been mooted since September for a Liverpool Political

Union of the middle and lower classes, initiated by the town's radical Dissenters. Meetings had taken place and plans hammered out in the autumn. Notable members of the Liverpool Political Union and most useful for political purposes were Egerton Smith and John Smith, joint editors of the *Liverpool Mercury*.[54] Another of the organizers, a shoemaker named G.P. Payne, emphasized that the purpose 'of societies like this [the Political Union] was to debate on the nature of reforms necessary and work so that the people at large, high and low, rich and poor, [would all] be effectively represented.'[55] Newspaper announcements promised that

> the subscription [to the Union] (which will be devoted to the conversion of Tories by means of publications, etc., tending to convince them of their errors,) will be but small, sufficiently small to be no hindrance to any one who desires to promote the welfare of his country; and the respectability of the society, if sufficient number of persons come forward to induce the most influential reformers in the town to join them, will be second to that of no party in Liverpool.[56]

Organizers recorded the names of 84 subscribers in September and October, before they presented any rules or manifestoes to the public, or made any formal announcement of Union's creation. Thomas Bolton, Thomas Thornely and James Cropper, all merchants, Thomas Smith, bookseller (and future parliamentary candidate for Bolton), William W. Currie, an insurance broker, and Colonel Williams, a gentleman farmer, framed the Union's constitution.[57] They became the Union Council and presided over an organization that looked very similar to its predecessors.

The Liverpool Political Union general membership adopted its rules in November 1830, formally defining Union members as one paying at least 1d per week or 1s per quarter. The Union granted the general management of the organization to a Council of 25, chosen at general meetings 'subject only to the control of such general meetings'.[58] The Council appointed all officers and spent the funds of the organization, uncontrolled between elections.[59]

More than most other Unions, the Liverpool Union suggested the adoption of the BPU model, both organizationally and in its commitment to keep middle- and working-class reformers harmoniously focused on a single objective. The Union membership voted this its primary objective at its inaugural meeting held on 24 November at the York Hotel. Samuel Tucker, a local liquor dealer chaired the meeting and summed up the members' primary objective: 'uniting for the exercise of a constitutional privilege – the vote.'[60] Other goals included the dissolution of the existing union between church and state; the election and payment of clergymen by their own congregations; a revision in the calculation of poor law payments; a substantial reduction in the Civil List; the abolition of all commercial monopolies, the East India Company in particular; a reduction in the half-pay list; a reduction in the standing army; and a revision or the abolition in the Corn Laws.[61] Attwood and the BPU would certainly have rejected these goals as too radical and the unity in the organization connecting Tories, Whigs and Radicals, not to mention the middle and working classes, would undoubtedly have ended in acrimony. Radicals in Liverpool, however, had long discussed free trade and the impact of expanding the home market on overseas trade as well as opportunities to challenge Corporation authority, so such objectives were not new.[62]

The Union drafted and forwarded a petition to the House of Commons in late December 1830 calling for radical reform including universal suffrage and the ballot.[63] One newspaper described the Union as having among its ranks 'a number of gentlemen of the first respectability and had, but the following year, over 4,000 members.'[64] But despite its upstanding reputation, presumably because it was a close Tory Corporation, the mayor and magistrates of Liverpool took every opportunity to cancel Union meetings and public rallies sponsored by the Union.[65]

In focusing on local political concerns, the Liverpool Union again demonstrated ties to the BPU. But the former's adoption of universal suffrage also reflected the great differences between parliamentary reformers who had no fear of a popular franchise, and indeed saw it as the key to end a whole host of political and economic abuses, and Attwood, who saw the vote as merely as a key to currency reform. While the Liverpool Political Union saw similarities between their organization and the BPU, the differences between them were clearly significant. In the first instance, Liverpool was a parliamentary borough whereas Birmingham was not. The long-standing power of the Liverpool Corporation and all the privileges of freemen and guild members coloured politics and political ideology far more than in Birmingham. A trading port, Liverpool felt the economic depression, but Birmingham's industrial community had few economic options beyond manufacturing. In short, Liverpool's reformers had far more to lose than their Birmingham counterparts in forming a Political Union and demanding parliamentary reform. The town would not lose its parliamentary representatives if legislation redistributed MPs, but a number of tradesmen might well lose their freeman status and their electoral rights. Like those in Nottingham, Liverpool's Unionists chose to fight 'Old Corruption' at the Corporation level in the form of a Union campaign for parliamentary reform. Their insistence that the government protect English constitutional rights and reform itself of its worst abuses linked their interests with the unrepresented of the north and midlands.

More Political Unions formed in the north. According to a Home Office informant, another Political Union began forming around Carlisle. Though there is little information concerning the goals of this mixed weavers' and master-manufacturers' Union, a petition drafted at a meeting of 4000 people indicated that they would only settle for Radical reforms, including universal suffrage.[66] The Union County magistrates and Council men intended to watch the Union's activities and membership drives carefully. In Mansfield, a Union also formed, calling specifically for universal suffrage and the ballot. Though there were only 35 enrolled members at the outset, the Union members resolved that broad changes were necessary in parliamentary representation.[67]

With every additional Union and the beginning of the Swing riots in the autumn, the Tories finally reacted to the increased 'outdoor' agitation. The first notice of the Political Unions in the Duke of Wellington's correspondence appeared on 1 October. Thomas Claney reported to Wellington that Henry Brougham's journey north had produced a political attack on the Duke. In Birmingham, Claney claimed that the BPU 'caused some difficulties' for the Duke in that it cheered Brougham, but he reassured Wellington that 'a mob can always be found for ale'.[68]

In November, the Home Office, under Robert Peel, began collecting reports from informants concerning Political Union activity. One informant assured Peel that 'the source of all this mischief that has already occurred and that may be apprehended lies in a nutshell. Put down with a bold hand, the Political Union Clubs and Trade Combination Societies which are one in existence and linked together by correspondence throughout the manufacturing districts . . .'[69] Peel also heard that the BPU member had 'the express intention of intimidating the Government' and appeared 'likely to become, indeed . . . a most dangerous body.'[70] But even with such information, the Home Office did not recommend that any action be taken against the nascent Union movement.

Nor did the Tories take any action towards reform. Frustrated members of the Liverpool Political Unionist Samuel Tucker, put it well: 'The ministry had become odious to the great body of the people; the head of it could not appear abroad in safety... In short, it was manifest that the ministers must go out.'[71]

POLITICAL UNIONS, THE WHIGS AND WILLIAM IV

The Whig ministry formed when Wellington's government lost on a vote on the Civil List. The Tories resigned and William asked Lord Grey to form a new ministry. The Whigs came to power and the Unions revelled in Lord Brougham's promise that he would support a reform motion and fully expected one from the new government. Reformers again saw the creation of Political Unions as an opportunity to show politicians and the King how committed they were to reform and the nature of the reforms they believed necessary to correct the abuses of power and 'Old Corruption'. William IV was also interested in reform – as an effective tool in maintaining peace and order in his kingdom. His concern that reform should not be interpreted as a weakening of the Crown was understandable and made this a criterion for any reform measure his new government might to present in Parliament.

Sir Herbert Taylor, the King's secretary, wrote to Grey: 'His Majesty feels the importance of introducing the [reform] measure, if it must be introduced, as a measure of the Government, divested, as far as it may be possible, of all that is calculated to deprive the Monarchy of its legitimate rights and attributes...'[72] The King also made plain to his new chief minister that he would not 'support measures of a democratic and revolutionary tendency... or vote for universal suffrage, election by ballot, annual Parliaments, further reduction of the Civil List, other popular measures leveled at the dignity of the Crown... [or any] destruction of the monarchy and of every existing establishment.'[73]

Grey tried to reassure the King that he would limit reform and enfranchise only the most respectable men: 'A great change has taken place in all parts of Europe since the end of the war in the distribution of property [and] this change requires a greater influence to be yielded to the middle classes, who have made wonderful advances both in property and intelligence.'[74] Others in office also made reassuring statements. Althorp talked of only 'placing the franchise as much as possible in the hands of the middle classes'. Lord Palmerston insisted that the Reform Bill must 'include a vast proportion of the more respectable of the middle classes of the country' in the new electorate.[75] Lord Durham also stressed that the proposal should 'attach numbers to property and good order' and a contemporary observer assured the government that 'any plan must be objectionable which, by keeping the Franchise very high and exclusive, fails to give satisfaction to the middle and respectable ranks of society . . .'[76]

The agreement to present a reform measure to Parliament thrilled the Political Unionists, but, ironically, the actual prospect of reform and the Unions' perception that they had persuaded the King to change his position only roused his suspicion of Unions. The King now had to consider what parliamentary reform might mean to the institution of the monarchy. He rejected the definition of Union as meetings 'of respectable men of means gathering together to discuss philosophical issues and pragmatic reasons for political and economic change.'[77] Rather he saw them as revolutionary gatherings of 'miners, manufacturers, colliers, labourers, form[ing] unions for the furtherance of illegal purposes, [which] would assemble on every point in support of a popular question, [and] declare [their] object of carrying the [reform] measure by intimidation.'[78] He remained convinced that 'many of these Political Unions . . . owe their origin to the Trades Unions, combinations formed for illegal purposes.'[79] The aristocratic Grey also believed this to be at least partly true, but chose to appeal to the middle-class constituency of the Unions, believing that that class alone 'form[ed] the real and efficient mass of public opinion . . . without whom the power of the gentry is nothing.'[80] Still, public assertions such as those in the *Examiner* claiming that 'at no time within the last century was ever such direct expression given to a determination on the part of the middle classes to obtain their rights by force, should their peaceable demands be rejected' were hardly reassuring.[81]

Lord Melbourne became the Home Secretary in the Grey government and began acquiring his own sources of information concerning the Unions and extra-parliamentary political activity in the provinces, displaying greater interest, if not necessarily concern, about the creation and operation of Political Unions. On the whole, the description of the Unions from Home Office informants presented a very tame picture of the membership. 'Political Unions are composed of persons who have long been Reformers and who have been at different times for some years,' reported J. Stafford to Lord Melbourne.[82] J. Ford described the Unions to Lord Talbot, who passed the information on Melbourne: 'the official character of "the Unions" are in general clerks in the manufactures and the manufacturers.'[83] Rather than persuading Melbourne to 'put down with a bold hand, the Political Union Clubs', as Peel had, this new information suggested that Unionists were not dangerous and were, in fact, so proper in demeanour themselves that they would 'denounce anyone who uses stronger language'.[84] Such information reassured the King. He did not trust the Political Unions, but, at least initially, he did trust his government to deal with them appropriately. And a government policy seemed all the more necessary as Political Unions formed with even greater frequency once the Whigs took over the government.

POLITICAL UNIONS AND THE WHIG MINISTRY

The first Union formed after Grey and the Whigs took office was in Newark-on-Trent. This Political Union focused mostly on the desire of the community to be able to vote without fear of retaliation by the Duke of Newcastle. Not surprisingly, the ballot dominated the discussion, the problem being given graphic illustration because the meeting was held at the Old Assembly Halls, the tenant of which, Mr Newton, had been given notice to quite the premises by the Duke, 'on account of his having thought proper at the last election to do what he pleased with his own vote'.[85] The only mention of the BPU was a reference made of its 'establishment of a tract society, which has published tracts containing all the information necessary to the society, and have thus diffused the sentiments of the Council to every member of the union. He [Newton] would suggest the establishment of a tract society in Newark, they would soon find the benefit arising from such a measure . . .'[86]

Another large Political Union formed in Manchester. Manchester faced rapid and overwhelming change in the early nineteenth century. Both the commercial capital of the cotton district of Lancashire and a factory town, Manchester was crowded with middle- and working-class advocates of representation for the town. Since Peterloo, Manchester's Radicals and reformers began to challenge the Tory oligarchy that dominated town affairs.[87] Middle-class reformers particularly sought free trade and factory workers protection as labourers. The first step in both cases was parliamentary reform and an independent representative for the growing industrial constituency. The politicization of labour union membership by John Doherty, the Irish newspaper publisher as well as secretary of the Manchester Spinners' Union, and co-founder of the National Association for the Protection of Labour, made parliamentary reform a prominent issue. William Cobbett was also influential in linking the two issues of labour interests and reform. As a result, Manchester reformers agreed that reform was necessary in order to accomplish several agendas – but agreeing on the nature of that reform or how to pursue it was another matter. Historian Nicholas Edsall has said that the Manchester Union was significantly different from the BPU in that Manchester reformers 'had not fixed idea of what they were gong to use their political union for'.[88]

In its original form, the Manchester Political Union arose from a public proposal by Jonathan Hodgins, the local cotton spinners' union leader in August 1830. While the suggestion to create a Political Union of the middle and working classes to demand parliamentary reform came from a working man, the middle-class reformers in the town soon took control of the process. Radical newspaper publisher Archibald Prentice set about creating a Political Union in which 'the people make themselves master of the arguments of universal suffrage, the vote by ballot, and against monopolies and restrictions of rights.'[89] Contacting radical London reformers and Henry Hunt, Prentice obtained the constitution of the Metropolitan Political Union and used it as a model for the Manchester Political Union, including specific radical reform proposals in the Rules and Regulations, namely universal manhood suffrage, the ballot and annual parliaments.[90]

On 24 November 1830, the Union met at the Manchester Mechanics' Institute and formally adopted a set of objectives for the organization. They included, apparently in order of importance, the extension of the suffrage for every male at least 21 years old, 'who contributes to the expenditure of the State'; vote by ballot; repeal of the Corn Laws; repeal of Taxes on Knowledge, among a number of taxes; the abolition of monopolies, the East India Company in particular; and the abolition of slavery.[91] In pursuing all these, the Union leadership promised that the organization would exhibit 'a strict and dutiful obedience to the Laws.'[92]

Like the BPU, the Manchester Political Union was to be 'essentially popular', allowing anyone to join the organization who could afford dues of one shilling per quarter. A general annual meeting would be held (on the second Wednesday in November), but the daily management of the organization would be the responsibility of the Council, 36 men chosen at the annual meeting and responsible for the employment of Union funds, as well as distribution of information to all Union members. Council members' duties included observing 'the proceedings of the Legislature, and the Local Authorities of this Town and Neighbourhood'.[93] Members pledged themselves to be 'good, faithful and loyal subjects of the King [and] to obey the laws of the land, . . . protect the Rights, Liberties and Interests of the Community, endeavour[ing] to get them changed by just, legal and peaceful means only.'[94] The Union's tactics included parliamentary petitions and the selection of delegates to establish connections with other Political Unions and observe affairs in London, reporting home on any developments affecting a reform measure.[95]

The first Manchester Political Union Council consisted of five industrialists, including Thomas and John Fielden, six shopkeepers of various sorts, six drapers, seven weavers and wool-sorters, a tea-dealer, a corn-dealer, a clerk, a gentleman, a printer and assorted craftsmen.[96] The Council would run the daily operations of the Union, promote reform, the activities of the organization and the continued discussion of further economic and political reform, and would scrutinize the membership of the Political Union so that the character of the organization remained respectable and peaceful.

At its 1 December meetings, the Council resolved that a membership oath be required of all prospective members. Drafted by the Radical Rowland Destrosier and Council members P.T. Candelet and Elijah Dixon, the procedure for becoming a member of the Manchester Union provided for the screening of individuals, by the requirement that all nominations come from the Union's executive body, and that applicants produce signatures from two householders attesting to 'personal knowledge that [the individual] is a man of good moral character and . . . a fit and proper person.'[97] No other Political Union required any scrutiny of membership, but objections from Nathan Broadhurst, a fustian cutter and representative of working men on the Council, were ignored. Though Broadhurst did not agree with most of the economic concerns of the industrialists and businessmen on the Council, he failed to understand why they would want to adopt a policy so potentially alienating to working-class reformers and detrimental to the idea of 'union' itself.

Prentice and other middle-class members of the Manchester Political Union clearly hoped to ensure that the Union did not become a haven for 'rag-tag revolutionaries'.[98] The ostensible argument for such careful selection of members was that a disreputable Union would not be taken seriously by the government. The Manchester Political Union was the only organization of its kind to impose such restrictions on membership. Character assessments by the Council were unique. In Manchester, 'unity' was part of the definition of the Union, but what might seem discriminating selection to some was bound to be seen as simple discrimination by others.

Nonetheless, it did not initially deter the working classes of Manchester from joining the organization, in spite of the membership fees. Within weeks the Union boasted approximately 3,000 members. Although there is no evidence that the Council ever rejected any prospective Union members, the scrutiny by the Council no doubt left an unfortunate impression on some of Manchester's working-class Union members. Still, Doherty threw his support behind Prentice's Manchester Political Union and this brought hundreds of spinners into the organization; and with the start of Doherty's new publication, the *Voice of the People*, there was a highly effective means of communication open to reformers in and beyond Manchester. Following the publication of the first issue in December 1830, membership in the Political Union rose by 1,000.[99]

Despite this outward success in joining reformers together in a single extra-parliamentary organization in Manchester, the attitude of the middle-class Council members would, not surprisingly, cause tensions between themselves and the working-class members of the rank and file, and ultimately result in a permanent rift in the organization. The Union circulated petitions to Parliament, but the tensions mounting between the Council and the working-class membership rendered it a largely ineffective organization.[100]

The founders issued a prospectus for the Sheffield Political Union in November 1830, although did not hold a public meeting until January 1831, thus allowing interested supporters to subscribe at the offices of the *Sheffield Independent*.[101] The Union's first meeting was in the Town Hall and more than 1,000 people attended.[102] Thomas Asline Ward, former editor of the *Sheffield Independent,* chaired the first meeting where numerous speeches were made concerning the necessity of parliamentary reform. One of the highest priority goals mentioned at this meeting was the Union's intent 'to prevent and redress, as far as practicable, all local public wrongs and oppressions, and all local encroachments upon the rights, interests, and privileges of the community.... If the Union promised nothing more than this, it would be sufficient to justify its establishment.'[103] Bramley pointed out that whatever the reaction to the creation of the organization, 'the objects of the Political Union... are conservatory and strictly legal.... It is no agitating society, its members are neither turbulent nor dangerous.'[104] After adopting a list of objectives such as universal suffrage, and rules that looked like most other Political Union constitutions, the iron manufacturer and Council member, Luke Palfreyman urged, and the Union accepted, the adoption of the ballot as a specific goal of the organization.[105]

The Union grew out of the town's largely Unitarian elite. Among its founding members were Asline Ward, Robert Leader, current editor of the *Independent*, Isaac Ironside, cutlery manufacturer, Radical, Congregationalist and future Chartist leader, Dr Arnold Knight, co-founder of the Sheffield Medical Institution Dr. G.C. Holland of the Sheffield School of Anatomy and Medicine; and cutlery manufacturers Benjamin Sayle, Ebeneezer Rhodes, Isaac Ironside and John Bramhall.[106] Rhodes, who had been master cutler in 1809, had turned to newspaper writing. (Ward had also been a master cutler and was a successful manufacturer who was very political and described himself as a democratic Bethamite.) These men promoted the Union to the townspeople as a necessity.[107] 'It appears', circulated printed reports declared, that 'we have within ourselves some eligible means of collecting and expressing the public opinion with energy and effect, now that Sheffield has not only attained to such commercial and intellectual importance in the scale of British towns, but when, to a moral certainty, it will be called upon to return its representatives to Parliament in a very short time.'[108]

The Home Office became aware of the Sheffield Political Union, but received assurances that 'there are good names in it, and men you can trust.... The Union's movements may do good by helping push reforms as a necessity.... The Union's objects are not incompatible with public security.'[109] The only mention of the BPU at this meeting was made by Palfreyman, who wondered if the Union should not follow the example of the BPU and provide its members with a distinctive means of identification. He advocated the adoption of a Sheffield Political Union badge.

Northerners formed another Political Union in Todmorden, thanks in large part to John Fielden, the Unitarian industrialist and factory reformer.[110] Both he and his brother Thomas were founding members of the Manchester Political Union, but their base was in Todmorden where they were pillars of the reform-minded Methodist Unitarian chapel.[111] They believed it in their best interests, and the best interests of a serious reform movement, to form another organization. An organization in their own town could address the concerns of local businessmen and workers in a way that belonging to the larger Manchester Union could not. 'Nothing [was] better calculated to promote the redressing of grievances, from both the middle and labouring classes, for petitioning the King and Parliament on the subject of reform, than a local Political Union, guided and directed by the town's best men from both classes,' wrote Fielden to his friend John Doherty, trade union leader, radical reformer and publisher of the *Voice of the People*.[112]

John Fielden became president of the Todmorden Union, and his brother named its treasurer. The names of 21 manufacturers and bankers, a surgeon, many members of the Methodist Unitarian Church, were registered as the members of the Council.[113] Other Council members represented both the town's middle class and skilled and artisan community: James Hardman, surgeon, and John Hill, cabinetmaker, for example.

In January 1831, the Union sent an address to the King pleading for mercy on behalf of those arrested for their alleged role in the Swing Riots of 1830.[114] In February, when it adopted its *Rules and Regulations*, the Union's objectives were nearly identical to those adopted in Manchester. Among the objectives the Todmordern Unionists shared with other Political Unions were a desire to repeal the stamp tax, abolish monopolies, advocate free trade and abolish slavery – concerns never addressed by the BPU. The Union also resolved to 'devise means to preserve the Peace and Order of the town and neighbourhood during any disturbances arising from political excitement.'[115] Religious equality was obviously important to the Nonconformist component of the Todmorden Political Union. John Mitchell pushed the Union to embrace the disestablishment of the Anglican Church as a Union objective, denouncing the 'spurious Christianity of the Church as established . . . [and the] ruby-nosed Bishops and dignitaries of our state-religion.'[116] Again, these reforms went well beyond the BPU's objectives and yet were part of the long-standing radical platform and goals long sought by generations of reformers. The Todmorden Political Union possessed a more encompassing vision of what parliamentary reform could change than many provincial Unions, but particularly surpassed Attwood's limited vision of paper money.

Perhaps it was a result of this more radical stance towards reform that the Todmorden Union became more and more removed from the Manchester Union. Fielden dissociated himself completely from the latter when the Union split and physical force was encouraged by the working-class Unionists.[117] Peace and order were of the essence to the Todmorden Political Union. Without them, the Union despaired of success of any reform measure.

The Worcester Political Union began to agitate for reform in December as well.[118] Its organizers, led by printer and businessman Isaac Arrowsmith, described it as 'a Union of the labouring and middle classes of the people' whose 'objects being strictly conservatory, are calculated in restoring the just rights and interests of the industrious classes, to confirm the constitutional privileges of the aristocracy and to preserve every class from the common anarchy which threatens all.'[119] The goal of the Union was 'an entire parliamentary reform . . . which shall make the House of commons in reality what it now is only in name, – a Reform which shall secure to every Member of the Body Politic, his full and free voice in the enactment of all Laws, the imposition of all Taxes, and in every other Act connected with the Government of his country.'[120] In this manufacturing town, the major cause for concern was economic, with production and wages low and unemployment high.[121] The Union's *Rules and Regulations* specifically called for the vote by ballot as a reform believed essential, though nowhere was there any mention of universal manhood suffrage or annual parliaments.

In contrast to Manchester, the Worcester Union made it a point to encourage reformers of all social classes and ranks to join the organization without any sponsorships and behavioural scrutiny. Its rules specified open membership, inviting anyone to join, but like other Unions, required a stiff membership fee of one shilling per quarter. The Union Council also encouraged 'subscriptions of noblemen and gentlemen' as it wanted, above all, to promote a reputation that reflected the goals of the organization: to secure, 'peace, order, unity and LEGALITY [*sic*] of our proceedings; and to consider all persons as enemies who shall in any way invite or promote violence, discord, or division, or any illegal or doubtful measures.'[122] It was the belief of those who joined the Union that 'the present distressed state of the country has its origin in the present corrupt and tyrannical abuses which have crept into the Peoples' House of Representatives.'[123] The Worcester Union's membership surged, with 1,500 dues-paying members, and more than 10,000 attending public meetings by mid-1831.

The communities of Huddersfield and Wolverhampton both established Political Unions in December.[124] The Huddersfield Political Union was the work of small shopkeepers and craftsmen. Founders and Council members included James Brooks, clothdresser, Thomas Vever, publican, John Heaton, grocer, and Samuel Dickinson, George Beaumont, John Hanson and Charles Littlewood, retailers.[125] They did not equivocate about what kind of reform in thought necessary. Their Political Union's objectives included universal manhood suffrage, annual parliaments and the ballot. The Union leaders also called for free public education for all and a restructuring of the Poor Relief system and 'a more equitable division of the burden among the richer parts of the community'.[126]

The town's bankers, specifically Alexander Horden and Richard Wightwick, formed the Wolverhampton Political Union. The Council, consisting of businessmen and artisans, met once a week at the Star Inn to discuss tactics for acquiring both parliamentary reform and grievances such as 'mis-spent taxes and the privileged status of the Anglican Church'.[127] Richard Fryer, a West Midlands businessman, was also a member of the Union. His concerns were economic and he concluded that parliamentary reform was the only way to achieve economic change. As he told the members of the Wolverhampton Union, 'Fifty years ago we were not in that need for representatives which are at present . . . we now manufacture for the whole world, and if we have not members to promote and extend our commerce, the era of commercial greatness is at an end.'[128] He was not especially concerned with 'all [the] fiddle-de-de about Old Sarum – Stick to the Repeal of the Corn Laws and vote by ballot.'[129] Finally, there was sentiment similar to Attwood's in the provincial Union leadership: reform was a means to an end. In Fryer's view, that end was broader economic rather than currency reform, but nonetheless expressed the same pragmatic, rather than ideological commitment to parliamentary reform.

The initial organization of the Leeds Political Union also occurred in December. The expansion of machinery and the factory system in the town's production of woollen cloth had had a profound impact on the economic and social systems of Leeds. Traditional spinners and weavers were in dire straits, and in the early 1830s industrial struggle between workers and employers was a dominant feature of Leed's life.[130] Some middle-class men also focused on the inequity exhibited in the enterprise and wealth of the town and its lack of parliamentary representation. Edward Baines, according to his son,

> centered his attention on political rather than industrial issues, crying abuses of the old system – the represented boroughs without inhabitants, the unrepresented boroughs with a population and wealth like those of capital cities, the extreme and ridiculous inequalities in the extent of the suffrage, the enormous expense and great temptations to corruption and debauchery attendant upon elections of seven to fifteen days' continuance, the inconvenience of having only one polling place for large counties, the heavy cost of out-voters . . .[131]

The Leeds Political Union began with Baines and a meeting of the towns Radicals – notably Dissenters and members of the Mill Hill Congregation (Joseph Priestley being a former minister). The founding members included, among others, Thomas Bischoff, a captain in the cavalry, the physician Bemjamin Hird, wool merchant Slater Milnes, James Mann, a bookseller, along with such notables as Joseph Brotherton, John Edward Taylor, editor of the *Manchester Guardian*, and William Wood, the minister of Mill Hill. Other known members included John Hebblethwaite, a shopkeeper, Richard Potter, a blacksmith, and George Philips, a tailor. All these men, with the exception of Baines, were also members of Mill Hill.

The Political Union at first appeared to be a reorganization of existing radical groups, known collectively as the Leeds Association.[132] The Association had called for extensive electoral reform, specifically a significant extension of suffrage (though not necessarily universal suffrage), annual parliaments, the ballot, as well as the elimination of trade tariffs and taxes and the abolition of slavery in British colonies. While the Leeds Association seems a BPU clone, its leaders did not intend that the Association would be such a public organization. The Association apparently disappeared as its leaders called a public meeting and announced plans for a Leeds Political Union of the middle and working classes which would 'promote peace and union, collect and organize the peaceful expression of public opinion, so as to act upon the legislature in a just, legal and effectual way . . . [which would] respect the preservation and restoration of public rights . . .'[133]

The Leeds Political Union did not do very much during the first phase of the reform agitation as its membership was divided about supporting a limited a reform measure. The working-class members wanted their middle-class counterparts to endorse their claims that only universal manhood suffrage would be acceptable. Baines and the others were unwilling to jeopardize the clear promise of a parliamentary voice for themselves, and no more wanted to see the working classes voting than they wanted to remain under the political authority of the aristocracy. The Union would eventually split and a more radical and predominately working-class union of the Leeds working population would form in November 1831.[134]

In addition to information sent to the Home Office about the Leeds Union, Melbourne had also received word from various informers regarding other Political Unions forming in the provinces, although there is no evidence to that effect in local newspapers or correspondence. According to R.J. Ford, a Political Union had been formed in the Potteries in February 1831.[135] He claimed that a group of 'deputies' had come from Lancashire and were trying to organize a Union among the 'miners and journeyman potters of Hanley and Shelton'.[136] Ford assured the Home Office that the Potteries were peaceful, but did claim that some master potters were frightened of reprisals if they tried to dissuade their workers from forming such a Union – 'a few are suspected of giving secret encouragement to their men to join the Union'.[137]

Joseph Haley was far more nervous about the prospect of a Political Union in the Potteries. His letter to Lord Melbourne requested a parish constabulary to be sent as he was 'considerably agitated by the political association who meet under the specious names of Union and Radical Union'.[138] He claimed the members were joining in considerable numbers and that they were all 'the ignorant and lower classes in this mining neighbourhood'.[139]

Still another Staffordshire Union was reported to have formed in the area around Wednesbury and West Bromwich in February. The informant warned the Home Office that the purpose of this organization was 'to excite a spirit of discontent, disloyalty, insubordination and even rebellion itself among the ignorant but otherwise good subjects of His most excellent Majesty'.[140] Letters to the Home Office described the formation of Political Unions in Durham and Bradford, but little information exists about the composition and goals of the organizations.[141] Indeed, other than a brief mention of the Bradford handweaver and comber, trade unionist and future Chartist leader Peter Bussey participating is a local Political Union, there is no additional evidence that these Political Unions actively functioned during the Reform Bill agitation.[142] A Union in Berkshire was also initially reported in a local newspaper.[143]

The government concluded that this was now a Union movement rather than merely localized actions of a few individuals. More Unions operated in the provinces and, as the Home Office archives reveal, the government was aware of their positions and rhetoric concerning reform, law and order, and loyalty to the monarch. For example, the Worcester Political Union stressed that its 'objects . . . were to confirm constitutional privileges of the aristocracy and to preserve every class from the common anarchy which threatens all.'[144] The Union was loyal to the Crown for the same reasons – 'to secure [the rights and privileges] of every Member of the Body Politic . . .'[145] Most Political Unions did not declare their open support of the monarchy, but no doubt blamed the government, not the King himself, for the continued existence of 'Old Corruption'.

Grey and the Whigs did not feel any more comfortable with the Unions than the King did, but they recognized that their presence and support strongly bolstered their claims that the public supported the government.

> That the public feeling [towards parliamentary reform] became more animated when the question was taken up by the Government, is indisputable. But this was a natural and unavoidable consequence; the associations . . . would now be called into action by a measure recommended by the Government, and supported by the King, which would be consonant to the wishes of the people. If, on the other hand, the present expectations of the public should be disappointed, there appears to me to be too much reason to fear, that, with the feelings which originally produced them, these associations will revive, that the peace of the country will be endangered.[146]

The link between reform and a strong and fair-minded monarch in the person of William IV was firm by the spring of 1831. Political Unionists and reformers generally saw the King as behind the Bill and the people's champion. This suggested to reformers, particularly advocates of the government's measure, that the King would not object to their organizing a campaign to support reform, similar to that in Birmingham. For many reformers, their organization and expression of public opinion on behalf of reform was an opportunity to express gratitude to the King. The Northern Political Union included in its list of objectives a desire 'to secure and extend, prudently, peacefully, and legally, the interests of the industrious classes and to strengthen the throne . . .'[147]

The general elections and Union activities connected with them worried the King. The 'popular demonstrations', he wrote Grey, were 'the seeds of Revolution, a disposition generally hostile to the aristocracy of the country, a strong inclination to introduce a form of Government purely democratical . . .'[148] But overall, there seemed little to fear from the Political Unions. With few exceptions, they supported the Bill, praising it and their King for the willingness to open up the political system voluntarily.

CONCLUSION

A total of 29 Political Unions formed between the foundation of the BPU and the Whigs' introduction of their reform measure in March 1831. These Unions generally modelled themselves on the BPU, in the sense of forming a union of the middle and working classes, and creating a Council and similar organization. In the *Rules and Regulations* of those Unions that drafted them, the criteria for membership, and the responsibilities for Union and Council members were almost identical in wording.

Many of the organizations acknowledged their debt to the BPU, but some seemed to follow the lead of Henry Hunt and identify with the MPU, defunct by the time the Whigs came to office. These, as well as many other Unions, adopted a far more Radical set of objectives than Attwood had. Though individual members might have supported currency reform as an issue, no Union adopted it as an objective. Many Unions, however, did talk of the economic distress facing England, but their solution was not paper money, but a resolution of the 'Old Corruption' complaints: parliamentary and electoral reform in order to expand the electorate and force the elimination of monopolies, reduction in taxes and trade restriction, abolition of the Corn Laws, and the general initiation of free trade policies in England. In addition, none of these Political Unions looked to the Blandford reform proposal as a serious option, although the BPU endorsed it and adopted it as the concrete reform proposal the Union had previously failed to offer its members. Generally speaking, their distinctly more Radical (not to say extreme) orientation very much set the other Unions apart from the BPU.

No real evidence of any significant contact between the great majority of these Unions and the BPU exists. The only effort at broader union that did take place was the short-lived connection between the northern Unions and the MPU. Attwood made no serious attempt at outside support, although Joseph Parkes certainly used the press to promote the BPU and its activities. If provincial Unions received assistance in drafting their constitutions, it was clearly at the initiative of the corresponding secretary of the Union assisted. As we shall see in the next chapter, more interest in reform at the provincial level meant more requests for assistance to the BPU, including one from Attwood's own brother Charles, writing for guidelines to create a Political Union in Newcastle. More than a dozen Political Unions wrote to the BPU to request copies of its *Rules and Regulations*. But to credit the BPU with forming a national movement is to ignore the fact that it departed significantly from what most other provincial reformers believed to be essential for the economic and political health of England. The BPU, the evidence indicates, for all its occasional outbursts of grandiosity, and its undoubted talent for great and dramatic demonstrations, was essentially a local phenomenon, without the will, even if there had been the way to create a great national movement.

As Political Unionists waited for the unveiling of the much anticipated Whig Reform Bill, Thomas Asline Ward of the Sheffield Political Union, not Attwood, warned the Political Unionists: 'we are now on the eve of the day of Parliamentary Reform; but we have too much reason to believe that it will not bring with it such a reform as will satisfy the people of England.... We are now to wait and review the deeds of the Ministers.'[149] The next act was about to begin.

LIVERPOOL
JOHN MOORES UNIVERSITY
AVRIL ROBARTS LRC
TITHEBARN STREET
LIVERPOOL L2 2ER
TEL. 0151 231 4022

3 Political Unions and the Introduction of the Reform Bill March–October 1831

> In the spring of 1831, the Reform Bill was introduced into the House of Commons. This bill was regarded as a mere compromise between wrong and right, yet, willing to secure the least extension of the franchised and desirous to save our country from civil strife . . . the [Political] Unions in general, resolved to waive our convictions, and acceded to the bill.[1]

The general election following George IV's death had produced a Parliament sufficiently sympathetic to allow Lord Grey to form a government committed to parliamentary reform and the new chief minister assured the King, 'that if he had not been convinced that a measure of this kind was imperiously called for by the circumstances of the times, and might be safely undertaken with a view to the security of your Majesty's crown and to the interests of your people,' he would never have proposed it.[2] The King fretted a bit about whether or not the Whig's Reform Bill would 'reduce the influence of the Crown and lower the dignity of the Monarchy' and insisted that the government protect 'those constitutional rights which had been transmitted to him by his ancestors'.[3] After assurances from the new government, however, the King accepted the necessity of a drastic reform measure and hoped that his willingness to do so would foster loyalty among reformers.

The Whig Ministry's Reform Bill called for some 60 boroughs to lose both their MPs while 47 additional boroughs were to lose one member. Eleven unrepresented boroughs would gain two MPs apiece and 21 unrepresented towns with a minimum population of 10,000, would gain one MP each. In the counties, Yorkshire would receive two MPs for each Riding. Another 26 counties would be divided into two constituencies with two MPs apiece. The Isle of Wight would gain one MP while Weymouth would lose two of its four MPs.[4]

As for the franchise, the Whig bill provided for the continuance of the 40 shilling freehold in the counties, with the addition of 10 pound copyholders and 50 pounds for leaseholders. In the boroughs, householders whose property was worth 10 pounds per annum would be enfranchised and all existing electors were to retain their vote, provided they were residents of the borough (that is, lived within 7 miles of its boundaries). Outvoters were to be disenfranchised. The length of Parliaments would remain the same at seven years. Polling would be made uniform in length, changing the ritual and behaviour of elections as a result.[5] Lord Durham was unsuccessful in his attempt to include the ballot within the bill. It was rejected by Lord Grey, at least in part, because it actually took away from the non-voter his only means of influencing the electorate.[6]

The Bill also significantly redistributed parliamentary representation. Fifty-six boroughs listed in the measure's Schedule A lost 111 members and another 30 boroughs on Schedule B each lost their one MP. Twenty-two previously unrepresented boroughs gained two MPs each, while another 21 unrepresented boroughs received a single representative. As for the counties, 26 of them were divided into two double member constituencies while each of Yorkshire's Ridings would receive two MPs.[7] In short, the Bill went well beyond enfranchising the northern industrial cities and the Blandford proposal. MPs and the general public alike were stunned.

Of the 27 Political Unions agitating for reform from towns without parliamentary representation, 11 of them were on one of the Bill's schedules to receive parliamentary representation.[8] Grey hoped to make the most of the situation politically. If the Unions trusted the King's ministers, Grey hoped they would drop the more radical reform proposals. Instead of insisting upon universal suffrage, annual parliaments and ballots, he convinced himself they would accept the more limited reform they were offered. Other Whigs also saw the importance of a good relationship with the Unions. Lord John Russell, when pressed on the floor of the House of Commons to defend his faith in the Unions and public opinion, came close to giving them a rousing endorsement by declaring that he

> saw no reason why he should say to thousands who had been awaiting with interest the result of this bill, 'you are unfit to be consulted by the King's government, and I therefore repudiate your praise.' On the contrary, he thought that he might notice [the] loyalty and good sense of the people in Birmingham.[9]

Grey and the Whigs did not feel any more comfortable with the Unions than the King did, but they recognized that their presence and support strongly bolstered their claims that the public supported the government.

> That the public feeling [towards parliamentary reform] became more animated when the question was taken up by the Government, is indisputable. But this was a natural and unavoidable consequence; the associations . . . would now be called into action by a measure recommended by the Government, and supported by the King, which would be consonant to the wishes of the people. If, on the other hand, the present expectations of the public should be disappointed, there appears to me to be too much reason to fear, that, with the feelings which originally produced them, these associations will revive, that the peace of the country will be endangered.[10]

With mixed feelings – the Bill did not include a single radical reform called for by most provincial Unions: universal manhood suffrage, annual parliaments and the ballot – Political Unions immediately set out to express their gratitude to the Grey ministry for keeping political promises and introducing a Bill at last.[11] The BPU Council held a special general meeting on 7 March to draft an address of thanks to the King and his ministers. Estimates claimed that 15,000 attended the meeting, all enthusiastic pledging their support for the Bill.[12] The Worcester Political Union sent 'a formal expression of their approbation of the new ministerial plan of reform and convey[ed] their thanks to the authors'.[13] Unionists in Sheffield sent a similar message. The Union in Liverpool, having just weeks earlier insisted the ministers include the ballot as one of the Bill's key reforms, met and discussed the 'very effective measure the government has proposed'.[14] Meetings of Political Unions in Coventry, Wolverhampton, Huddersfield and Todmorden produced more addresses of thanks, assuring the Whigs that public opinion, at least that represented by the Unions, was solidly behind them.[15]

A few Political Unions focused on this as they called public meetings to discuss the Bill and the role the Unions would play in supporting it. The Nottingham Political Union met on 2 March at the Exchange Building with 600 members in attendance. Robert Sutton praised the ministerial reform plan, as 'he did not doubt but that they should find a large extension of suffrage and, perhaps, an annihilation of the rotten borough system', but he also pointed out that the government needed to be shown that 'one reform was greater than all put together – the Vote by Ballot'.[16] The meeting adopted a petition to the government congratulating them on their efforts to enact reform, but urging them to extend their proposals to include universal suffrage and the ballot. While the Nottingham Political Union decided to publicly support the Reform Bill, it vowed to continue to agitate for the inclusion of the ballot by parliamentary petition and addresses to the King.

John Doherty of the Manchester Political Union urged working-class Unionists to support the Bill as it was a good first step towards further reform. 'There is one clause framed for the benefit of the workman,' though he never specifically pointed to it in his statement. He simply urged Political Unionists to support the Bill because 'something will be obtained from the borough-mongers, if the Bill is not suffered to be frittered away'.[17] Presumably Doherty believed that an attack on 'Old Corruption' was better than none at all. Blackburn Unionist George Dewhurst reasoned the same way. 'Simply because we cannot attain all of what we want,' he urged his fellow Unionists, 'we ought not to refuse partial reform.'[18] Something was gained: both towns were slated to become parliamentary boroughs and send representatives to Parliament for the first time in modern English history, but the Unions' leaders still saw the Bill as only a partial measure, though, and supported it as a promising first installment.[19] All Political Unions, whatever reservations they might have, decided to support the Bill. William Carpenter, the London radical and publisher of the *Political Magazine*, urged endorsement, 'because the "lower orders" must support the middle class in the demand for reform; and even for the reform bill, although the latter are likely to be greater gainers by the measure than the former, in order to secure the future of the entire reform movement.'[20]

Some Unionists may have believed that with constant public pressure, the government might add at least the ballot to the Bill in committee. But even as it stood, no Political Union rejected the Whigs' impressive attempt to fulfil their promise to the English people. The King's apparent support for his government and the Bill made him the people's champion. This suggested to reformers, particularly advocates of the government's measure, that the King would not object to their organizing a campaign to support reform, similar to that in Birmingham. For many reformers, their organization and expression of public opinion on behalf of reform was an opportunity to express gratitude to the King. The Northern Political Union even included in its list of objectives a desire 'to secure and extend, prudently, peacefully, and legally, the interests of the industrious classes and to strengthen the throne . . .'[21]

While the Unions praised their reforming monarch, William IV concentrated solely on their potential for destruction. The 'popular demonstrations', he wrote Grey, were 'the seeds of Revolution, a disposition generally hostile to the aristocracy of the country, a strong inclination to introduce a form of Government purely democratical . . .'[22] Yet, there seemed little to fear from the Political Unions. With few exceptions, they supported the Bill, praising it and their King for the willingness to open up the political system voluntarily. They did not espouse democratic rhetoric or openly discuss revolution. The most fearsome thing the King could say about them in the spring of 1831 was that they were multiplying.

NEW POLITICAL UNIONS

There were only a few Political Unions founded in the days immediately following the Bill's introduction in Parliament.[23] The Reform Bill scheduled the town of Halifax to receive two MPs and be represented as a borough in Parliament for the first time. Though there is no evidence to suggest that popular organization prompted the Whigs to include Halifax in this schedule, that fact that it was included prompted reformers in that town to immediate form the Halifax Political Union.[24] Its chairman, B. Baker, believed his organization to be formed upon the principles of the BPU, but used criticisms against 'Old Corruption' rather than currency as justification for reform. 'The source of all evils entailed on society', the Union's first resolution read, 'was an unjust and vicious constitution of that House [of Commons] . . . the practical representative of fewer than two hundred nobles and influential individuals.'[25] And, grateful to the Whigs as Halifax reformers may have been, the Union also sought the ballot as an additional reform not included in the Bill, claiming, 'voting by ballot appears in the present state of society, to be a most essential if not indispensable branch of effective reform.'[26] The Halifax Union hoped for inclusion of this radical reform at some later point, but in the meantime, enthusiastically supported the Bill.

Dudley and Walsall in the Black Country both appeared on schedule D and thus slated for one parliamentary representative each.[27] They too formed Political Unions, although the Reform Bill agitation in the Black Country is far better known for its strikes than for its cooperative efforts in achieving parliamentary reform.[28] Troops were stationed throughout the area, including in the town of Dudley itself, to deal with the constant threat of collier strikes.

Evidently not fearing the Home Office and claims that the Unionists and striking colliers were one and the same, the Dudley Political Union formed in April 1831, organized by Samuel Cook and Thomas Parkin. Cook, originally from Trowbridge, was a draper and active radical since the French revolution when he formed an extra-parliamentary organization in Dudley, the Friends of Liberty in all Ranks of Society.[29] His efforts to continue organizing radicals in the 1820s led to his arrest for sedition.[30] On his release, Cook continued his radical political action. The Political Union appeared to be a continuation of those political efforts. The Home Office viewed all activities in the area as potential sedition and had informants keep a watchful eye on the Political Union when it formed. In addition, another Union was established in Walsall, although nothing is known of the leaders or members of that Union.

Though both Unions were geographically very close to Birmingham (approximately 10 miles northwest of the city), there was little contact between the Political Unions. Dudley reformers explicitly chose the Birmingham organizational model with a Council, though with different goals. The Dudley Political Union sought parliamentary reform, and specifically called for 'real representation of the Lower Classes' and an inquiry into 'the rights and liberties of the industrious classes'.[31] It also sought tax reform, specifically a progressive tax, but primarily sought the passage of the Bill as the means to economic reform and improvement for the industrious classes. There was no mention of currency reform.

But where the Dudley Union differed most dramatically from the BPU was in its more democratic rules of membership. This organization, unlike most, demanded nothing more of members (save dues) than that they register their names in a book. They were not required to agree with or follow the directives of the 18-member Council, to be elected at the annual general meeting. Cook was undoubtedly disappointed at the Union's first meeting when he remarked, 'not a decent mechanic was seen'.[32]

There is no evidence that connects the Political Union and the striking colliers. It is doubtful that any of miners could have afforded the one shilling per quarter membership dues required of Unionists. Nor is it likely, with immediate economic problems, that colliers would be willing to take the time to discuss the prospects of a Bill that would not enfranchise them or give anyone but their employers a greater parliamentary voice. Whatever the government's fear, the colliers were silent, and the new Unions took the field without them. The new Unions, as did those created the previous year, watched and waited to see how the Bill would fare in the House of Commons.

THE REFORM BILL GOES FORWARD

As anticipated, anti-reformers were determined to defeat the Whigs' attempts to restructure parliamentary representation. Sir Robert Peel began his attack on the Bill within days of its introduction, despite Lord Wharncliffe's attempts to persuade him to let it go to committee and then dismantle it, step by step.[33] On 23 March, the government only got the Bill through a second reading by one vote (302 to 301), but it went to committee nonetheless.

The House then adjourned for the Easter recess. On their return to Westminster, many MPs scrabbled to remove particular boroughs (namely those they represented) from the Bill's first two schedules and to reduce the number of overall reductions. General Isaac Gascoyne, a veteran ultra-Tory sitting for Liverpool, moved in the committee that each part of the United Kingdom should retain the proportionate share of the representation derived from the Act of Union.[34] The cabinet responded by trying to reduce by half the proposed reduction of seats and raising the total number of representatives to 627 MPs. Only two of the proposed 31 boroughs slated to be cut were outside of England. Lord Althorp could not find any additional seats to cut, though some shifting of boroughs on schedules took place.

Political Unions, both old and new, were not particularly concerned that the Bill might not make it through committee without significant amendment and quietly went about the business of acquiring more members, drafting more petitions and addresses of support, and discussing what long-term reforms might be possible with the return of a new Parliament returned on terms proposed in the Reform Bill.[35] The Duke of Newcastle, for the first time, evidenced a keen interest in the Nottingham and Newark Political Unions.[36] Though both Unions had functioned for nearly a year, it was only when Newcastle determined that they might sway voters against his chosen candidates that he asked agents to forward information to him concerning the Unions' activities.[37]

Then, on 18 April, Gascoyne proposed an amendment to the Reform Bill that, departing slightly from his original intent, forbade any reduction in the number of MPs for England and Wales.[38] Two days later the amendment passed, 299 to 231. The cabinet met a few hours after the vote, fearing popular unrest. They hesitated to ask for a dissolution of Parliament, as did the King to grant one. But when informed by Grey that the Tories were searching for precedents for delaying a prorogation, the King, angry with Lord Wharncliffe and the Tories move to circumvent constitutional procedure, agreed to a dissolution. The King, attending Westminster in person, prorogued Parliament and called for a general election. The Whigs promised to reintroduce the Bill if the election went their way.

THE 1831 GENERAL ELECTION

The May 1831 parliamentary election was important for both the Whigs and the future of parliamentary reform. It was really a referendum on the Reform Bill and the election was decisive. Candidates opposing the Bill dealt with criticism and hostility during the election. A number of constituencies simply rejected their MPs in favor of a candidate pledged to support the Reform Bill. Not only was this important in that politicians became aware at first hand of the extent of public support for the measure, it was also the first opportunity for Political Unions in already represented constituencies to prove themselves a force MPs had to take seriously in their election.[39]

The results were an overwhelming endorsement of the government and its Reform Bill. The government had a majority of 130–40.[40] Of the 82 English county MPs, only 27 voted for the second reading and 34 voted for the amendment. Of these, only six were returned in April. There was little violence at the polls and a reporter from *Blackwood's*, analysing the elections, concluded: 'the strength of government, the protection of property, the authority of the . . . constitution . . . the habits of obedience, order, and submission to which the people have been trained . . . the moral awe in which the lower classes have been educated, the veneration with which they have been accustomed to regard the institutions of their country' brought a peaceful result – but not always a deferential one.[41] Liverpool voted General Gascoyne, its representative since 1796, out of his seat. Electors in Newark ousted the Duke of Newcastle's candidate. The Duke had played an active role in the general election, seeking to undo any Union influence that might turn his candidates out, but a combination of Union support for his opponents and hatred for the Duke were probably responsible for his defeat.[42] Though detailed evidence is lacking of the extent to which the Political Unions in both areas helped to defeat these anti-reform candidates, there is much more proof elsewhere.

In the case of Coventry, the election itself demonstrated an opportunity for the Union to play a significant role in the rejection of one of the town's MPs in favour of another whose commitment to the Reform Bill was strong and whose reaction to the local Political Union was one of respect and an awareness of their political power. The Coventry Political Union had closely followed the actions of its MPs from the introduction of the Bill. Initially, the Union was satisfied with the performance of both its MPs, Edward Ellice and Thomas Bycliff Fyler. Ellice was the Whig whip and thus responsible for securing the votes in Parliament to pass the Bill. Fyler, an army officer and Tory MP since 1826, had given the impression that he too supported the Bill. He wrote to Richard Marriot, corresponding secretary of the Political Union, assuring him that he would vote for its passage.[43]

The Union Council sought greater reassurance before recommending that the Unionists who were also electors should vote to return both Ellice and Fyler. The Union had already called upon the electors of Warwick to oust King as their MP as he had voted against the Bill.[44] The Council did not take its duty lightly. 'In a matter of such extreme moment,' explained Marriot in an open letter to Union members, it was deemed proper to have an explicit pledge from Mr. Fyler that he would support the Bill.'[45]

Marriot wrote to Fyler, asking for such a pledge. Fyler instead offered an address to the freemen of Coventry, not to members of the Political Union, explaining that 'his future conduct, if re-elected, was to be a matter of inference from his past'.[46] Marriot and the Council, offended by the slight as well as unnerved by this possible negative vote on the Bill, wrote their letter to the freemen of Coventry. 'Our local affairs have taken a course we did not anticipate,' the letter read, recounting the request and Fyler's slight of the Union and his failure to pledge himself to the Bill. It continued:

> Mr. Fyler having voted against General Gasgoyne's motion, we [the Union Council] inferred that he was favourable to the ministerial bill of reform, and so did the reformers generally in the city. When a candidate asks for the confidence of a constituent, they have a right to demand the fullest explanation of the principles by which he will be guided. Mr. Fyler would not give this explanation [therefore, the Council decided to] procure a candidate who would conceal none of his intentions and who would pledge himself to support 'the Bill, the whole Bill, and nothing but the Bill.'[47]

It was not difficult for the Council to find another candidate.[48]

Henry Lytton Bulwer sat for Wilton, thanks to the patronage of the anti-reform Earl of Pembroke. As a reformer and ambitious young politician, Bulwer felt he had no choice but to abstain on the second reading of the Bill, inform Lord Pembroke he intended to support it and look for another parliamentary seat.[49] He found it in Coventry. On 28 April, the Political Union called a meeting at the Craven Arms to introduce Bulwer to some 4,000 present.[50] Bulwer spoke with confidence:

> I came to support that which the unanimous voice of nearly all the intelligence, talent and pure disinterested patriotism of the nation had declared good, and which it was in vain for fools or knaves to attempt to counteract. In a word, he came as a real reformer, determined, if he should have the honour of representing them, to support the measure which have now emanated from the councils of his Majesty and which he believed to be indispensable necessary, as the first and great means of relieving the people from the system of oppression under which they laboured.[51]

In spite of Fyler's efforts to prove himself a reformer, the remarkably united reforming vote returned Ellice with 367 votes and Bulwer with 361 to Fyler's 123. As much as this was a victory for reform, it was an even bigger success for the Coventry Political Union. It was the Union that had demanded pledges from candidates before endorsing them for re-election. Fyler had refused to give one and had been humiliated at the polls as a consequence.

The Bristol Political Union formed on Monday, 30 May 1831, immediately following the general elections.[52] It was a direct response to the victory of Edward Protheroe Jr, the pro-reform, anti-Corporation MP who had, in 1830, run successfully for one of Bristol's parliamentary seats in a scandalous election. Then, Protheroe had lost to J.E. Baillie, who became the Whig MP for Bristol, by 700 votes.[53] The Bristol Radicals and reform Whigs were encouraged. But elections in Bristol were highly partisan affairs and manipulated by the Corporation. For the 1831 election, Whigs and reformers came together to support the government and the Bill, and defeat Bristol's Tory MP, Richard Hart Davis. The Whigs put up Baillie and Protheroe and, in spite of traditional links between particular trades and the Tory Party, received support from nearly all the pro-reform freemen and tradesmen. Hart Davis withdrew from the race on 29 April, having received only 200 votes and freemen and tradesmen throughout the city drafting reform declarations and voting for reform candidates.[54] Baillie and Protheroe were returned and a chairing took place on 4 May with a procession of 10,000, including all the Bristol trades.[55]

The Bristol Reform Association, a loose-knit organization of radicals and Whigs drawn from electors outside the West Indian trade monopoly (which had supported Protheroe's candidacy in 1830 and again), now joined with the West Indian Whigs. In 1831, the Association saw the results of the general election as a local mandate to organize more efficiently in its efforts to support the Reform Bill. In the latter election, the Association, led by some of the most successful manufacturers in Bristol outside the West Indian trade, including E.P. Fripp, Richard Ash and W.E. Acraman, following the Birmingham model of organization, threw all their influence behind the government's reform measure and the candidates who supported it. They formed the Bristol Political Union at a meeting of trade groups on 30 May.[56]

Bristol's Mayor, Charles Pinney, said that the Union's formation was 'in consequence of delegates from Birmingham having been here in this town . . .' and claimed that 2,000 persons were at the inaugural meeting at which reformers decided to 'unite in one bond of the Union with Birmingham and other places by which they would become one great force that would be able to resist the yeomanry'.[57] John Eagles, a Bristol printer, criticized the organization's formation, claiming, 'At the election, the Bristol reformers were in perfect accordance with those similar meetings throughout the kingdom, clearly proving that not [the Bill] only, but ulterior measures were the objects for which these Unions are formed . . .'[58]

The Unions' founders and officers included George Edie Sanders, merchant and banker, named President; William Herapath, chemist and a professor of toxicology at the Bristol College of Medicine and committee member of the Mechanics' Institute, served as Vice-president; George Wright, a banker, was Treasurer; John G. Powell was Secretary; and James Hare served as Corresponding Secretary.[59] Hare, a flourcloth manufacturer, was also a leading abolitionist in Bristol, a good friend of Francis Place, and had been the campaign manager for Protheroe's ill-fated candidacy. Another prominent member was Harman Visger, a radical and later the leader of the Bristol Liberal Party.[60]

The Bristol Political Union's objective was to organize the 'freemen householders and others of the City' in order to preserve every right already possessed by them as citizens and subjects . . . keep a watchful eye over the conduct of the Representatives of the City in Parliament' and provide 'mutual protection of those mechanics who might suffer from voting too conscientiously'.[61] According to reports received by the Home Office, allegedly from the Union itself, and certainly repeating the same language, its objectives were 'the mutual protection of those mechanics who might suffer from voting conscientiously and to keep a watchful eye on the conduct of the representatives of this city in Parliament.'[62]

The Bristol Political Union adopted a radical platform of goals. While it supported the Whig Bill, its ideal reform measure would include universal manhood suffrage, annual parliaments, the ballot and a redistribution of parliamentary representation based upon population. But the Union, chastened by numerous defeats against the Bristol Corporation's control of local politics as well as parliamentary elections, was entirely pragmatic in its immediate goals. As Powell put it, 'our principal efforts ought to be against corporation abuses', as from that evil, all corruption and bad government followed.[63] The Unionists advocated economic reforms such as free trade, the abolition of monopolies, a reduction in tariffs and the abolition of slavery in British colonies.

The Union members included middle-class professionals, businessmen, artisans and small shopowners. Reports also claimed that wage labourers from the docks and manufacturing also joined the Union, but with annual membership dues of one guinea, that is doubtful.[64] Estimates of Union membership range from, 1,000 to 2,000, depending on the date one is examining the organization.[65] The Council members were concentrated in the educated and wealthier ranks of the Union membership. The Council met weekly at the Cat and Wheel on Castle Green, advertised meetings, distributed parliamentary information and discussed long-term reform goals once the Bill became law.

Essentially, the Political Union represented a new political force power in Bristol: the new manufacturing Whig opposition to a coalition of anti-reform Tories and old West Indian Whig merchant interests. Embracing the Reform Bill, the new Whigs split with the old Whigs, weakening whatever opposition to the Tory Corporation existed even further.[66] In early August, a meeting in Queen Square, attended by many 'mechanics', categorized the Union as a working men's Union, but by October, whatever had been the case earlier, the rank and file was made up of mostly middle-class reformers with a few working-class members.[67]

The 1831 elections also had an impact in the market town and port of Bridgwater in Somerset, near Bristol. Bridgwater was a scot and lot borough, allowing anyone paying poor rates to vote. Though unaffected by the Reform Bill's schedules, 'nearly two hundred voters subscribed their names and cash' to the creation of the Bridgwater Political Union, under the presidency of the town's Mayor, John Evered, Esq., 'for the purpose of promoting purity of elections, and prosecuting and destroying by all legal means, bribery and corruption.'[68] Clearly, the recent contest of William Astell and Charles Kemeys Tynte, Whigs standing for Parliament as reform candidates stirred up reform sentiments.[69] The Union endorsed the Bill, but also expressed the strong belief that the ballot was another necessary element to be added to the reform measure and sent an address to that effect, to the King as well as Parliament.[70] The Union clearly sought the uniformity in electoral qualification promised in the bill as a means of ending the confusion and less than honourable voting behaviour in the borough.

The relationship between MPs, though not the election *per se*, had an important impact in the formation of the Northern Political Union (NPU) in Newcastle upon Tyne. A freeman borough, Newcastle returned both incumbents, pro-reform Sir Matthew Ridley and John Hodgson.[71] Both had voted with the government on the Reform Bill and there was little reason for the reformers in Newcastle not to return them. Upon their return, the radical community in Newcastle called a public meeting to discuss a 'Plan for the Northern Political Union'.[72] As the Union's founder, Charles Attwood, the younger brother of Thomas, declared: 'The recent elections have taught the people a lesson. They have revealed to them the secret of their power.'[73]

The plan and the meeting were the work of Attwood, a glass manufacturer from Gateshead; James Losh, a businessman and lawyer, whose radical activities and Unitarian background had placed him in many extraparliamentary reform organizations since the 1790s; John Fife, a surgeon and freemen of the Incorporated Company of Barber-Surgeons; Charles Larkin, a manufacturer; and Thomas Doubleday, a businessman, Quaker and early admirer of William Cobbett.[74] Thomas Hepburn, leader of the Newcastle trade union of pitmen, was said to be among the organizers, although there is only one source for this.[75] They invited members from the already existing Friends of Reform organization in Newcastle which, though supportive of the Reform Bill, did nothing in the way of campaigning to secure its success, as well as the town's freemen, pitmen and business community to attend a meeting on Monday, 27 June 1831. The more than 1,000 participants created the Northern Political Union, the goals of which were to 'unite the higher and middle classes; soften the asperities of one, and increase the independence of the other . . .' as the classes, united, would 'watchfully guard the principles of the Reform Bill and support the Friends of the People in both Houses of Parliament.'[76] Its objectives were 'to urge the middle and working classes to increased interest in political affairs' and 'disseminate useful political information'.[77] The resolutions, rules and objectives, all, not surprisingly, identical to those of the BPU, were unanimously adopted.[78]

That sense of power in the people, Attwood noticed, would grow more pronounced as the Whigs reintroduced the Reform Bill. It passed its second reading on 7 July by a decisive 367 to 231 vote. The NPU expected Newcastle's MPs to recognize the Union as a political ally, one that would be useful in securing support for the Bill by public opinion. When both Ridley and Hodgson voted against the government on a particular of the Bill, namely the disenfranchisement of Appleby, the NPU Council challenged them on their votes.[79]

An enraged Ridley wrote an open letter to the Union, published in the Newcastle dailies:

> I have the honour of being chosen to represent Newcastle upon Tyne by the independent electors of that town, to whom alone I consider myself responsible for my parliamentary conduct, and I cannot admit the right of any other person to call me to an account which they alone have the power to do. I must beg respectfully

to decline answering the question proposed to me. I cannot (by acceding to the request) consent to acknowledge the right of a body, of whose existence as part of the constitution I am not at present aware of, and whose authority if acknowledged must tend to supersede and abrogate that of my constituents . . .[80]

Hodgson was willing to respond to the Council's questions, writing to Doubleday that he voted against the ministry on the Appleby question because he supported 'to the utmost the principle of disfranchisement laid down by his Majesty's ministers, but when they appear to me to violate that principle, I cannot give them my support'.[81] He added that he was prepared to defend every vote taken on the Reform Bill 'as consistent with the principles that I professed at the last election'.[82]

The NPU Council was furious with Ridley and responded with another open letter in the press attacking his position on the constitutionality and authority of the NPU.

In taking the liberty of respectfully asking the question embodied in their [the Council's] letter . . . they certainly did not expect a reply as a matter of right, but they did expect it as a matter of courtesy. The Council of the Northern Political Union, in behalf of the members of that Union, beg to assure you that they neither assume themselves to be a body to which you or any other person ban be accountable for your or their political opinions or acts; nor is it their intention, were it in their power, to interfere in the slightest degree with the rights either of your constituents, or of those of any other member of parliament. That they can have no such intention, is evident in the fact of many of the Free Burgesses of Newcastle upon Tyne being themselves associates of the Unions. They are fully and entirely aware that the controlling power is, in the instance of Newcastle upon Tyne, at present vested solely in the Free Burgesses; that those only who have the privilege to elect have the privilege to question – and if they even venture to assume that the members virtually represent the entire community, they will readily consent to assume it as a pleasing theory rather than as a necessary fact.

The Council in conclusion beg to state, that the Northern Political Union is a body of persons associated legally, and therefore constitutionally, for the promotion of certain legal ends and purposes; nor do they claim for themselves any other than the right common to all Englishmen, of forming for themselves their own opinions of public men and public measures, and of lawfully acting to the best of their ability in accordance with those opinions.[83]

The relationship between the Union and Newcastle's MPs was similar to the one in Coventry. While the Newcastle Political Union did not see itself as so powerful as to make MPs responsible to them, they did expect their representatives to recognize that they would be very useful in rallying public opinion for the government and the Bill because, although it was once again in committee, it was hardly secure. In Coventry, the success in ousting Fyler for Bulwer fostered a sense that the Union had enough local authority to make politicians beholden to them. An alliance that could have developed in Newcastle became instead a hostile relationship between an organization and two men who shared a common goal and a good relationship in Coventry which would sour when the Union demanded too much from its MPs.

The Political Unions became an important element in the Whigs' successful return to office and their strengthened support for the Reform Bill. While many Unionists questioned and cajoled parliamentary candidates as to their current position on reform, others provided the newspaper-reading public with a history of their past deeds to better inform the electorate. Assuming that the King and government appreciated their efforts, the Political Unions were very public in their efforts to see only supporters of the Whig reform measure would be returned to Parliament. Still, the Unions did nothing more than demonstrate on behalf of the government's efforts. Fears that they were secretly organizing a revolution to establish a democratic republic were nothing more than Tory paranoia. In April 1831, Political Unions wanted the Reform Bill and little else.

THE REFORM BILL REINTRODUCED

Following the election, the Whigs returned to the fray. On 24 June, Lord John Russell once again introduced the Reform Bill in the House of Commons. To the public, it seemed certain that the Bill was secure. Reform had proved popular in 1831 elections, demonstrating support for the Whigs' proposal, specifically. It would be difficult for the Tories to defend borough-mongering and electoral corruption by continuing to attack the Reform Bill. Even Peel hinted that he might change his position when he told his constituents at Tamworth in May, 'there is no dishonour . . . in relinquishing opinions or measures and adopting others more suited to the altered circumstances of the country.'[84]

Members of the House of Commons debated the Bill and a large majority of reformers on the backbenches made it clear they would not compromise any further. At the second reading on 7 July, it sailed into committee with a comfortable majority of 136. Then, there were battles over Schedules A and B, 16 amendments introduced in committee (although ten of them were tabled by 21 July, having been proposed by those who voted with the government on the second reading), and heated discussion as to the problem of borough freeholders who owned property valued at less than ten pounds and residence qualifications.[85] But some of the amendments were simply promises MPs had made to constituents and not a serious threat to the measure. For example, E.J. Littleton, MP, promised Staffordshire supporters that he would propose changing the one MP slated for the Potteries to two MPs.[86] The only committee defeat for the government came on an amendment proposed by the Marquess of Chandos that fifty pound tenants-at-will could enjoy the franchise in the counties.[87]

As the Bill progressed through committee, Political Unions became increasingly confident and increasingly popular. New Unions formed in a diverse array of towns. The Wakefield Political Union was apparently meeting and organizing in a manner to warrant a letter to Lord Harewood, the Lieutenant of the West Riding, indicating that 'upwards of 103,000 inhabitants [in the area] . . . from several ebulltions [*sic*] of public feeling, electioneering, etc. . . . made for an inability to preserve the peace and safety of the town [neighbouring Leeds] . . . in the face of [political] organization and association.'[88]

In August, the potwalloper borough of Preston, the parliamentary seat of Henry Hunt, formed a Union.[89] Hunt had condemned the BPU soon after its creation because of its failure to embrace radical reform. The failure of his own MPU in London did little to shake his faith either in the Bill or in the Political Union form of organization.[90] Still, it was local Radicals Joseph Hanson, a master weaver, and John Taylor, a clogger, who actually organized a Political Union to support the government, the Bill and 'the Patriot King'.[91] Another Union formed in neighbouring Padiham as well.[92]

The Brighton Political Union formed in early September 1831.

According to the *Brighton Gazette*, 'operatives of this town form[ed] themselves in a Political Union, as a branch of the London Union . . . [the NUWC].'[93] Brighton was well known throughout England for its political inclinations and, in fact, the London correspondent of the *Brighton Herald* commented that the capital was quite surprised that a town so prosperous and so dependent on the higher classes should contain even a single Radical, let alone that they should be so active.[94] In spite of reports that it was largely composed of artisans, the Union was, in part, the work of Brighton's middle-class Dissenters, led by George Faithfull, an attorney as well as a Baptist lay minister. Its objectives, beyond the Reform Bill's passage, were the repeal of the malt, hop and soap tax, the repeal of the Corn Laws, the abolition of church tithes, assessed and stamp taxes, and universal suffrage, shorter parliaments and the ballot.[95] As with the Bristol Union, there were long-term goals, as opposed to the short-term goal of carrying the Whig Bill.

The situation was similar in the northern town of Oldham. The Political Union there formed in August, created by long-standing Oldham Radicals. Also Dissenters, these local Radicals had been part of the Hampden Club movement in the 1810s and would continue to work for factory and economic reform in the late 1830s long after the Bill.[96] These tireless reformers were the Methodist lay preacher William Knott, Samuel Bamford, whose autobiography has made him famous, James Halliday, a leading Radical, Joshua Milne, a cotton spinner and manufacturer who employed more than 700 people in four factories, the grocer/orator Alex Taylor, and John Knight, a cotton manufacturer turned schoolmaster, and dedicated to the Radical movement. Knight was an untiring advocate of the political rights of the working class, influenced by trade unionists John Gast and Thomas Hodgskin on the subject of the value of labour. He served as the Union's secretary brought workers into the Union, including James Greaves, an operative cotton spinner, and William Fitton, a weaver.[97] Along with the middle-class radical/artisan connection in Oldham, there was a strong link between the Political Union and the Methodist Unitarian movement. Among the congregation's members were John Fielden, the patron of the Methodist Unitarians as well as of the Political Union in Todmorden. Seven of the 27-member Union Council in Oldham were Methodist Unitarians.[98]

The Union met in rooms in Yorkshire Street, used during the week by John Knight as schoolrooms, espoused a radical programme of reform based on Cartwright's principles of electoral reform. The Union condemned 'Old Corruption' in the form of excessive taxation, sinecures, pensions, places and other appointments. Knight proposed that the Union, whatever the state of the Bill, demonstrate its commitment to radical reform and moved a resolution in favour or annual parliaments and the ballot. While he had support, the Union ultimately voted to support the government's Bill.[99]

As well as inspiring the creation of new organizations, the second parliamentary presentation of the Reform Bill prompted Political Unions to became more active in their support for its passage. In Coventry, a petition of support was sent by the Union to both its MPs, Ellice and the newly elected Henry Lytton Bulwer, for presentation in the House of Commons. It expressed the Union's concern over the delays and obstructions slowing the progress of the Bill. It warned the government that 'giving to that minority of your Honourable House a control over the majority, and thereby overthrowing the high and cherished hopes of a long oppressed but loyal people', would jeopardize popular support.[100] George Edmonds of the BPU was present at the Union meeting that drafted the petition. He complimented the organization on its 'prompt and spirited manner . . . [in alerting the government to the reality that] it must either go along with the people, or sink into everlasting contempt and infamy.'[101] The Union pledged to continue in its keen observation of the government.

The committee stage of the debate on the Reform Bill ended on 7 September after 40 nights of debate and negotiation. The ministry then prepared its report, making final adjustments to the Schedules. The third reading was held on 22 September and the Bill passed, 345 to 236. The Bill then went to the Lords. The government believed that after the general election, the Lords would support the Bill, Grey remarking, 'I hope that what has taken place in the elections may have its effect on the prudence of that body'.[102] There had been some new creations in the Lords in June to remind them of the possibility of more if they were recalcitrant. But by August, the cabinet was fearing it had weak support. On 5 September, the cabinet discussed more creations, and even resignation before a humiliating vote occurred. Wellington was only too aware that a defeat of the Bill in the Lords might antagonize the public. Still, he believed that such an act would be the Lords' constitutional duty. He sought and received information about the popularity of Political Unions and the influence they had on public opinion. Much of it was incorrect. Lord Elgin indicated that only towns with Unions, namely Birmingham and Manchester, were committed to the Whig Bill at any cost.[103] As Wellington put his conclusions, 'We think that there is a very prevailing change of opinion in the country upon the subject of the Bill. At all events we think that the House of Lords ought to give the country a change of being saved by affording further time to consider of this question . . .'[104]

The second reading debate began on 3 October after some days' wait following the death of Grey's grandson and Durham's son, Charles Lambton. On the first day of the debate, the BPU held a meeting a Newhall Hill with some 15,000 in attendance.[105] Over 120 petitions of support for the Bill were brought to the House. But other petitions and a likely Tory victory in the Dorset by-election suggested to Wellington that the public was not fully committed to the Bill.[106] The debate lasted four days and on the 7th, the roll was called. The opposition had a majority of 41: 199 to 158.

When the Lords rejected the Whig Reform Bill, there were 35 individual Political Unions in the provinces supporting it, petitioning Parliament on its behalf, and sending addresses, approved at large public meetings, to William IV. From the introduction of the Bill to the end of September, 13 new Political Unions had formed (three scheduled to receive two MPs, two to receive one each) without a hint of violence or hostility. Political Unions responded to the Bill's defeat in much the same way with large public meetings and addresses and petitions, to the King as well as the government, blaming the vote on Tory aristocrats and the Anglican bishops. They laid no blame on the champions of the reform measure. All expressed thanks and devout loyalty to the King. Typical was an address sent by the Leicester Political Union expressing regret that the King's efforts had been thwarted by the Lords:

> Your Majesty's gracious intentions towards your loyal subjects, although seconded by the efforts of an honest, a patriotic and enlightened Ministry, have been however unhappily defeated by a majority of the House of Lords. Under these circumstances, alike distressing to your Majesty's paternal feelings, and destructive of your people's hopes, we deem it our sacred duty to offer to your Majesty our earnest prayer, that your Majesty will be graciously pleased to continue in office your present Ministers, in whom, we, your Majesty's loyal subjects place our entire confidence, and in whose firmness and integrity we have the fullest reliance.[107]

Other Political Unions reiterated this message. Upon receiving word of the Bill's defeat, the Coventry Political Union Council forwarded a petition to Westminister expressing the assurances of loyalty from the organization:

> we approach your Throne with sentiments of the most profound veneration and attachment to your Majesty's person, and with gratitude for the paternal solicitude which your Majesty has evinced for the welfare of the subjects, the amelioration of their condition and the restitution of their political rights.[108]

The Union promised the King that his continued support would 'render your Majesty's name truly illustrious and shed a glory upon your reign brighter than the greatest victories or the most extended foreign conquests could bestow.'[109] The Bath Political Union's petition thanked the King for his 'gracious intentions' and 'deem[ed] it our sacred duty . . . under these circumstances distressing to your Majesty's paternal feelings and destructive to your people's hopes . . .' that he support his Ministers and continue demonstrating 'firmness and integrity [in which] we, your Majesty's loyal subjects place our entire confidence'.[110]

But in spite of protestations of loyalty, the relationship between the Whigs and the Unions changed after the Bill's defeat. Political Unionists and the public generally were confident that the Reform Bill would succeed in spite of the setback. They could not conceive that such a strong public sentiment, demonstrated by the efficient but peaceful organization of extra-parliamentary Unions throughout the country, could be ignored by the aristocratic members of the upper House. Political Unionists and reformers throughout England were about to realize how wrong they were. Not only would the fight be escalating, but the King's fear of the Union would be as well. William IV's demand that his ministers eliminate the Unions and their potential for violence prompted a new stage in the development of the Political Union reform campaign.

4 The Reform Riots and Political Unions as Peacekeepers: October–December 1831

Political Unions ought to be formed in every parish in order to control the government and Parliament and to keep the peace.

Joseph Hume, MP for Middlesex[1]

I believe if the Unions had not been formed as a nucleus for the people to gather round, there would have been bloodshed. The men who formed Unions acted with wisdom, with judgment, acted with propriety; they afforded the people an opportunity of giving vent to their feelings . . .

Colonel Jones, MP for Bath[2]

The Political Unions, which had usurped the voice of the nation, now stood forward with that assurance with confidence of support, or rather, permission in mischief . . . they declared what sort of reform they required, and they commanded the minister to produce such a bill, and called upon the parliament, at its peril, to reject it.

The Duke of Newcastle[3]

After earnestly assuring His Majesty that tradesmen and small proprietors, not mere rabble, were already either in Unions or on the eve of joining them, I glanced at the propriety and prudence of some measure . . . to give the Government or Civil power the appointment of officer and the control of any voluntary association formed with a professed view of keeping the peace.

Lord Holland[4]

England was not really on the verge of a dreadful catastrophe, but many feared that it was as rioting began to break out after the House of Lords rejected the Whig ministry's Reform Bill in October

1831. Disturbances occurred in London and throughout the midlands, but the worst were in Derby, Nottingham and Bristol.[5] Most historians have correlated the violence in those towns with political disappointment and frustration that the aristocracy had so lightly dismissed the will of the people.[6] Others have examined the riots from the perspective of the local tensions, specifically between the Corporations and their political opponents.[7] Nearly all the studies, in some way, have used the riots to argue that England's potential for revolution was growing, giving William IV a taste of what could come if the Bill was rejected again – a lesson he did not learn very well initially. Many scholars argue it was Grey and the wisdom of the King that saved the country from chaos, but the Home Office's records made clear that the people and their extra-parliamentary organizations had much to do with the maintenance of order and good will. According to Francis Place:

> the proceedings of the people during the short period from the rejection of the Bill by the Lords [to its passage] . . . were such as had never before been known, such as never perhaps could have been made in so short a time. As fast as the news of the rejection spread, meetings were held, in Counties, in Cities and of promiscuous bodies of people . . . the tone was the same: to support the King and his ministers in every way and at any cost of money, time or life.[8]

Still, few historians seem to concur with contemporary views. Lord Holland admitted, 'The Unions even at Birmingham and elsewhere were composed and composing of those who must stand between us and the plundering mobs . . . No army could keep them down with the assistance and cooperation of those who now formed or were forming Unions.'[9] John Stuart Mill enthused that England was 'indebted for the preservation of tranquillity solely to the organization of the people in political unions.'[10] But there is a much neglected truth in what he says. Political Unions contributed to the maintenance of law and order, particularly following the defeat of the Bill in October. The events in Bristol and the actions of its Political Union made clear what the next role could be for these organizations in helping the government pass its reform measure. Political Unions that were critical of the government's Bill and insistent that more radical reforms be included in the measure, dropped these demands in lieu of the real opposition to the more moderate Bill. Reformers throughout England looked for ways to show their support for the government. They created new Political Unions in order to muster a universal public demand for the Bill's passage in the hopes this would make anti-reformers think twice about the consequences if the Bill was defeated again.

But the development of the Political Union movement and some of its tactics in preserving the peace also encouraged the perception, among many opponents of reform, that they were fomenting a political and social revolution. Some Political Unions did discuss the possible use of physical force in their campaign, but, as Charles Tilly claims, 'if in 1832 withholding of taxes, a run on the banks, or armed insurrection had actually occurred under the control of radicals and reformers, that might have brought Britain into the red zone.'[11] They did not occur and no revolution took place. As a result of such a peaceful popular campaign, Jonathan Clark's assumption that during a political crisis 'populist radical attention meant that the common man was still presented with relatively simple options of obedience and revolt' is somewhat exaggerated.[12] In order to understand the contribution of Political Unions and the riots' impact on their numbers, tactics and influence, it is necessary to examine the riots, the part taken by Political Unions and the public reaction.

THE MIDLAND RIOTS AND REACTION

News of the Bill's defeat reached Nottingham by Pickford's Van at 8:00 pm in the on Saturday, 8 October. On Sunday, following failed attempts to get the Corporation to call a public meeting to petition the government, crowds gathered, setting off window-breaking and an attack against known anti-reformers. As a result, the Riot Act was read. The details of the riots have been examined at great length elsewhere, so I will not repeat them here, other than to say that throughout the three days, crowds attacked the House of Correction, Colwick Hall (outside the city), burnt down the Duke of Newcastle's unoccupied Nottingham Castle and a silk-factory at Beeston, and attacked Wollaton Hall – all buildings associated with prominent Tory anti-reformers.[13]

When Colonel Thackwell finally received a request from the town magistrates to use the force of both the Yeomanry and the 15th Hussar division at his disposal, they had already deputized hundreds of special constables, including members of the Political Union

Council, and had directives from the High Sheriff to assist in re-establishing order with citizen's arrests.[14] The riots were over by Tuesday evening, but the unrest continued. The Duke of Newcastle accused the Political Unionists of instigating the riots.[15]

The Home Office, however, completely dismissed the accusation. Communications between the military officers called to put down the riots and Lord Melbourne, as well as communications between the mayor, magistrates and Melbourne, kept the government aware of the details of the riots and the activities of all those involved in trying to stop them.[16] According to a report in the Home Office papers, 'Nottingham like every other populous and manufacturing town contains a considerable number of poor, desolate people who are at times ready for mischief. The mayor and gentlemen who must have know this well, ought to have formed a constabulary to preserve the peace. If they had one this and continued it only for a few days, no mischief could have been perpetrated.'[17] There was no mention of those special constables that the magistrates had recruited to prevent the riot.

Rumours circulated that the Political Union had armed itself and practised drilling after the riots in order to maintain the peace in case the Reform Bill was defeated again. Lancelot Rolleston, a magistrate, reported to the Home Office that the Union now solicited subscriptions for the purchase of arms and that coaches arrived daily with supplies from Birmingham.[18] Melbourne ordered an investigation and happily reported the results to Grey: 'A gentleman of credit . . . reported that the arming Branch [of the Political Union comprised] five men and a driller' and that the rumour about guns from Birmingham was untrue.[19]

Rumours of large numbers joining the Nottingham Political Union, however, were well founded. It established branches in Carrington and New Leaton in the following few months.[20] By the end of November, the Union's membership list totalled just over 1,800, nearly triple what it was prior to the Bill's defeat and the riots.[21]

In addition to Nottingham, rioting broke out in Derby.[22] On 8 October, when the news of the Lords' rejection of the Bill arrived by way of the London dailies, anti-reformers, not reformers, took to the streets. Apparently in retaliation, a crowd of reformers formed, began throwing stones, breaking windows of businesses owned by anti-reformers, and finally pulled up all the shrubbery along the palisades in the town centre. Local authorities arrested three men.

When the mayor and magistrates held a public meeting the following day to consider what measures should be taken to prevent further rioting, the crowd demanded the prisoners' release. Ignored by officials, the crowd attempted their own rescue. They fired guns at the jail, accidentally killed a bystander and finally smashed the gate and released 23 prisoners. A cavalry troop arrived on the afternoon of the 9th, dispersed the crowd at the county jail and attempted to clear the streets.[23] Many of the crowd went on to Little Chester, where they broke windows and made a general ruckus before returning to Derby in the evening. Once again, the crowd threw stones at windows, pulled up iron grates and now attacked houses of reformers and anti-reformers indiscriminately. But when the crowd marched on the Post Office 'the military began to act, and with so much success, that before nine o'clock, the town was pretty well cleared.'[24]

The next day, the mayor of Derby rejected a request for a public meeting to discuss the Lords' rejection of the Reform Bill, but instead proposed sending a town petition. Mobs immediately tore down the stalls set up later in the day to collect signatures. Once again, magistrates called in the troops. An innocent man died in the mayhem and another was wounded. Soldiers and special constables finally cleared the streets by evening and began patrolling to prevent any recurrence. Only the soldiers, not the constables, used firearms, leaving the constables worried that another crowd would form, using weapons against them. Most of the damage and violent behaviour occurred before the soldiers arrived in Derby from Nottingham.

Derby did not have a local Political Union at the time of the riots, so there was no accusation that the Union had prompted the disorder. Nor was there any new branch of special constables formed to appease supporters of the organization.[25] All that the sources specify is that respectable men paraded the streets and, in this case, checked public houses once the military had stopped the rioting.[26] There is no evidence as to who volunteered as special constables or was among the crowd asking the mayor to call a public meeting to discuss the state of the Reform Bill. There is also little evidence as to who the rioters were. *The Times* suggested that the rioters were not the mature adults of Derby, but youths.[27] A witness at the subsequent trial of the rioters testified that at least 20 or 30 in the crowd were country people, and another claimed that the rioters on 10 October came from neighbouring villages.[28] Nowhere in any of the newspaper accounts, Home Office reports or trial transcripts was there a suggestion that any reform organization existed in Derby, let alone was in any way connected to the rioting. The Derby riots grew out of frustration with the failure of the Reform Bill. No Union existed to channel public disappointment or to participate in the quieting of the crowds on the street. That would soon change in Derby and dozens of other towns throughout the country.

The reaction to the riots in Nottingham and Derby was not as dramatic or decisive as one might imagine. Neither the government nor anti-reformers, except for the Duke of Newcastle, reacted with horror or demanded special measures from the troops already garrisoned in the area. Nor did other Political Unions pay much attention to the events. Disappointment at the Bill's defeat and the targeting of Ultra-Tories property did not, Unionists believed, warrant more than recognition of that fact that the people were frustrated, and that frustration could turn to violence if not alleviated.

Nor was the government unduly worried about these riots. Melbourne, in reviewing the reports of the mayors, magistrates and military officers, concluded that there was no real political or social threat posed by the Nottingham and Derby riots. He was more concerned about the overall state of law and order, agreeing with Lord Brougham's remark that the system was failing. As for any fears that the violence was in some way connected to extra-parliamentary political organization, nothing suggested it. The Nottingham Political Union appeared to be unconnected to the riot, which magistrates and the officers who put down the riots seemed to feel was in response to the Bill's defeat in the Lords, and perhaps against the exacting political and economic control exerted by the Duke of Newcastle. There was no Union in Derby and the Home Office did not even inquire as to whether a Union functioned in the town and might be linked to the disturbance in any way.

Historians and contemporaries have compared the midlands riots to the notorious Bristol riots later in the month. The latter were more dangerous than the stoning and firing of property in Nottingham and Derby. These riots erupted a few weeks after the first rage at the Bill's defeat had had time to subside and the government had pledged to reintroduce it in the House of Commons as soon as possible. They began by targeting an anti-reformer, but soon turned into the destruction of property and institutions that represented government and law, not just the property of ultra-Tories holding back passage of the Bill. Still more frightening for some was the very active role played by the local Political Union. Francis Place assessed the connection between Political Unions and the October riots. He incorrectly concluded that 'the mischiefs which took place at these towns [Nottingham and Derby] and the City could have been prevented. There were no unions at either Derby and Nottingham and though there was one at Bristol, it was at variance with the Corporation and few in number.'[29]

THE BRISTOL RIOTS AND REACTION

There are a number of accounts of the Bristol riots, both contemporary and historical, the most recent and comprehensive by Jeremy Caple.[30] While I have relied on those previously published studies of the riots, perhaps the most significant work utilized in this discussion is a forgotten, but extraordinarily detailed narrative of the riots written by a Mr Ham, the former secretary of the Bristol Political Union, whose work Francis Place requested in February 1836 in order to write a history of the riots himself.[31]

Bristolians braced themselves for rioting with the news that 'the Recorder of Bristol', Sir Charles Wetherell, was coming to town to attend the assizes at the end of October. This tension was primarily thanks to the fact that Bristol's Ultra-Tory alderman and Recorder had accompanied his violent opposition with pronouncements that Bristol was indifferent to reform. Wetherell's scheduled appearance guaranteed a public response as anger was high, particularly among members of the Bristol Political Union.[32] Anticipating trouble, Christopher Claxton, acting for the Corporation, tried to gather a guard of sailors to protect Wetherell when he arrived, but as the sailors pledged their loyalty to the King, they also pledged that they would not be 'the cat's paw of the Corporation and its agents'.[33] The Bristol Corporation failed to win support from property owners in forming a special constabulary to protect Wetherell. It drafted ordinances designed to coerce reluctant volunteers, providing fines of five pounds and up to two months imprisonment for anyone convicted of refusing the request of two or more magistrates to act as special constables.[34]

The Home Office was also made aware of the potential for rioting on the part of the Bristol Political Union. Claxton wrote to Lord Melbourne that the Political Union had held a meeting attended by more than 3,000, and reported that the chairman's speech was inflammatory, calling upon those assembled 'to remember what pressure would do with the law and . . . [and to establish a] bond of Union with Birmingham and other places by which they would become a great force that would be able to resist the yeomanry . . . [but that] they [the government] had nothing to fear from the King's troops . . .'[35]

Tensions were clearly high. Bristol Political Union Vice-President, William Herapath, declared, 'he did not regret the conduct of the Lords for the longer reform was delayed, the **more** would the people *demand* from them . . . [and] they had now [an opportunity] to *deliberate* upon the rejection of the bill by the Lords – to give them the earliest opportunity of expressing their wishes upon the subject, and to enable them to take such measures as seemed necessary for their future protection.'[36] The Political Union Council refused to allow its members to be sworn in as special constables as well, but promised that the organization would not interfere with Wetherell's appearance in the town.[37] Finally, the Corporation hired sailors of the merchant fleet to serve as bodyguards, or 'bludgeon' men, to put down any potential riots. Mr John Reynolds acted as go-between for the Bristol magistrates and the Political Union in order to 'reach some constructive arrangement with the Union prior to Wetherell's visit'.[38] He urged Herapath to 'do a most essential service to the city and the cause [of reform] . . . by using the whole of his influence [he could] prevent a tumult.'[39] Herapath in turn contacted Alderman Henry Daniel, who offered the opportunity for the Union to serve as Wetherell's bodyguard when he came to town.[40] He declined the invitation for the Political Union to act as Wetherell's bodyguard. He explained that Union members would stay away from the assizes, 'because if they were present and any breach of the peace were committed, it would by their enemies be attributed to them.'[41] Herapath assured Daniel that he was also 'anxious that the peace of the city should be preserved'.[42] Daniel informed Herapath of the magistrates' plans to protect Wetherell by the use of the sailors (temporarily authorized as constables) and troops, if necessary.

Herapath took this information back to the Political Union Council and assured Daniel that 'no member of the union will be found committing outrages on that day [Wetherell's arrival].'[43] But the Council also informed the Corporation, and everyone else in the town, that 'if the magistracy of the city feel themselves incompetent to preserve the public peace without being supported by the military, they should resign their offices, and suffer the civic authorities to be elected by a majority of the votes of their fellow-citizens.'[44] The Political Union Council denounced the use of the military against citizens and urged its members, 'at all times of popular excitement, [to] use their most strenuous endeavours for the preservation of the public peace.'[45]

Wetherell's arrival resulted in three days of rioting which included mobs storming and burning the Mansion House, Customs House, the Bishop's Palace, a number of private homes and emptying and firing three gaols. Wetherell barely escaped the crowd, which seems to have fluctuated between 400 and 2,000.[46] As soon as the crowd began attacking property, 'Mr. Williams [a magistrate] proceeded to summon such of the [Political Union Council] members as lived in the vicinity of Queens Square and about 10:00 James Ven, the secretary and Mr. Chamberlain arrived at Mr. Herapath's.' They informed him that from 'the intelligence they had received and the firing of the soldiers, they concluded that lives had been lost and that unless an immediate stop could be put to such proceedings, serious calamities would result.'[47] The Council drew up a handbill and had members distribute it through the mob on Sunday morning. It read:

> The Council of the Union knows that Sir Charles Wetherell has left the city and that the assizes are postponed. They earnestly entreat that every man will immediately return to his own home . . . [and not] outrageously injure the cause of reform.[48]

Later that morning, the Union Council met and resolved that J. Withers and Herapath should call upon the magistrates, 'and offer them the services of the Union, with the proviso that they should not act under the command of the military'.[49] Evidently, the mayor declined the services of the Union as a body, but said he would be grateful 'if the council would send some of their members to protect the persons of the Magistrates'.[50] Ven commented later that this 'was another chance thrown away by the Corporation . . . three of four hundred men, known as members of the Union, could have commanded the obedience of the mob, one fourth of the number would have induced the citizens of Bristol to take part with them and rioting must have ended.'[51] But the Union's reluctance to intervene on behalf of the Corporation left the mayor and magistrates with only one solution: the cavalry.

When the troops arrived in Bristol, they found chaos. The gaol, Bishop's Palace, Mansion House, toll house, Bridewell, customs house, excise house, docks and several private houses in Queen's Square had been burned or demolished.[52] Colonel Brereton's concern for safety and his fear of civilian deaths as a result of gunfire, prompted him to adopt a cautious role for the military. He refused Mayor Pinney's request that the troops take any action necessary to disperse the mob and his reluctance allowed the crowds – whose dominant sentiments were a dangerous combination of anger and fear – to swell. As a result, the crowd became more desperate and reckless and Brereton's fears of another Peterloo mounted. The crowd stoned the soldiers, injuring three of them and prompting gunfire from the troops. One rioter was killed.[53] It became very clear that only the withdrawal of the troops would restore peace to the city. The magistrates solicited special constables to provide civil policing after the troops' removal and hundreds volunteered. By the time it was all over, official estimates were 12 dead and 94 wounded.[54] Of the 102 arrested during the riots, 81 were convicted in trials that produced a trunk full of transcripts and documents.[55] Brereton was court-martialled and before his trial was completed, committed suicide.

The role of the Bristol Political Union in maintaining the peace was less successful than its leaders and the town magistrates would have wished. But that was in part because Herapath would not formally commit the Union as a body once he knew that the military had already been called in. When the troops arrived, Herapath did not want any misconceptions, on any side, as to what role Unionists were playing.

Critics accused the Political Union of instigating, rather than trying to quell the riots. Those on the streets during the looting and destruction saw little evidence that the Political Union was present. In the trials of those arrested during the riots, descriptions of the rioters did not match Union membership.[56] One witness testified that not only did members of the Political Union not incite or encourage those on the streets, but 'a man who appeared a mechanic (and from his conversation with me I believed to be a member of the Political Union) said that the soldiers had been sent for . . . [but] that the Political Union were to meet on Monday and the magistrates would see that "we can put it [the riots] down".'[57] Another claimed that Herapath and Ven had been in front of the Council House just prior to its burning.[58] The *United Service Journal* reported that 'The Unionists . . . armed with white favours suddenly swarmed in the streets like butterflies after a shower.'[59]

The Political Union did replace the soldiers on the streets, but the magistrates did not recognize the usefulness of the Union. On Monday, 31 October, a frustrated and very nervous group of magistrates summoned Herapath to the Council House. After considerable conversation, not all of it pleasant, Herapath finally called upon Political Unionists to be sworn in as special constables. By the end of the day, about 300 of the 2,819 men patrolling the streets of Bristol were Political Unionists.[60] It was significant that the magistrates still negotiated with Herapath for Political Union participation in policing the town. Evidently, the majority of special constables did not command the same respect from the people as members of the Political Union.

The Bristol Political Union had turned into a recognized and apparently trusted authority among ordinary Bristolians. If Unionists, who had always urged peace during Wetherell's visit as well as rejected the idea of any military presence in the town, were willing to patrol the streets with the authority to arrest those disturbing the peace, the magistrates could feel more secure that their authority would be respected and that law and order would be restored. Writing to Francis Place a few years after the riots, Union secretary John Ham remained 'quite convinced that the Union *could* and *would* have preserved the peace of the city . . . had the magistrates given them sufficient authority.'[61] The Bristol Political Union had the people's respect and that made it the most effective source of authority in the town.

OTHER RIOTS AND TROUBLE SPOTS

Perhaps in response to the riots in Bristol, crowds took to the streets in Worcester on 5 November. Historians have speculated that the cause was Wetherell's marriage into a Worcester family.[62] The combined circumstances of the County Reform Meeting on 7 November 1831, also being market day and the anniversary of the Gunpowder Plot, led to further rioting. Windows were broken in Foregate. Handbills were immediately distributed inviting inhabitants of the city to enroll themselves as special constables. As in Bristol, the Political Union volunteered for the job and had 'tendered their services to the Magistrates in the course of the evening and been sworn in.'[63] The constables were sent out, and the rioters began to attack. 'Several blows were exchanged on both sides.'[64] The mayor, Henry Clifton, swore in 400 special constables, many of them members of the Political Union Council, and sent a request for the 7th Hussars, stationed at Droitwich. The Hussars arrived at 1.15 am, to be greeted by a mob throwing stones. Thirty people were arrested, most released on their own recognizance and a promise to keep the peace.[65] Days after the rioting ceased, local officials noted that 'those present at reform meetings' or Political Unionists 'had done a great deal to keep the destruction and violence to a minimum'.[66]

Henry Hunt also reacted to the Bill's defeat and the use of the military to put down the riots in Bristol. Mindful of the Peterloo massacre, Hunt reacted to the news by going north and stirring up the masses. He prepared a series of addresses and began a tour, presenting plans to create a union of workers to fight for nothing less than universal manhood suffrage, annual parliaments and the ballot. Hunt condemned the Reform Bill and urged his audiences to cease supporting it.[67] The tour took Hunt through Macclesfield, Stockport, Manchester, Bolton, Blackburn, Preston, Leeds and Huddersfield – all sites of Political Unions. He assured the workers of the north and northwest that the Bill would not enfranchise them. At his meeting in Bolton, Political Unionist William Naisby, by using the tax rolls, showed that only one adult male in 30 would meet the new qualification in that town.[68]

Hunt's cultivation of discontent among the workers in the north prompted fears in the government that a revolution was at hand. In Preston, which Hunt represented in Parliament, he called for the 're-formation of the great Northern Union', an organization that would turn the current crisis into a campaign for a reform measure that would not make men the 'dupes of the Whigs'.[69] His visit to Preston accomplished two things. First, he helped organize a working-class Union with delegations representing the north of England in a new Radical reform campaign. This Union of the Working Classes worried the government and Political Unionists alike in its demand for universal suffrage at a time when a moderate reform measure had just failed. Second, Hunt's visit resulted in riots in Preston, with 25 arrests and the billeting of troops in the town for the rest of the winter.[70] Though his Radical rhetoric worried the government, Hunt was hardly a successful revolutionary. His own economic and social standing, combined with his demagogic tendencies, alienated most of his supporters in time.

The reform riots, wherever they took place, represented the people's anger and frustration over the aristocracy's failure to accept their will on reform. The Bristol riots and the role of the Bristol Political Union had an impact on public perception. The defeat in the Lords, news reports of the riots and the Union's attempt to police the streets all helped clarify the true state of reform, the threat of revolution and the practical value of popular organizations. Lord Althorp assessed one side of the issue in writing to his father that 'leaders of Political Unions are . . . frightened as they have set a machine in motion which they cannot control.'[71] Perhaps most troubling about events in Bristol, unlike the earlier riots, at least for critics of Political Unions, was that magistrates had had legitimized these extra-parliamentary organizations by requesting their assistance as special constables. The rioting heightened fears of revolution. But the local authorities' acceptance of – in some cases reliance on – Political Unions was even more threatening.

The 'official' use of the Political Union to bring order to the town, the notion that extra-parliamentary organizations had so much authority among the people of Bristol – and that the magistrates had simply handed their power over to the Union – terrified politicians. The Union had even drafted a three-point message to the government that claimed 'that the Unions and no other power whatever could prevent the greatest mischief taking place.'[72] The King, coaxed by his Tory brother, the Duke of Cumberland, the Duke of Wellington and anti-reformers, demanded the end to Political Unions as a threat to the existing English constitution and the safety of the kingdom.[73]

The actions of the Bristol Political Union invigorated reformers as they responded to the events in Bristol and public reaction. Though the Union did not prevent or ultimately put down riots, they played a prominent part in calming things down. They embraced the responsibility of maintaining order and protecting life and property as one of the primary objectives of Political Unions. The incorporation of the Bristol Political Union into the special constabulary, according to Captain Bowles, who had also been among those called in to put down the riots in Nottingham, had created, 'feelings [of fear which] brought volunteers from the population to join special constabularies' thus bringing them into the process of peacekeeping and policing and avoiding any reliance upon the Political Unions.[74]

In spite of Lord Melbourne's report which suggested the Bristol

Political Union's role in trying to end the riots was 'confined to the issue of placards', the government was, no doubt, motivated to introduce legislation creating a municipal police force in England.[75] The government looked at the events in Bristol and saw that Political Unions actively involved in policing as well as dutifully protecting the government and its reform measure from attack. A Home Office memorandum claimed that 'the institution of Political Unions which now [following the Bristol riots have] become general . . . convinced the Government that they were taking risks that could not be justified and compelled them to attend to important matters: first, that the Unions, and no other power, whatever, could prevent the greatest mischief taking place.'[76] Those politicians who had feared that the Political Unions were too radical were reassured that their members were responsible and level-headed men, not the violent revolutionaries they so feared. Adding strength to that conclusion was the knowledge that the Bristol magistrates had, to some degree, legitimized Political Unionists by turning to them for assistance in the first place.

There were, of course, those who feared the worst. The Tory, Lord Talbot, was one of those 'urg[ing] the government not to rely [on the Unions] for the passing of the Reform Bill' and recommending that Lord John Russell not openly welcome the Unions' assistance in carrying the Bill.[77] Other contemporary observers declared that 'even in Bristol, peace might have been preserved if the Tory junta [and West Indian Whig interests in the Corporation] had only accepted of the assistance of the Unionists.'[78] Such affirmation of their potential strength further legitimized Political Unions as respectable, law-abiding and a necessary ally to secure peaceful reform. Melbourne's Home Office reports affirmed this, claiming: 'if the peace should be broken . . . the government would have no power to put it down. Whatever regulation or control there was would lie in the Unions.'[79]

Political Unions also recognized that the government faced a difficult battle in convincing the King and anti-reformers that the public deserved a hearing and participation in government after the violence in October. Connections between the events and Political Unions only added to the anti-reformers' belief that the extension of the franchise would only assure such behaviour, and lead to the masses taking over the governmental process. Reformers, determined not to let the Tories win this battle of perception, formed Political Unions throughout the country. As Edward Ellice put it,

'The Bristol affair seems to have produced one good consequence – rallying the supporters of peace and the men of property and industrial pursuits all over the Kingdom, for the maintenance of order and quiet.'[80]

THE CREATION OF THE NEW PEACE-KEEPING POLITICAL UNIONS

The creation of new Political Unions took off after the rejection of the Reform Bill and the rioting in Bristol. The BPU claimed to have received over 50 requests for copies of its *Rules and Regulations* from provincial reformers.[81] The creations of Unions was so widespread and numerous, that Grey found himself explaining the phenomenon to the King as proof of public support for the Bill. 'It is not the less true that these Unions have received a great impulse and extension from the rejection of the Reform Bill,' he wrote, 'and that many persons, not otherwise disposed to do so, have been induced to join them for the purpose of promoting that measure.'[82] The King became more and more convinced that, despite their protestations to the contrary, Political Unions were not loyal organizations of reformers, but dangerous and seditious conclaves of revolutionaries.

The Home Office alleviated some of the King's fears when it issued an official report stating that Political Unions had played no part in any of the riots in the midlands and that 'the members of the [Bristol] Political Union came forward bodily to serve as special constables in re-establishing the peace.'[83] Grey offered assurances that, 'if further outrages of this nature [the riots] should occur, [he would seek] the means of making some addition to the military force of the country.'[84]

While this may have calmed the King's fears of revolution somewhat, it did little to address what he saw as the far more pressing problem – the growing influence of the Political Unions. Whether or not directly responsible for the events in Nottingham and Bristol, the King held the Unions indirectly responsible, for their very existence represented defiance of the law. The Unions were defying statutes concerning extra-parliamentary political associations from 1799 and 1817. William understood why Grey had not utilized the existing law to disband the Political Unions – they were useful demonstrations of public support when they endorsed the Bill. But the government's toleration of the Unions, the King believed, had opened a Pandora's box of activity among the people, legal and illegal, which, based on the government's lack of action against the Unions, they had every reason to believe would also be tolerated. In short, the King believed that the Unions' operations, free from government restriction or interference, was the catalyst for more popular action – including the October riots.

The King's fears were also those of the Duke of Wellington, who expressed them to His Majesty at every opportunity and no doubt fanned the flames. Major General Fitzroy Somerset, former Military Secretary, and Lord Granville Somerset kept the Duke informed of the military's operations in Bristol as he accumulated evidence of communications between the BPU and the government.[85] Having been told prior to the riots that representatives of the Home Office had met BPU delegates in London, Lord Bradford assured Wellington that, legally speaking, such communication was at best 'improper'.[86]

After the Reform Bill's defeat in the Lords, Political Unions responded with mass meetings and addresses and petitions, to the King as well as the government, blaming the vote on Tory aristocrats and the Anglican bishops. They laid no blame on the champions of the reform measure. All expressed thanks and devout loyalty to the King. Typical was an address sent by the Leicester Political Union expressing regret that the King's efforts had been thwarted by the Lords:

> Your Majesty's gracious intentions towards your loyal subjects, although seconded by the efforts of an honest, a patriotic and enlightened Ministry, have been however unhappily defeated by a majority of the House of Lords. Under these circumstances, alike distressing to your Majesty's paternal feelings, and destructive of your people's hopes, we deem it our sacred duty to offer to your Majesty our earnest prayer, that your Majesty will be graciously pleased to continue in office your present Ministers, in whom, we, your Majesty's loyal subjects place our entire confidence, and in whose firmness and integrity we have the fullest reliance.[87]

Other Political Unions reiterated this message. Upon receiving word of the Bill's defeat, the Coventry Political Union Council forwarded a petition to Westminister expressing the assurances of loyalty from the organization:

> We approach your Throne with sentiments of the most profound veneration and attachment to your Majesty's person, and with gratitude for the paternal solicitude which your Majesty has evinced for the welfare of the subjects, the amelioration of their condition and the restitution of their political rights.[88]

The Union promised the King that his continued support would 'render your Majesty's name truly illustrious and shed a glory upon your reign brighter than the greatest victories or the most extended foreign conquests could bestow.'[89] Grey believed that the Unions might attract those frustrated by events and channel the energies of potential rioters into constructive action for the government measure, rather than into destructive behaviour that would jeopardize the Bill. Second, if rioting did break out, the Unions could serve as a special constabulary and work with local magistrates to restore order quickly. This would, many hoped, alleviate the fears of those who, despite the published evidence to the contrary, were convinced that Political Unions formed to instigate such events. Policing became a primary purpose for a number of provincial reformers forming Political Unions after the Bristol riots.

There was a change among existing Political Unions as well. Those that had not endorsed the government's Bill because they believed it too moderate, now became painfully aware of the reality: anti-reform forces were a much more serious obstacle than they had previously appreciated. It was now clear to reformers throughout the country that they needed to concentrate all their efforts on the Whig measure and simply postpone indefinitely the campaign for universal suffrage, the ballot and annual parliaments. They too took it upon themselves to defend and protect their citizens and property from riot and other disturbances that might develop as the Reform Bill was reintroduced.

Thirty-six Political Unions formed between the end of October and the end of December 1831. Some of these Unions we know little about: they called a first meeting for which there was a public notice or newspaper advertisement (indicating the date of that meeting), but we know little or nothing about them thereafter, if indeed they long survived their formation. Among the 'unknown' Unions were those in Alfreton, Belper, Hales Owen, Heywood, Hinckley, Holt, Hulme, Ludlow, Macclesfield, Merthyr Tydfil, Ramsgate, Reading, Swanwick, Thanet, Tilbury and Torrington.[90] Nonetheless, the founders consciously chose the name 'Political

Union' for their organizations, linking them with the Union movement and its goals, regardless of how long they lasted.

For other Unions, more but still quite limited information exists. Often, there is one detailed account of the formation of the Union, with speeches, objectives, resolutions and parliamentary petitions. In such cases, the leaders, or at least those speaking at Political Union meetings and recorded in the newspapers, can be identified, but no information as to the overall Union composition or whether, like the BPU, these were Political Unions whose goal was to join together the middle and working classes has survived. What is clear from the language of these Unionists as well as their rules, regulations and objectives, when available, is that they knew that they must present a unified front against the House of Lords and opponents of the Bill if they were to foil their efforts to defeat it. Second, they were clear that they must also stand for peace and order, for the same reason.

As a direct result of the riots and the growing belief that Political Unions could be an effective peacekeeping tool, one of the first towns to create the newly redefined Political Union was Derby. Led by William Baker and Mr Vickers of Belper, the Union resolved to support the Bill although it was 'not what all the people had asked for, [and] while it might not satisfy them, and establish their happiness, he [Vickers] thought it would save them from a national convulsion.'[91] Vickers also argued that had a Political Union existed in the town weeks earlier, the riots could have been prevented. 'If the men who committed such outrages had been better informed they would not have acted as they did. It was a lack of political focus', he claimed, 'which resulted in violence rather than the peaceful expression of political concern upon the defeat of the Bill.' It was for this very reason that establishing a Political Union was so 'manly, patriotic and Christian'.[92] Though the Bristol Union could not stop the rioting, the public perception seemed to be that had the military not made matters worse, Unionists serving as special constables would have commanded the respect of the rioters and restored the peace without violence. One Mr Meakin also pointed out to new Unionists that keeping the peace was not their only mission. He listed a set of objectives, including the repeal of the Corn Laws, games laws, laws protecting monopolies and those which particularly discriminated against 'the lower orders'.[93]

The Gloucester Political Union, it appears, was a largely middle-class organization, its members being clients and associates of the

Union's founders, local solicitors R.H. Carter and C. Parker.[94] The Union declared its support for the Bill and pledged itself to 'protect the people and [their] property from all violence and disorder and assist civil authorities in the suppression of any local disturbance of the peace.'[95] Of course, it supported the government and the Reform Bill as well by petitioning the government and attending rallies and meetings.[96]

A Union in Hanley and Shelton also formed for 'promoting the passage of the Reform Bill' and 'to furnish a means of protection both to persons and property in the event of a sudden commotion.'[97] This Union, composed of 'manufacturers, tradesmen and workmen from the Potteries', focused on securing the Bill and the representation for the Potteries which members believed so vital to their political and economic interests. The Union was also concerned about presumed ties, particularly from the Home Office, between the Political Union and disorder among local miners.[98]

The Boston Union organizers, including the printer and journalist for the *Stamford Bee,* John Noble, Sr, established their Union 'on the same principle as that in Birmingham'.[99] The Union would 'aid in the cause of constitutional reform'. But unlike anything that the BPU had included in its *Rules and Regulations*, this Union intended to serve as a police force.[100] 'These societies, it is believed, may save the country from anarchy and riot; they have been found to check the wild spirit of plunder.'[101] In Somerton, the newly formed Political Union's goal was 'to circulate political knowledge by means of pamphlets and other publications, among all classes of society . . . so that they may know their rights and privileges as men and their duty as subjects and secure the peace and prosperity of all.'[102]

Solicitors Samuel Lucas and Joseph Jenkinson established the Union at Dronfield. They recorded 80 paid-up members at the first meeting.[103] Its Council, chaired by A. Wolstenholme, endorsed the Reform Bill, pledged to fight 'any society which had a compulsory objective in view – the arbitrary and illegal attack against the individual', and rejected criticisms that 'such political societies [as the Union] in general supported and encouraged men of deceitful or suspicious characters.'[104] The Union began to focus on such concerns as whether or not its working-class members were objects of suspicion and prompted others to distrust the Union's cause. Debates on the abolition of taxes on knowledge and the worthiness of mechanics and labourers to be afforded free access to the political information and displaced discussions of universal suffrage.

Creating informed and responsible electors was, Union leaders believed, the best way to assure critics that reform would not open the door to revolution or political corruption on a mass case.

The Yeovil Political Union formed in late November.[105] At its inaugural meeting, the chairman contended that the Union was created, 'not for the purpose ... [of] opposing the spirit of the Constitution, but to put down anarchy and confusion, in whatever form it may appear ... We are ready, like every other good and loyal subject, to place ourselves under the command of the civil authorities, should the riotous scenes that have lately convulsed the town and neighbourhood ... happen here.'[106] The Yeovil Union Council took it upon itself to report to the Home Office, informing its officials that 'we are reformers, but not revolutionaries. We demand only the just restoration of our rights, nor will we cease from our endeavours, or be diverted from our purpose till a thorough Reformation in Parliament is accomplished ... and England will be happy old England again.'[107]

In Shepton Mallet, the objects of the new Political Union, under the leadership of T.H.H. Phipps was 'to support the King and his ministers in accomplishing reform and preserve peace and order in town.'[108] Bury's foremost radial, Matthew Fletcher, considered to be 'intimately connected with every aspect of working class political life', was the organizer of the local Political Union.[109] The new Political Union at Heanor sought 'peaceable and constitutional means to effect parliamentary reform' with the help of Mr. Vickers of the Derby Political Union.[110] A Union formed at Bradford-on-Avon 'on the principle of the Birmingham and National Political Unions'.[111]

The Taunton Political Union, also called the 'Loyal Political Union', met for the first time on 11 November under the leadership of Dr Kinglake, George Stone and attorneys H. Leigh and Mr. Snowden. It described itself as an organization of 'wealth and influential characters in this town'.[112] The Taunton Union was so concerned with its reputation that the Council sent an open letter to the *Bath Chronicle* declaring its objectives, in order to end 'any suspicion that it [the Union] is anything else but that which it professes to be: a united body for securing the accomplishment of parliamentary reform, by loyal, peaceful means.'[113]

The Union also made clear that it believed it was the fault of the Bristol magistrates and their failure to heed the advice of the Union that the riots escalated with the entrance of the military. The Union Council drafted and sent a petition to the Home Office, criticizing the use of the military in Bristol. The magistrates gave 'unnecessary insult to that powerful and respectable assembly [the Bristol Political Union] and hostility to the people and to their popular rights' when the cavalry was called in.[114] It urged its members to restrain themselves from any physical violence, lest it resulted in the drastic measures taken in Bristol. It warned, 'be wary and watchful – patiently mark the progress [of the Bill] and be prepared for any stratagem of its implacable and unprincipled enemies.'[115]

Rochdale's Union was the work of James Taylor with help from J. Toft. Taylor, a follower of William Cobbett and a Methodist Unitarian minister, brought artisans, small shopkeepers and his religious community into the Union.[116] They advocated universal household suffrage, but in spite of the unity between the middle and working classes, did not advocate universal manhood suffrage or any radical reforms. Rochdale worked to achieve cooperation between the middle and working classes, but focused more on removing the abuses of 'Old Corruption' rather than any sweeping economic reforms that would give the workers greater control over industrial production. James Taylor led the organization with another Radical, Richard Pilling, a powerloom weaver, who had been part of the organization of the Political Union in Stockport.

The Home Office received word from some of the new Unions directly. Melbourne received handbills concerning the creation of the Frome Political Union from its chairman, George Porch, along with a personal letter assuring him that the organization would cooperate with the authorities in maintaining the peace as the bill was reintroduced.[117] It also received the Union *Rules and Regulations* from a revived Padiham Political Union which, although forming the previous May, apparently had not met since the riots. There was as well information on the long-established (but not very active) Blackburn Union, and new organizations in Briercliffe and Burnely.[118]

There were a few Political Unions that formed after the Bristol riots about which we do know a fair amount. These included Unions in Bath, Leicester, Hull and Norwich. For example, the Leicester Political Union, perhaps the group of provincial reformers most concerned about public order, was a long time in the making. Leicester had boasted a Reform Association since the Whigs came to office. Composed of mostly middle-class radical reformers and members of the Unitarian Great Meeting Chapel and other Dissenting congregations, Association members were primarily concerned with parliamentary reform that would eliminate the monopoly of power enjoyed by the close and corrupt Corporation of Leicester.[119] The Association's goal, aside from rallying public support for the Reform Bill, was beginning the process of transforming the Corporation into a body representative of the new industrial manufacturing interests. It held public meetings to discuss economic conditions, including the benefits of the elimination of tariffs, monopolies, the repeal of the Corn Laws and an overall reduction in taxes. Members included the hosiery manufacturers John Coltman and Joseph Whetstone, worsted spinners turned manufacturers, William Brewin, and William and John Biggs, as well as the bankers Thomas Pare and Thomas Paget, Jr, elected in that year as MP for Leicestershire. The core of the Leicester Political Union Council came from was the Unitarian Great Meeting, although the minister of the Harvey Lane Baptist Chapel, James Phillippo Munsell, the Congregational minister, Hugh Worthington, Joseph Winks, a printer specializing in publishing Baptist and political reform tracts in Loughborough and pastor at the Carley Street Baptist Church, also served on the Council.

By the spring of 1831, the middle-class radicals of Leicester recognized that the Grey ministry needed all the public support possible for the Reform Bill. William Biggs and Robert Brewin, leaders of the Reform Association, argued that a more inclusive organization, like Daniel O'Connell's Irish Association, was necessary in Leicester if reformers wanted to maintain a sense of urgency about reform. Cooperation with the working classes, through the trade unions, was now a necessity. It also looked promising as Edward Sansome, chairman of the Leicester branch of the National Association for the Protection of Labour, and a Mr Seal, head of the framework-knitters union, tentatively supported the Reform Bill. They regarded it merely as a first instalment towards further reform, but they understood the need to present a united front to anti-reformers.[120] Then the Reform Bill failed to move through committee in the spring of 1831. Biggs wrote to the BPU Council requesting a copy of the *Rules and Regulations.*

Close enough to both Nottingham and Derby to worry about the impact of the riots in Leicester and aware of the mounting frustration over the Bill's defeat, the town's Radicals and reformers decided to transform the Reform Association into a Political Union. At a meeting of 'over 100 respectable inhabitants held in open area by bazaar, Humberstone-gate', Biggs and Brewin 'proposed that a

Political Union be formed in this town.'[121] The Leicester and Leicestershire Political Union held its first meeting at the Bell Hotel on 2 November 1831.[122] Approximately 800 local trade unionists and members of the predominantly Dissenting Reform Association members enrolled prior to the meeting, but, by the end of the evening, the Union membership list boasted 4,466 names.[123] Those attending elected Biggs secretary.

The Union's first tasks were in the areas of publicity and public relations. Biggs decided that the nascent organization owed concerned citizens a full accounting of the Union's objectives and tactics. He hoped to solicit their support, and more importantly, restrain any riotous impulses a frustrated population might have over the Bill's defeat. The Union published and widely distributed its first official broadside, introducing the organization and calling upon citizens to attend a public meeting:

> Fellow-townsmen and neighbours! – in uniting together under a more complete and effective organization, our principles are still the same. The motto of our union is peace and reform, reform, without which there can be no lasting tranquillity. – peace, without which there may be devastation, there may be slaughter, there may be despotism, but there can be neither political improvement nor social happiness. It is because we believe that every hope of liberty must vanish is a state of domestic discord, that we solemnly enjoin on the members of our union, and conjure our fellow-countrymen in general, to refrain from all language and all conduct calculated to create alarm, to disturb tranquillity, and to avert the stern, steady gaze of the nation from that small but desperate faction, who are at length compelled to fly before the justice of the sovereign and their country.[124]

Nearly all the speeches of the middle-class Union Council leaders, and the employers of knitters and spinners, alluded to the Nottingham and Bristol riots. Speeches condemned 'brute force, not guided by reason, nor wielded by principle', and reminded Union members that the reason behind these organizations was to unite individuals in support of reform because, though 'the physical force of an united people is tremendous, it is irresistible, but to render it so, it must be concentrated by union, it must be directed by reason, it must be sanctioned by public opinion.'[125] It was made clear that by joining the Union, reformers could both promote the Bill and preserve the peace. Brewin contended that 'to preserve the public peace, and to prevent the sacred cause of reform from being wrecked by anarchy, treachery, or discord . . . we invite all those to whom these objects are dear, to swell our numbers and increase our usefulness.'[126] Biggs pointed to the sites of rioting, sympathizing with the crowds that he, too, 'should not hesitate to employ physical force if necessary, as I have no more inclination than yourselves to die a slave of boroughmongers'.[127] But he also reminded them that, 'the disturbances we lament in the neighbouring towns have been provoked by the infatuated folly of individuals whom no dangers can warn, nor any experience instruct . . . it is like raising heaven and earth to kill a fly . . . It [violence] brings distrust and discredit on the character of the people. It spreads alarm, and from alarm, disunion.'[128]

The Union Council also put the main responsibility for maintaining the peace and the securing the future of the Bill squarely on the workers:

> Fellow-countrymen of the working classes! Your fate is in your own hands. None but yourselves can now prevent reform. If you follow the safe guidance of your friends of the middle classes, you will be free, and enjoy those blessings which freedom invariably brings in her train. But if you distrust their sincerity, or despise their caution; if you suffer yourselves to be diverted by speculative theories from securing the prize which is within your reach, and the value of which you may learn from the efforts made to prevent your obtaining it: still more, if you allow yourselves to be seduced by ruffians and villains from the path of honesty and of honour; you will find that you have not only lost the substance in grasping at a shadow, but that the thunders preparing for the heads of your enemies will fall with destructive force on your own. The scale of victory in this contest is in the hands of the *middle classes*.[129]

It was also made clear that the middle classes too had their own duty and responsibility:

> And you who belong to that important, numerous, and influential rank of British society, to whom the first appeal has been made by your patriot king and his ministers for the salvation of your country, show yourselves worthy of the trust reposed in you. Let not your calmness and presence of mind desert you amidst the present agitations; nor the fear of the popular violence cause

you to throw yourselves into the ranks of the enemies of reform, or to seek that protection from coercion which you will much more effectually obtain from conciliation. Do not confound the honest and intelligent people with the knaves and ruffians who are taking advantage of their justly irritated feelings to accomplish their purposes of villainy and mischief. While you strike down the one, neglect not to soothe, to support, and encourage the other: and when the present clouds shall have passed away, and a more fair and smiling season returns, the sunshine which illumines your country will be reflected from your own bosoms in the proud consciousness of having saved her best interests from destruction.[130]

Above all, Biggs and other Union leaders stressed that violence jeopardized the Bill as it would weaken the main argument used by Grey and the government: that public opinion was solidly behind the reform measure and, its passage would, in no way, open the door to a violent overthrow of existing society. 'Above all,' Brewin warned, violence 'places a friendly government in a situation of peculiar embarrassment.'[131] The solicitor and Council member Samuel Stone also admonished, 'nothing but our own misconduct could prevent our victory.'[132]

As for the political objectives of the Leicester Political Union, the chief goal was to dismantle the monopoly of power enjoyed by the Corporation. The Bill's creation of uniform electoral qualifications began this process, but it was clear from Union speeches and Biggs's handbills that municipal reform was their next objective. Not surprisingly for this Unitarian-led organization, the end of Anglican religious privileges and tithes was also on the agenda. The Union also sought all economic reforms which would bring free trade, and in turn improve the foreign market for manufacturers and allow higher wages for their employees. Not surprisingly after the October vote on the Bill, the limitation of the power of the House of Lords became an objective as well. While these were future goals, the minutes of the Political Council meetings recorded by Biggs reveal that the Union's leadership was almost exclusively concerned with the passage of the Reform Bill. The Council rejected most petitions drafted by the Political Unionists as too critical of the bill's limited reform and did not wish to 'embarrass the government in attempts to pass the reform bill'.[133]

It was the Lords' rejection of the Bill which brought discussions about the creation of a Bath Political Union at a public meeting on 13 October.[134] *Bath Journal* editor, John Keene, and longtime local Radical J. Hawksey Ackersley organized the meeting and urged those attending to establish a Union like the BPU, a Union of both middle- and working-class members whose express purpose now was to support the government.[135] 'In consequence of the rejection, by the House of Lords, of the Reform Bill, which was submitted to Parliament by his Majesty's Ministers,' Keene told the crowd, the meeting's 'resolutions will state the course which it is thought advisable should be adopted'.[136] 'Let us then use all our efforts to support the Government in the exercise of its just authority, and the Bill on which you have set your hearts on will undoubtedly be passed,' he urged.[137] The leaders asked that everyone should do whatever was necessary to 'show by our conduct that we deserve [the Bill] . . .'[138]

> Let us show by our patience, our calmness, our strict adherence to good order; our implicit obedience to the laws and our respect for the decrees of the magistracy . . . let us not by any thoughtless conduct put those excellent friends [the government] to shame and make them regret that they took it upon themselves to advocate our cause.[139]

On 7 November, 3,000 inhabitants of Bath joined together and formed the Bath Political Union. Delegates from Bristol and Birmingham, according to one source, came to give advice and assistance.[140] James Crisp, Radical and master hatter, became the Union's first chairman, followed by J.T. Mayne, a local barrister. Within six weeks, 1,500 artisans, manufacturers and other residents of Bath joined the Political Union for a subscription fee of one shilling per quarter. The Bath Union committed itself to 'an uncompromising stand against the borough oligarchy' and support for the Whig government.[141]

As urgently as the new Bath Political Union leaders discussed the need to see the Reform Bill enacted, they also stressed the need for peace and order during the remainder of the campaign:

> Remember, that if we break the peace, it is the King's peace which we shall be violating. Shall we disturb the public quiet? No! for we should then be playing the game of our political opponents, and annoy, in the severest degree, the honest and patriotic Ministry who are straining every nerve – using all possible

endeavours to serve us . . . The Ministers have given us a good character, let us show by our conduct that we deserve it.[142]

This self-ascribed role prompted serious criticism of the Bath Union. An open letter to the inhabitants of Bath condemned this 'self-constituted political body', calling members 'political monsters' and declaring the Union illegal, and not 'consistent, either with the preservation of the Constitution or the common peace and security of Society,' representing as it did the most 'pernicious [of] busy-bodies in the social state'.[143] The author of the open letter was far more concerned than the Home Secretary, who also knew of the Bath Union's creation.[144]

James Acland and Joseph Noble, the printer and publisher of the *Hull Portfolio*, organized the Hull Political Union.[145] Plans began just days after the Reform Bill's defeat to form 'a "Union" of men determined to free themselves from the persecution and their common country from the domination of our National and Local Aristocracy.'[146] The Lords' vote outraged Hull's reformers. They would not tolerate 'a refusal of justice to the people and fatal evidence of the utter indifference of the higher classes, to the wants and claims of the millions, upon whom they perpetuate the oppression, to which they have so long subjected them'.[147]

The members of the Hull and Sculcoates Political Union hoped 'to obtain by every just and legal means . . . a full, free and fair representation of the People'.[148] In spite of the evidence demonstrating that perhaps not even the Bill itself, and certainly no larger dose of reform was going to pass the Upper House, the Hull Political Union called for the ballot and shorter parliaments in addition to passage of the government's measure. James Acland's argument, the author of the Union prospectus, was that if the King and his ministers were made to distinguish 'the loyal people from the iron sway of an unprincipled and heartless oligarchy', additional reforms to preserve the purity of elections would not be objectionable.[149] Acland invited everyone to join the Union 'who dare attempt the regeneration of our political powers, the renovation of our acknowledged rights, the redress of our manifold wrongs!'[150] Though there was an emphasis on the defeat of the Reform Bill by the House of Lords, the Hull Political Union used the same 'Old Corruption' arguments and justifications for their reform objectives as Political Unions had from the beginning.

By December, however, the Union readjusted its position and

resolved that 'the Reform Bill in progress . . . deserves the most earnest support of the country . . . and we express our hope that His Majesty's ministers will not pause in their glorious career, until they have cleansed the stable of National and Corporate corruption.'[151] The Council, prompted by concern over the perception by many in authority of the Unions as connected to violence and riot, publicized the role of the Union in the town: 'notwithstanding the exasperating tendency of conduct on the part of Local Governors, [Unionists] are determined to devote themselves generally and collectively as unsworn protectors of the public peace, and of private rights, [and] to the maintenance of the laws of the realm and the support of right principles, and of the social order and happiness of the community'.[152] It had also published Union hymns, manufactured and sold Union memorabilia and increased its membership to over 400.[153]

Economic concerns as well as fears of public disturbances prompted the creation, in November 1831, of the Norwich Political Union. Founded by William Enfield, Jr, a worsted woollen manufacturer and a prominent Unitarian, and J. Dawson, a printer, the Union was to serve as a means of 'reason and moral influence . . . [rather than] physical force . . . [which would] bind the middle and lower classes together for the purpose of securing, by peaceful and legal means only, the great Measure of Reform.'[154] Their intent was that manufacturers and weavers should be 'drawn closer and rendered indissoluble, by the perception of their common interest and mutual support', and use extra-parliamentary pressure to ensure that the large Norwich electorate would return representatives committed to economic reform.[155] The Union leadership welcomed all 'gentlemen of talent, energy, and respectability able and willing to step forward and take the lead' and ensure that weavers 'get political knowledge . . . and procure a restoration of civil rights by being admitted a share in the choice of Representatives, and the framing of those Laws by which we are to be governed.'[156] The Union could achieve this by 'ensuring the return of upright and intelligent, active and efficient, representatives . . . [and then to] direct the Members [of Parliament as to] the best means of securing a fair remunerating price for Labour to all the working classes . . . [through a] fair reduction in the whole system of Taxation, so that it may press less severely upon the industrious classes of the community.'[157]

Public order was also a concern for founders of the Norwich Political Union. Local newspapers such as the *East Anglian* accused the leaders of forming the Union because prospects of violence had made it necessary for some sort of body to channel the energies of the people into something productive. 'We would observe with regard to the Political Union . . . that it is only in times of very great excitement when they can be wanted . . . Public danger is their cement.'[158] The Union itself talked about keeping an eye on those they suspected of the rick-burning in the countryside. After Bristol, there seemed every possibility that economic and political frustration might erupt in East Anglia.

Perhaps the best example of a Political Union created to maintain public order as well as support the Reform Bill was the London-based National Political Union, founded by the middle-class reformer Francis Place in response to the Bill's defeat and the riots.[159] When the rejection of the Reform Bill made it clear to Place and his fellow Westminster Radicals that 'the aristocracy would not spontaneously renounce their power', he proposed the creation of a Union 'to give a definite form to public opinion, to create an organ through which that opinion could be efficiently transmitted . . . to put the wishes of the people at large in organized array: to give them by Union, so imposing an appearance, that denial of their demands should be hopeless and direct oppression dangerous.'[160]

He began to 'concoct a scheme for a metropolitan Political Union on a large scale . . . on the plan of the Birmingham Union omitting only such matters as related to the particular views of Mr. Attwood respecting the currency.'[161] The NPU was also Place's attempt to undercut the support the National Union of Working Classes received throughout the greater London area. The NUWC openly scorned the Bill and by August 1831 when it passed in the Commons, had persuaded an increasing number of Londoners to withdraw all support for a measure that would do them no good at all. Indeed, Henry Hunt announced in the Commons that 'The people felt much cooler towards the measure. It was now, in fact, a dead letter.'[162] Place set out to demonstrate just the opposite to the government and anti-reformers alike.

On Wednesday, 12 October, representatives from many of London's parishes assembled at the Crown and Anchor Tavern in the Strand at 6:00 to decide on 'the best means of giving effectual support to the King and Government, and on the measures necessary to secure the peace and safety of the metropolis.'[163] Place's thinking was pragmatic. If his organization was going to succeed, it needed to play up this issue of revolution and the Political Union's role in suppressing it. Gibbon Wakefield, a friend and political associate of Place, published a pamphlet, widely circulated in London, warning householders that the NUWC were attempting to organize a 'revolutionary outbreak' in which they would call upon 'the most dissolute elements of the metropolis' to bring this to pass and urging people to join the more moderate National Political Union instead.[164] According to Place, 'the NPU differed very much from the BPU. The Council of that Union assembled only when it had some important business to transact, and it called the general membership together only on still more important occasions. In the NPU, it was absolutely necessary that the Council should meet at least once a week, and a portion of its members still more often as a business communication that its officers should attend at some known place as an office all day long, and that some of its members should be frequently, if not continually there during the hours of business . . .' no doubt to help broaden membership.[165]

The 2 November NPU Council meeting finalized the *Rules and Regulations* which the committee would present to the general membership for approval at the Union's first meeting. The NPU was designed to support the government. Rules concerning the frequency of general meetings, subscription fees and the appropriate role of a Union member were the same as most other Political Unions.[166] The only difference was that the NPU intended to create branches in order to direct the London metropolitan area with greater effectiveness. There was also a greater concern for peaceful organization following the Bristol riots. Prior to the first NPU meeting, Place had placards posted on the streets of London reminding people they could ill 'afford the Boroughmongers a pretext for saying that we are not of one mind . . . but also [could] not [afford to] suffer other Bristols.'[167] Other placards were posted to assure the government that the Political Union was in solid support of their Reform Bill. 'Reformers,' they read, 'nearly to a man, have been unanimous in their acceptance of the Ministerial Measure.'[168]

Place called the first public meeting of the new NPU for 10 November. The radical surgeon Thomas Wakely chaired the event. Hundreds of members of the NUWC and Rotundanists attended, demanding that the organization pledge itself to universal manhood suffrage and reject the government's measure. Place began to fear a riot as the crowd was enormous and Wakely could not maintain order.[169] The meeting was moved to Lincoln's Inn Fields and Place compromised with the Rotundanist leaders, agreeing that half the NPU Council would be composed of working men (many of them members of the NUWC), but that the objectives of the NPU would remain as they were – completely supportive of the Whig reform measure and committed to its peaceful passage. Place commented that he was not worried about the working men joining the NPU as 'it was most fully demonstrated that they were willing to cooperate with those called their betters and to place sufficient reliance in them . . . They were very generally desirous that ministers should be supported . . . and the Reform Bill carried. They were ready to associate with great men, if great men would come among them.'[170] William Lovett and Richard Cleave of the NUWC made several attempts to amend the proposals for the new organization. Lovett complained that Place and his friends 'had [so] arranged themselves that they drowned by their noise and clamour every effort that Mr. Cleave and myself made in proposing our amendment to the meeting.'[171] Cleave, Lovett and Wakley were, however, selected to sit on the NPU Council, much to Place's annoyance. But by early in the new year, Place had gathered together enough supporters on the Council and within the general membership to consolidate his own position. In any event, Place was able to carry his case for support of the Whig Bill rather than universal suffrage. Struggles with the Rotundianists for control of the NPU would continue to be a problem through February 1832, but Place and advocates of the Bill succeeded in taking a majority of the places on the Council in the first election for that body.[172]

The NPU would continue to promote itself as the peaceful supporters of the Bill, composed of concerned radicals from both the middle and working classes. As resolved at the first NPU meeting, the NPU was 'not a Union of the Working Classes, nor of the Middle Classes, nor of any other class, but of all Reformers, of the masses and of the millions. The National Political Union is essentially a Union of the People.'[173] The NPU signed up 300–400 members that very day and 5,000–6,000 in the next few months of 1832.[174] Place's concern for the preservation of public order was met. When the Whigs reintroduced the Reform Bill on 12 December, the public and members of the NPU were quiet and peaceful. Riot and disorder, at least for the time being, were not issues troubling Place.

ESTABLISHED POLITICAL UNIONS RESPOND TO THE RIOTS AND THE 'ARMING OF BIRMINGHAM'

The surge in Union formation and the recognition that Political Unions and public opinion were essential to carry the Bill re-invigorated those Political Unions created before October 1831. The Northern Political Union recommitted itself to the campaign, resolving that the Council would take 'such steps as be advisable for ensuring and hastening the success of Reform, for upholding his Majesty's Government [and that] the cause should triumph without so much as even the smallest Infraction of the public Peace.'[175] It urged members of the Northern Political Union and all citizens of Newcastle and its surrounding regions to 'show them [the government] that Political Power and Liberty should be trusted [to the industrious classes] because they know how to act with Reason, with Methods, and in Harmony.'[176]

In Worcester, the Political Union changed its position on radical reform. The Bill was imperative and its cavalier dismissal by the Lords the single greatest cause of danger to the peace of the kingdom. The Political Union recruited members by playing to the public's fear of violence. 'Let not your calmness and presence of mind desert you admidst the present agitation; nor the fear of popular violence cause you to throw yourselves into the ranks of the enemies of reform, or to seek that protection from coercion which you will much more effectually obtain from conciliation.'[177] In urging the Bath Political Unionists to remain peaceful and orderly, Council members reminded them, 'if we break the peace, it is the **King's** peace which we shall be violating . . . No! we [cannot] annoy, in the severest degree, the honest King and patriotic Ministry who are straining every nerve using all possible endeavours to serve us.'[178]

In Todmorden, Union leader James Hardman called upon his fellow Unionists to demonstrate complete loyalty to the King as they did not want to be considered among those 'who are driving the nation to revolution, bloodshed, and irretrievable ruin.'[179] The Yeovil Political Union sent the Home Office and King copies of the speeches made at its inaugural meeting describing the new Union as a gathering of loyal subjects of the Crown meeting, 'not for the purpose . . . [of] opposing the spirit of the Constitution . . . We are . . . like every other good and loyal subject place ourselves under the command of the civil authorities.'[180] The new Union in Shepton Mallet sent a petition to Westminster announcing its determination 'to support the King and his ministers in accomplishing reform and preserve peace and order in town.'[181] The Taunton Political Union called itself the 'Loyal Political Union' and sent an address to William IV saying so.[82]

The Huddersfield Political Union sent a formal address to Lord Wharncliffe which informed him that its members 'have now sufficient confidence in their own talents and energies, and are determined that no other class shall be entrusted (or ought to be relied upon) to redress their wrongs or obtain their rights.'[183] The Union assured Wharncliffe that its aim was not revolution, but to 'display an irresistible front, steady in conduct and fixed in purpose; demonstrating that one grand simultaneous movement is sufficient to renovate the most perverse state in which society ever existed.'[184]

Wharncliffe was hardly assured when, in Sheffield, upon receiving word that the Reform Bill had been defeated in the House of Lords, he witnessed 'thousands flock[ing] to Paradise Square, with black flags, contemptuous effigies and the sound of muffled peals from the church bells.'[185] Sheffield Union Council member, Robert Leader, observed that the defeat was particularly hard for the town's reformers as it 'added a touch of personal poignancy that the fatal blow had come from the hand of a familiar friend and neighbour. For it was Lord Wharncliffe, the recipient of many eulogies during his representation of the County of Yorkshire from 1818 to 1826, who had moved the rejection of the measure.'[186] If not before this exposure to Political Unions, then after, Wharncliffe joined the Duke of Wellington in his convictions that Political Unions were intent on destroying the English constitution.

When the colliers in Dudley went out on strike in December 1831, adding to the government's concerns of violence and disorder, the Dudley Political Union also adopted policing as part of its role in assisting in the passage of the Reform Bill. When the local magistrates made arrangements to protect the colliers from violence and made arrangements for them to return to work with minimal delay, they asked the local Political Unionists to serve as the protecting force.[187]

The Unions, immediately following the riots, had professed their loyalty to His Majesty's government and commitment to peaceful agitation and a proactive role in maintaining order. The Unions had done their best to reassure the King of their true intent, a fact not lost on Grey. For example, at the inaugural meeting of the Leicester Political Union, William Biggs, one of the founders, reassured subscribing members that the Bill was not lost. He specifically credited the King and his government for remaining steadfast on the issue. 'With a patriotic king at their head, a House of Commons like the present, and with such a feeling as now existed throughout the kingdom, their cause must ultimately succeed.'[188] The Reverend Charles Berry also praised 'one of the most glorious and good kings since the days of King Arthur' for his faith in Grey and the Whigs.[189]

The Leicester Political Union's royal petition read:

> We, your Majesty's faithful subjects . . . humbly beg leave to offer to your Majesty the expression of our heartfelt gratitude for the sanction which your majesty has afforded to the sacred cause of reform under circumstances the most trying to your Majesty's feelings. We rejoice to believe that your Majesty's confidence in your present able and faithful ministers, continues unshaken, impressed as we are with the conviction that their continuance in office is essential to the internal peace and security of the county; and we hereby entreat your Majesty to strengthen their hands . . . [against] all persons whatever who are opposed to their patriotic measures, and to your Majesty's gracious intentions in favor of the liberties and happiness of your loyal and affectionate people.[190]

Attwood added to the unfolding drama by staging parades with a reported 100,000 participants, earnest speeches and the draping of public buildings in black crepe.[191] The Bill would be secure, he assured the public, 'unless their own violence should rashly lead to anarchy and place difficulties in the way of the King and Ministers.'[192] He admonished his followers to 'be patient – be peaceful – be strictly obedient to the laws, and everything is yet safe.'[193]

Rumours of the BPU's arming itself spread throughout the country. A National Guard, devised, allegedly by Charles Jones, a Council member as well as gun manufacturer, was supposed 'to preserve the peace of the town' and avoid riots such as those in Bristol. To that end the Political Union was to divide the members into sections which would 'act as an efficient body of the Police'.[194] The plan called for Birmingham's division into seven districts, then again into units of ten with a hierarchical organization of 'tything men', ten of whom were to form a unit led by 'a Constable of a Hundred'. Five such groups were under the direction of a 'Marshall of a Subdivision' and all marshalls, one for each of the seven districts, were to be under the supreme command of a Political Union Council appointee, the alderman.[195] The plan was complicated in structure, but its advocates believed such a system of defence was far preferable to the recent events in Bristol.

As far as arming the BPU, the plan never mentioned how this would be done in practice or paid for. The Home Office worried that the Union Council planned the purchase of weapons on the basis of an anonymous letter which explained the Council's increase of the subscription rate as being directed to that purpose.[196] Subsequent reports indicated that rumours of the BPU's arming amounted to little more than the Union distributing copies of Colonel Macerone's *Defensive Instruction for the People*, which described tactics for street fighting and the home manufacture of weapons, and that some unarmed practice drilling took place in a field outside the city. But an informant in Birmingham, Francis Lloyd, assured the Duke of Wellington that the press and the government had 'confuse[d] the acts of the Birmingham Political Union with the opinion of the town . . . [when in fact] people in Birmingham do not consider it worthwhile to show contempt for the Union . . . [as] the government corresponds with the Political Union.'[197]

Grey needed to defend, or at least explain, the ministry's lack of action against the Unions in light of these rumours. He assured Sir Herbert that 'the government should neglect no means of discouraging the Unions', but he also hinted at their usefulness in maintaining public pressure.[198] 'I cannot shut my eyes to the danger which may result from a second rejection of the Reform Bill,' he wrote to Sir Herbert.[199] A second defeat would, in Grey's opinion, cause Unions to multiply, perhaps 'receiv[ing] great additional strength from being joined by a description of persons who have hitherto kept aloof from them.'[200]

The King wrote to Wellington, assuring the Duke that he

> cannot possibly have viewed with greater anxiety and uneasiness than has the King the establishment of Political Unions in various parts of the kingdoms, not deprecate more strongly than does His Majesty the intention of assuming arms and forming national guards which has been expressed at some of the meetings of these political unions . . . His Majesty is indeed so much alive to the vital importance of counteracting such designs and he is so well assured of the entire and cordial concurrence of his government in this feeling, that he does not hesitate to declare that they

> shall not be entertained, nor tolerated, but on contrary that they shall be resisted to the utmost while he holds the Crown of these realms, confident as is His Majesty that the formation of national guards under the influence and control of the combinations which are taking place under the name of Political Unions, would not only be incompatible with the existence of the monarchy, but subversive of all government, law and authority.[201]

But the King took no action. He seemed to have accepted the Whigs' assessment that the Unions reflected discontent, but were not creating it. This, no doubt, frustrated the Duke and other Tories.[202] The Duke of Gloucester had already decided that 'the King and his government are in league with, and the protectors of, those [Unionists] who are . . . undermining the constitution of the country.'[203] The Duke of Buckingham voiced similar concerns. He argued that the government was intimidated by the Unions and 'the first business was to unite with ministers in these measures which were necessary to make them a free deliberative assembly which they are not while the Political Unions exist.'[204]

Grey also wrote to Wellington concerning the rumours of the Unions' forming a militia, asking him that 'no such information having reached any department of the King's government I think it my duty to request that Your Grace will have the goodness, if it is in your power and you see no objection, to furnish me with the means of ascertaining the accuracy of a fact which is of a nature to call for the most careful attention on the part of His Majesty's ministers.'[205]

But it was not entirely true that the government had no information concerning the formation of Union militia. Grey was in contact with Sir Francis Burdett, an honorary member of the BPU and NPU, which formed following the Bill's defeat in the Lords. 'I hope you are satisfied with our Birmingham Union,' Burdett wrote Grey, referring to the Union's peaceful reaction to the defeat and its continued and strong support for the government.[206] Grey also received a note from Thomas Attwood immediately following the riots, pressing upon him, 'the absolute necessity of not considering this great subject as a matter to be treated with strictness and severity', on the ground that the mischief had arisen from 'the gross imprudence of the local authorities'.[207]

Grey was not the only member of the ministry in touch with members of the Union movement. Lord Althorp was in correspondence with Joseph Parkes of the BPU. 'I shall perhaps again trouble you', Althorp wrote, 'from your position you can give me the best information as to the feelings of the Unionist reformers and I feel great confidence in your judgment.' He wanted to know the state of Birmingham and whether rioting was likely to break out in the midlands.[208]

A detailed correspondence followed and Parkes freely offered advice to Althorp concerning the 'circumstances and difficulties of the Ministry, (on which I am well aware the Public cannot be fully informed and on which Ministers are the *best* though not the *only* judges,) [as it] will re-introduce the Reform Measures without the exercise of the Royal Prerogative and the creation of new Peers.'[209] Parkes suggested some specific modifications in the Schedules and restrictions in town franchises, and particularly urged the rewriting of the measure to read 'enfranchisement' rather than 'disfranchisement', a term he felt would 'build a pyramid by reversing [the Bill's] form . . . [alleviating] the minds of the great body of Reformers with deep suspicions of the integrity of the Ministry and no little contempt for their judgment.'[210] He expressed his opposition to 'the selection of House and Rent as the standard of qualification . . . [as unconstitutional, and ill advised, equally with reference to Reformers and Anti-Reformers', alluding to 'the injury [Henry] Hunt already does and what [William] Cobbett might do . . .'[211] Nonetheless, he recognized that 'any material alterations founded on that standard, however insignificant will be judged harshly and jealously. It would probably wreck the Bill with the People.'[212]

Stressing practicality and political necessity, Parkes put a number of issues to Althorp, including his fears that 'Grey's Cabinet will be torn in pieces by its enemies and pretended friends, or rent by reaction and divisions among ourselves . . .'[213] As he pressed Althorp to deliver a message to Grey and his ministers as they prepared to go back into committee: 'no mark of a new form will ever blind or satisfy the People if any *material* sacrifice of those essentials is made in the forthcoming measure . . . [and] if Lord Grey's Cabinet *in* or *out* [of office] loses the confidence of the People *it is all over*.'[214] He offered ten pages of specific amendments to the Bill, which he believed would secure both its passage through the Lords and the support of the people.

There was no denying that the government was in contact, if not in cooperation with the BPU. How many people knew of this working relationship between Parkes and Althorp is not clear, but a number of anti-reformers suspected Parkes's association with the Whigs and did their best both to discredit Parkes and the Grey ministry for this link. According to Sir James Scarlett, Parkes had been the benefit of a 50 pound contribution to the Union for Lord John Russell, and indeed, Parkes and Russell had corresponded some weeks earlier.[215] Rumours flew and Grey needed to act in order to maintain the King's confidence. Satisfying the King without jeopardizing this relationship was a difficult, but important matter.

Grey followed his 10 November letter to Wellington with another to the King, thanking him for his confidence and assuring him that he was fully aware of talk concerning 'the arming of those Bodies which are known under the name of Political Union... [although] there have been no direct measures for the organization of armed bodies and the maintenance of your Royal authority and the protection of the peace and safety of your Majesty's people' were well in hand.[216] But pamphlets and petitions circulating in the country which seemed to confirm Wellington's scenario of impending doom for the British constitution. In Norwich, one pamphlet argued that 'the formation of any independent body in the State [such as a Political Union], which is not recognized by the Constitution... is in itself an utter subversion of all the established institutions of the country. It matters but little under what pretext associations of the people are formed, or under what particular denomination they many be brought together: if their object be the carrying into effect any great political measure, the danger is equally imminent and the result no less positively certain.'[217]

Another pamphlet published in Bath also denounced the Unions:

> as temporary Unions for carrying the measure of Reform, they furnish an evil precedent for the future, whilst they are uncalled for, and therefore useless, for that particular object... But as permanent bodies, organized to watch the Government, and overawed, by the display of physical force the Legislature itself, they are not only pernicious; but if not technically illegal, are manifestly opposed to the spirit of the Constitution; which supposes the House of Commons to be the alone legitimate organ of the national will.[218]

Even a parliamentary petition from Cambridgeshire specifically denounced the Unions, calling their existence 'deprecate' and 'promise[ing] co-operation in the suppression of Political Unions.[219]

Grey now had to convince the King that his government was

better informed than that the Duke and they had nothing to fear from the Political Unions. If the BPU undertook military exercises with arms, the government was ready to use troops stationed outside the town to disband the whole organization. Grey simply told the King that the dreadful events in Bristol, when both the military and local magistrates failed to deal decisively with the rioters, not surprisingly (if not necessarily wisely) prompted the BPU Council to prepare in case of a similar emergency.[220] Grey was aware that the financial condition of the Union did not allow either a rise in dues or the expenditure of the amount it would take to arm a National Guard of the size discussed in the plan.[221] It was, after all, economic distress which had prompted the creation of the BPU and that condition had not been ameliorated during the Reform Bill debates.[222]

Grey was persuasive and the government still had the support of the King, and, for better or worse, the Political Unions. But that put Grey in a difficult position. He needed to demonstrate to the King and his critics that the government was not pandering to Union demands, sacrificing both public order and the constitution simply to get the Reform Bill through Parliament.[223] Nor could he jeopardize public goodwill for the Bill that the Unions fostered.[224] The King's fears mounting, he insisted that Grey do something – anything – to check the further growth of the Political Union movement and to curtail their increasingly bold public activities. The Riot Act certainly gave magistrates and sheriffs the power to disband Union general meetings and rallies. They could break up a Union meeting by reading a proclamation in the King's name and 'command all persons there assembled to disperse themselves and peaceably to depart to their habitations or to their lawful business . . .'[225] This was the law, whether or not the Political Union was rumoured to be arming or peacefully gathering in support of the government and the Reform Bill.

The King, however, was still not satisfied. He believed the Unions posed a different kind of threat from that of the mob. However much the Unions claimed to be supporting his government, the King feared the potential existed to turn their 'national movement' against his authority. He wanted more than just the large public meetings to cease, but every aspect of Political Union organization: Council meetings, press coverage, the growing ties between individual Unions and – most importantly – the growing public perception that they were a legitimate avenue for political participation

with authority sanctioned by the King and his government.

After lengthy discussions with Grey, the government decided to reassert the legal position concerning extra-parliamentary political associations and seditious behaviour by way of a Royal Proclamation. Lord Holland admitted that, on this matter, 'he silently acquiesced, though in truth neither opinion nor proclamation nor even indictments for conspiracy, even if followed by conviction, amount to more than scolding and railing . . . utterly unequal to prevent the formation of unions or disperse them when formed, if there be a determination in the people to persist.'[226] The King and the Attorney-General and Solicitor-General of England began a thorough legal examination of the Political Unions. Grey carefully examined the statutes as well.[227] The arming of organizations, and the presentation of organizations as civil authorities independent of the government, were considered seditious activities and, therefore, illegal under the statutes 39 Geo. 3 c. 79 and 57 Geo. 3 c. 19.[228] Under the same statutes, Unions large enough to require sub-divisions or branches for managerial purposes, as well as those in communication with other Unions, or assisting in the organization of other Political Unions, were also determined to be illegal.

Needing to maintain the trust and support of the King, Grey agreed to His Majesty's request. On 21 November 1831, William IV issued a Royal Proclamation against Political Unions. 39 George III c 79 had defined as unlawful societies that required 'unlawful oaths and engagements of fidelity and secrecy, used secret signs, appointed Committees, Secretaries and other officers in a secret manner and . . . were composed of different divisions, branches or parts, which communicate with each other by secretaries, delegates or otherwise . . .'[229] Some of the criteria did not apply to the Unions, but the statutes specifically mentioned the London Corresponding Society, United Irishmen and United Englishmen as examples. Clearly, William IV did not distinguish between extra-parliamentary groups. The Unions did not, in any way, act in secret or require secret oaths, but the argument was made that they were part of a national movement, not individual provincial organizations, and as a result, the second part of the law applied. Many believed that the Unions fit the 1799 law which ordered 'the suppression of societies established for seditious and treasonable purposes.'[230]

In addition, 57 George III, c 19, enacted 31 March 1817, further defined illegal activity. In an attempt to maintain the public peace and prevent 'riot, tumult and disorder [that] may become the means

of producing confusion and calamities in the nation', any meeting exceeding 50 participants (other than those called by county riding or division officers), held 'for the purpose or pretext of considering of or preparing any petition, complaint, remonstrance or declaration or other address to the King . . . [or] either House of Parliament for alterations in matters established in Church or State, or for the purpose or on the pretext of deliberating upon any grievance in Church or State' were rendered illegal. Exceptions would be made when announcements cited the names of seven individuals responsible for the specific event, the notice of intention of the meeting and its time and place.[231] According to these laws, Political Unions were illegal and their meetings, unless small or Council meetings, not permitted. Even at such meetings, petitioning the Crown or government on behalf of the Reform Bill was defined as sedition. The Proclamation, Wellington hoped, 'will separate the government from the radicals'.[232] He praised Grey for his work 'to prevent much of the evil which might have expected to result from their [the ministry's action] by making it know His Majesty's opinion . . .'[233]

But local officials and the government did nothing to implement the reissued laws. There was no reason to believe that the Unions were seditious organizations and much flurry of Union activity was a response to the Bill's defeat – all of it fully supportive of the government. Political Unions were a crucial means of demonstrating widespread public opinion and support for the Bill. Grey continually referred to this when he and the King discussed the steps necessary to pass the Bill as the will of the majority of the people, as represented by the House of Commons and the King's government, could not be dismissed. To enforce the Proclamation, arresting Union leaders and reading the Riot Act at meetings, Grey was convinced, would turn the rumours of revolution into a certainty. As he explained after the Reform Bill's passage, 'the Proclamation . . . was directed against an attempt to convert the Unions into armed and disciplined bodies, under the pretext of preserving the public peace . . . nothing further was required with a view to the purpose for which it had been issued.'[234]

Even though the Proclamation primarily had targeted the BPU, Bristol, and the few others that had openly spoken of arming themselves to serve as a special constabulary force in town, Union Councils registered some objection to it – be it anger or a bemused dismissal. Thomas Attwood took the Proclamation to be a 'friendly

warning', but believed that in reality little would change as long as the Union did not engage in any violence.[235] Place and the NPU Council interpreted the Proclamation as more of a threat than warning, but dismissed it nonetheless.[236] They publicly declared that the Proclamation 'did not prohibit societies which had no secret proceedings, divisions or branches . . . [nor did it prohibit] the appointment of delegates, nor meetings of delegates.'[237] An NPU handbill also pointed out that the Acts did not prevent any Union from recommending the establishment of other Unions. 'They do not prohibit any Union from sending instructions to any body of persons for the formation of other Unions; they do not prohibit any Union from appointing delegates to meet with persons desirous of forming Unions, and assisting to conduct their proceedings, to the moment the Union is formed but all such interference must cease before such Union is declared to be in existence.'[238] Still, the NPU advised branches to create independent organizations by adopting their own constitutions, registering members and collecting dues as an independent organization. In Lambeth and Clerkenwell, independent Unions formed.[239]

The Northern Political Union took a more defensive position than the NPU, as its rules specifically stipulated that the members of the Union may 'form themselves into Classes . . . and elect annually a Conductor' for administrative tasks such as collecting dues.[240] It contended that because the division of the Union was optional and left to the discretion of members, the Proclamation did not apply to the Northern Union, but that Unions such as the BPU and NPU should ignore it. Members distributed handbills which not only stated the laws which prohibited political seditious associations, but argued that the Unions were very different and, in fact, had only formed as a direct result of 'Tory Malevolence and Tory Lawyer-craft'.[241] One unnamed Political Union in Lancashire claimed it would march, 10,000 strong, and 'give the BPU a good thrashing, if they do not ignore the Proclamation.'[242] There were similar letters published in numerous provincial newspapers.[243]

Some Political Unions were worried as to whether or not their organizations' activities fell within the Proclamation's definition of sedition. The Derby Political Union published an open letter in the local newspaper rejecting any notion that the organization was an illegal body because it espoused reform and sought to prevent any future rioting in the town. The entire letter pleaded the case of the Unions, insisting that the King's Proclamation only applied to the large Political Unions, such as those in London and Birmingham, which had branch affiliates.[244] Likewise, William Herapath, Vice President of the Bristol Political Union, personally wrote to Lord Melbourne to persuade him that his organization was not subject to the criteria stipulated in the Proclamation. 'I beg to say that as our intentions were almost confined to a desire to ensure the passing of the Reform Bill, it shall be dissolved the moment it becomes obnoxious to the government.'[245]

With the Unions focusing on the details of the Proclamation and seemingly dismissing as preposterous the notion that members might be arrested and tried for treason as the result of campaigning for the passage of the government's legislation, the Proclamation failed to instill the fear in Union leaders that the King had hoped. Nor did it have much impact in slowing down the formation of new Political Unions, now numbering in the sixties. The Proclamation might have irked some of the Political Unions, but it did not undermine their overall loyalty and respect for the King or the institution of the monarchy, in spite of continued worries concerning this.

CONCLUSION

There was a flurry of Political Union formation after October 1831. The 'people' clearly recognized that Political Unions were useful in organizing and clearly demonstrating the widespread popular support which existed for the Whig Reform Bill. Many also saw Political Unions as useful and effective tools in securing peace and public order. Although it was rare for Unions to discuss publicly policing techniques or the possibility of arming, the example set by the Nottingham and particularly the Bristol Political Union, whose members came forward to serve as a special constabulary on behalf of local magistrates, inspired the new Unions to do the same. The result revitalized the Political Union movement. The Unions took the opposition of the Lords very seriously and thus dropped reform objectives and radical positions that would fuel the fires of opposition. Their primary goal became supporting the government and the Reform Bill at all costs. The Unions also took on another responsibility: watchman in preserving the peace and protecting property from rioting and violence. Shrugging off criticisms of their motives and methods, Political Unions' decisive action in helping secure the peace throughout the kingdom – preventing further rioting while alerting many to the danger that another defeat in the Lords posed for the whole country – demonstrated that they were respectable and loyal in both their support for the Reform Bill and the King's peace. Union leaders knew arguments proclaiming the organizations 'useless', 'illegal', or 'threatening' had been disproved to the public as well as the King and his ministers. The Unions rallied their forces and plunged into a widespread and united public campaign for the Whig Reform Bill. It would not be a certain success. Nor would it be the last of the new Political Unions. The final phase of the Political Union campaign saw Unions assuming another self-selected role as the pressure mounted against the Tories and enemies of reform.

5 Political Unions and the Final Campaign: Agitation, the May Days and Victory, January–June 1832

> Go on with your Unions. Be orderly and prudent, and you will baffle your enemies . . . Not only men of character and men of property . . . will join your proceedings, but those in office and authority will soon recognize and sanction them, and lend their aid . . . It is the duty of those who are in authority to move with the people; to unite with the people in one common good . . . [1]

> England is now actually governed by Political Unions. The parliament of Birmingham issues edicts. There is little law, little punishment (how long none!). Revolution is openly sought; if by intimidation, and the form of law, well; if not, by violence. What encouragement, if we can call the inactivity, the paralyzed stupor of fear in a government, encouragement, has been given to this feeling . . . the Political Unions, and branch Political Unions did their work well.[2]

> Nothing but the establishment of Political Unions has prevented us from becoming the victims of the dreadful catastrophe.[3]

The Whigs reintroduced the Reform Bill in the House of Commons on 12 December. It passed on the 18th, 324 to 162 and the government prepared for another showdown with the House of Lords. It was apparent to Grey that the Lords would continue opposing the measure unless something drastic was done. The people had already taken to the streets following the Bill's first defeat. Clearly they would not tolerate the aristocracy once more obstructing the will of their elected representatives in Parliament, as well as the wishes of the King and his government. The Whigs could not back away from enacting the Bill, or even tolerate much amending of the measure, without courting a popular revolution and jeopardizing the whole structure of the English constitution.

The solution for the government was a large enough creation of peers to insure the Whigs the votes necessary to pass the Bill in the Lords. But after lengthy discussions with the King, Grey decided that any 'addition [to the numbers in the House of Lords] shall be deferred till it may appear certain that, without such addition, the strength of the government would be insufficient to bring the measure of parliamentary Reform to a successful issue.'[4] While Grey and the King wrangled over the number of creations that might be required, others put together lists of names to present the King.[5]

Grey was even more hard-pressed to justify his position of waiting out the Unions, rather than order magistrates to arrest the leaders. He insisted that what was required of everyone was patience. He was in discussion with his cabinet and the King about a creation of peers to secure the Bill. There was no question that nothing good would come from any further attack on the Unions. He convinced the King that the Unions would no longer be in existence, let alone a threat, once the Bill became law. 'When the great object of Reform is carried,' Grey wrote to Sir Herbert, 'I have a confident belief that the middle and more influencing classes of the community would be separated from them; they would then become powerless and more easily dealt with.'[6] He also pointed out that the Lords' rejection of the Bill had created a loyalty among the Unions hitherto absent.

No further steps were taken against the Unions and as a frustrated Wellington concluded, 'I don't believed that there is any separation between the government, the radicals and the Unions . . . [as] the conduct of the press for the last three weeks [indicates] . . . there is some communication between His Majesty's most honourable Privy Council at St. James' and their brother council of the Union at Birmingham.'[7] The Duke of Buckingham and Chandos expressed his concern that 'the prolonged existence of Political Unions in the Country, acting under no authority of law . . . has led to a state of things deeply affecting the independence of Parliament, and the permanence of the Monarchical authority within the Realm.'[8] Citing the London NPU as a particularly egregious violator of the Proclamation, Buckingham urged Grey to act more aggressively to implement the spirit and the letter of the law. Grey chose not to act, as the Unions were maintaining a low profile and acting in a lawful manner.[9]

Some Tories appeared to be in as much anxiety as the Whigs.

Moderates or 'waverers', such as Lords Wharncliffe and Harrowby, became convinced that defeating the Reform Bill again on the second reading would be a disaster and result either in a blow to the aristocracy and the sanctity of the Upper House by a creation of peers, or possibly a political and social revolution among the people, if some reform measure was not enacted. The waverers formulated a strategy whereby they would vote for the Bill at the second reading and then execute carefully planned efforts with the Ultras to reform it in committee. Lords Harrowby and Wharncliffe and the other waverers, however, could not persuade Wellington to act with them and support the Bill on the second reading. On 19 January, Lords Wharncliffe, Harrowby and Haddington decided to go ahead with the plan on their own, drafting their plans and publishing them in a circular, hoping their fellow Tories would see the wisdom in their proposal and support the Bill at the vote.

During the early months of 1832, the King was still urging Grey to suppress the Unions: 'His Majesty has always viewed the power which Mr. [Daniel] O'Connell and other agitators have occasionally exerted in dispersing mobs and sending them peacefully to their homes, to be which must be considered as most pregnant with danger to the State . . . [therefore] His Majesty looks to the early suppression of these Political Unions with continued anxiety.'[10] But Grey warned the King that 'if some measure is not resorted to put an end to these Political Unions, they will destroy all government.'[11]

Recognizing the legal restrictions placed on them in the Royal Proclamation, the Political Unions curtailed their activities so as not to antagonize the King and opted to wait and see how both the government and the anti-reformers would fare after the third introduction of the Reform Bill. According to Francis Place, 'The BPU was in a state of abeyance, millions of people had their attention strongly drawn towards that union, but I knew from the leaders that they were at the moment undecided what to do and were waiting to see what course things might take.'[12] Place went so far as to claim that 'from the meeting of the Parliament on 6 December 1831 to its reassembling after the Christmas holidays on 17 January 1832, there was little excitement among the people.'[13] His records indicated that 'Political Unions continued to be formed but these were all intended for prospective exertions, [and] public meetings were very few.'[14] There is little evidence of any new Unions until after the Reform Bill began to be seriously debated in the House of Lords.

Some opponents sensed that Unions were preparing themselves for a fight. A few Political Unions certainly found ways around its restrictions to communicate with one another and some simply ignored the law and waited for the government to take legal action against them. The Bristol Political Union was so bold as to defy the Proclamation by leaving a petition for the King at the door of Sir Herbert while with the King in Brighton, pleading the case of the five Bristol rioters convicted and sentenced to death for their crimes in October.[15] A note to the lieutenant in the West Riding of Yorkshire asking for assistance for the magistrates of Leeds evinced more than a hint of fear. The writer described a 'deplorable spirit which is now rife for rebellion, rapine and plunder . . . a crisis is at hand which only a kind Providence and the use of proper means to prevent our long-tried and venerable institutions from being shook to their foundations by these associations [the Political Unions] can avoid.'[16] But these were the exception, not the rule.

REINTRODUCTION AND DEFEAT OF THE REFORM BILL

The Reform Bill finally came out of committee on 10 March and passed on the third reading in the House of Commons, 355 to 239. Once again, reform was in the hands of the Lords and it had been rumoured by the end of February that the waverers had the numbers they needed to see the Bill carried on the second reading. Whigs and Political Unionists knew that many Tories feared that to vote with Wharncliffe and Harrowby would be political suicide and end their hope of a government position under Wellington some time in the future. Even if they wanted to vote for the Bill, many Tories would not openly defy the Duke.

Thomas Attwood begged Grey to do all he could to secure a promise from the King to create enough peers to secure the Bill as he would not be able to dissuade a frustrated public from taking to the streets if the Bill went down again.[17] Charles Larkin of the Northern Political Union concurred. 'Revolution', he said, 'is the alternative of reform. But, while I shudder at the contemplation even of the probability of revolution, dreadful as it is, I should rather infuse the spirit of wisdom into councils of our legislators, than depress the people into a tame, quiet submission to tyranny and oppression.'[18]

As if to secure the government's position against any compromise, the Northern Political Union held a mass meeting in Newcastle in March. Members discussed the prospects of the Bill and of an increased property qualification as a possible offer to the Lords. It is here that the Political Unions first embraced a new and effective tactic of support for the government and the Bill, as it stood: immediate stoppage of all direct or property tax payments until the Whig Bill became law. John Fife, speaking for the NPU Council, put it simply: 'if this bill be not passed, the people, feeling themselves not to be represented, therefore [are] not morally and constitutionally bound to pay taxes.'[19] Though the Unions did not take it up at the time as a plan should the Ultras reject the Bill again, it would become a significant strategy for the Northern and other Political Unions during the May Days crisis.[20]

The following month, Fife and Charles Attwood sent Grey an address from a meeting of the Advocates and Friends of the Newcastle district of the Northern Political Union, in which they assured the prime minister that the Union supported him and the Bill, a decision they believed 'a subject for exultation and for Hope, but not for over-confidence or security'.[21]

> Contemplating then, as we [the Northern Political Unionists] do, with deep alarm the probable fate of the Reform Bill in the Committee of that House [of Lords] and aware of the momentous nature of the impending Crisis – knowing the excited feelings of the people at this eventful period of our country's fate – we deem it our bound duty earnestly but respectfully to urge upon your Lordship the necessity of advising His Majesty to call up into the House of Lords a number of additional Peers sufficient to ensure the safety and integrity of the Bill in its passage through the Committee.[22]

Grey replied that he was pleased with the 'reaffirmation of my countrymen', but did not enlist the aid of the Northern Political Union in passage of the Reform Bill.[23] Grey had assurances from the King that if there was no other way, he would create peers, although he was never comfortable with the idea and Grey's use of this private agreement so infuriated the King that it almost lost them his support.[24] The creation of more Political Unions only strengthened Grey's resolve that the government should deal with the Tories without the direct support of the Unions. In late February, the Stratford-upon-Avon Political Union appeared.[25] Northampton reformers established another Union.[26]

Debate on the Reform Bill began in the House of Lords on the 9th. On 14 April, by only nine votes, the Lords passed the Reform Bill at the second reading (184 to 175). Grey, fully aware that there was a limit to the number of peerages the King was willing to create, conceded that parts of the Bill, such as the number of boroughs in Schedule A and the monetary figure for electoral qualification in the boroughs, were still open to change in committee.[27] As the Whigs congratulated themselves, messengers set out at tremendous speed to the north, throwing placards out the windows of carriages which announced the vote, and according to witness John Bright, 'the glorious triumph of popular principles even in the House of Lords'.[28]

The committee stage of the Bill was postponed until after Easter. The government needed time to prepare, for it had reason to worry. First, this was the stage at which the waverers intended to make changes to the Reform Bill. Second, the King was very irritated at Grey for not having fully warned him that the Bill again faced serious trouble in Parliament. Nor was the King happy with the methods with which the cabinet intended to confront the Tories: namely, the threat of a large creation of pro-reform peers.

It was thus with strained support from the King that the Whigs entered into committee struggle with the Tories over the Reform Bill. The government informed the waverers that if they accepted the principle of disenfranchisement, it would be willing to negotiate on which boroughs appeared on Schedule A. The cabinet, in the meantime, tried to work out modifications to the Bill itself. Althorp asked Joseph Parkes as representative of the BPU about the waverers' proposal to restrict borough voting by changing the qualification from a ten pound value to a ten pound rating. Parkes thought that Political Unions would find this acceptable. Union reaction in Birmingham and elsewhere let him know he was quite wrong. Cobbett accused him of abandoning the cause of reform.[29]

Even more damaging criticism came from Charles Attwood, Chair of the Northern Political Union. He loudly denounced any attempt to raise the borough qualification.[30] Both the BPU and the Leeds Political Union (Baine's organization) Councils were willing to see the qualification altered, but the younger Attwood's impassioned speech prompted such a strong public response, that neither openly endorsed the proposed change, leaving the government to conclude that the Unions would not tolerate the raising of the property qualification without a fight.[31] In Leicester, Council member and Baptist lay minister Winks warned against violence, but not very emphatically, in reacting to the anger in the Union ranks when they feared the Bill might be amended.[32]

At the point when the committee was due to vote on the Bill, Grey did not realize that the waverers and Ultra-Tories planned to call for a postponement of the vote concerning the disenfranchising clauses. The cabinet, when finally aware of the plan, agreed that any attempt to postpone should be resisted as strongly as possible. But a creation of peers or resignation of the government seemed inevitable. The waverers never seriously believed the government would resign over the issue, and the Tories could hardly have been optimistic about having the support necessary to form a government of their own if it did. Wellington and the Ultras, particularly the Duke of Cumberland and Lord Eldon, were blind to these realities, unlike the Tory moderates. They also did not seem to realize that those who had been promised the vote would not allow the property qualification to be raised, in order to exclude them. The reform issue would not be settled at all, but the Tories did not seem to recognize this truth.

The Political Unions certainly recognized it. True, on 27 April, the BPU Council drew up resolutions that in the event of the government's defeat on this issue the Unions would accept a smaller reform measure from the Tories.[33] But the BPU Council, in spite of its belief that the BPU led Political Unions throughout the country, did not speak for the rest, as would soon be demonstrated.

On 7 May, Lord Lyndhurst called the question on postponement and this, as everyone knew, amounted to a vote of no confidence in the government. Grey made it clear that, if defeated, the government would either secure enough peers from the King to reverse the vote, or he would resign. The Tories hoped that the King would refuse to create peers on the grounds that the Tories' postponement motion was not intended to defeat the bill. Amendments were, therefore, put forward in order to demonstrate that the Tories were merely trying to change aspects of the measure they found problematic. The Tories put Lord Ellenborough up to the task of announcing that he and his colleagues were prepared to abolish all 113 seats in Schedule A.

That day, the BPU held a massive public meeting at Newhall Hill.[34] By 10 o'clock in the morning, crowds had gathered outside the Union offices, while a number of Council members rode to the outskirts of the city to escort visiting Political Unions from other towns. Shortly before noon, Attwood and the rest of the Council led the procession from Great Charles Street to Newhall Hill. About 100,000–150,000 individuals, many of them visitors from nearby Political Unions and non-Union spectators, waved banners and flags. Attwood and other members of the Council made speeches, George Edmonds' being the most notable. He warned that 'their Lordships had better take lessons of the dancing masters, to qualify themselves for situations on the continent and their ladies should become proficient at the wash tub.'[35]

The Lords voted against the government and for Ellenborough's motion by a vote of 151 to 116. Grey left immediately for Windsor after meeting the cabinet. He presented the King with the cabinet's request for a creation of 50–60 new peers and was promised a response the following morning. Early on the 9th, Grey learned that the King had accepted his and his ministers' resignations. William IV came to London to persuade Lord Brougham and a few others to remain in office, but none would accept. Althorp announced his resignation in the Commons that evening to great cheers, and the following day, Lord Ebrington made a motion supporting the Whigs.

William IV then asked Wellington to do the impossible – form a government pledging to carrying substantial reform. Peel had refused to be a part of one even before the Whigs had resigned. Peel's reluctance spilled over to other Tories such as John Wilson Croker and John Charles Herries, former President of the Board of Trade. Wellington had only Lord Lyndhurst and, what is more important, no one at all capable of controlling the House of Commons. In addition, a motion was made in the Commons that no one who had voted for the Bill could be expected to give the Wellington ministry any support.

When the King left London on 13 May, there was little likelihood that Wellington could form a government. He had agreed to carry a substantive reform measure, but without Peel, who (still haunted by his decision to support Catholic Emancipation) refused to join him. There was therefore little hope. To make sure that there was no question at all, the Political Unions did their utmost to make clear to Wellington and the King that the people would not accept the Duke as Prime Minister. No longer perceived as the 'Patriot King', William IV's worst fears were realized: Political Unions continued to form and became even more active than ever before.

STILL MORE UNIONS FORM

Another half dozen towns formed Unions following the Bill's defeat. A 'branch' of the Northern Union formed when Charles Attwood contacted the Reverend Mr Wright in Sunderland. 'The branch was formed during a crisis the most eventful in the history of the country when a collision seemed pending between the men of wealth and the multitude sunk in poverty – between the people who sought for power and the people of the nation. It was under this impression that a few friends to reform in Sunderland came to the resolution to put their shoulders to the wheel.' There were some 1,000 members enrolled on the Union's register.[36]

On 18 May, reformers in Barnstaple formed the North Devon Political Union.[37] The meeting, organized by Messrs Meliss, J.C. March, R. Vernon and other local businessmen, registered 150 members on the first night and an equal number in the week following the first meeting.[38] The Union had its own view of the crisis and discussing its plan should Wellington form a government and call an election. 'If any person presents himself as a candidate to represent the people in Parliament, who will not pledge himself to assist in restoring the lost rights of the people, he shall be considered by the North Devon Political Union, not only as an enemy to the comfort and well-being of every individual of the community, but as a person unworthy of the support of this Association.'[39]

Insisting that reformers could stop a Tory government, the newly formed Warwick Political Union drafted a petition to the House of Commons urging them to take strong measures to force Wellington to withdraw and lead the Tories in accepting the inevitability of the Reform Bill.[40] In Salisbury, a Political Union held its first meeting in the second week of May.[41] William Fawcett, the town's mayor, chaired the meeting where the Reverend Mr Good proposed the establishment of the Union, 'now that it was time to enter on the career of exertion'.[42] Speakers condemned the actions of the Tories, both waverers and Ultras, and declared themselves unwilling to live under Wellington as they could expect nothing more than 'chain, fetters and swords . . .'.[43] The Union drafted a petition to the Commons to stop all supplies (i.e. to stop voting money for the government) until Wellington withdrew, and Mr Stokes called for the new Union to act on its own – 'namely a firm resistance in their own persons to the payment of taxes.'[44]

In Sittingbourne, there was 'an enthusiastic determination made on the spot to form a Political Union and to use any institutional means to forward the great measure of reform and expressing their unabated confidence that the peace and happiness of the country could only be insured by the return to office of Lord Grey and his colleagues.'[45]

Another new Political Union formed in Trowbridge, 'under the sanction of the major part of the trading community'. [46] Lichfield established its own Union, as did the town of Reddtich.[47] Unions also formed in Stapleford, Crameote, Sutton-in-Ashfield, Edinstowe and Surrey.[48]

R.E. Heathcote in Staffordshire organized a Political Union because he was

> aware of no other mode in which the people's voice can be so peaceably, and at the same time so forcibly expressed, as under the direction of Political Unions . . . that I have ventured to recommend the formation of one in this neighbourhood. The plan, you know, is not new – it has been tried in Birmingham and other great towns with the most beneficial effect. Let any one put it to himself. What would have been the state of those towns during the last eventful fortnight, but for the salutary control and direction of such institutions?[49]

Heathcote and the other Union organizers, including Ralph Stevenson, William Ridgway and other local notables, were very clear on how such an extra-parliamentary organization would be perceived by local officials following the reinstatement of the Royal Proclamation against extra-parliamentary organizations and in light of mounting tensions. Many of the Union organizers had been active in forming a local police force a decade earlier.[50] Respectable and moderate, these reformers were finally convinced that the best way to show their support for the Bill would be to form a Union and petition the King. William Ridgeway spoke for many when he declared: 'If I thought for a moment the object of the Union was to encourage disorder, confusion or anarchy, I would not join it.'[51]

Union membership consisted mostly of master potters and manufacturers, owners of local mines, bankers, lawyers and doctors, and even a few local landowners, Simeon Shaw, George Miles Mason and Isaac Broad among the businessmen. John Bouton, the Chief Bailiff of Stafford, chaired most meetings. The creation of their own Union was one of the few things they could do that would both support the Whigs and remind the King and the Tories that the people were watching them, and preparing for ways to challenge their rejection of reform.[52]

ATTEMPTS AT A TORY MINISTRY AND THE MAY DAYS: ECONOMIC RESISTANCE

The King was rightly concerned about the increase in Unions and Union rallies after he called Wellington to form a government, but his fears of Unions' potential to foment revolution appeared real. Frustrated and angry over the Lords' obstructionist politics and what they saw as a betrayal by the King of his Whig ministry, Unionists began to talk, for the first time, about revolution and a republic. The greatest crisis of the entire Reform Bill campaign had come. Historians have seen the May Days as the closest thing throughout the whole two and a half year reform period to a real revolutionary threat to peace and order in England.[53] Contemporaries certainly felt that it was the final hour. Place later bragged that had Wellington formed a government, 'I and two friends should have made the Revolution, whatever the cost.'[54] Upon hearing that the Political Unions were discussing a run on the banks, Hunt remarked, 'the feelings of the people were so worked up, and so excited that no Administration could possibly be found, except the late Ministry, calculated to satisfy and tranquilize the country.'[55] The *Coventry Herald* reported that 'since the resignation of Earl Grey and his colleagues . . . this city presented a scene of excitement and agitation unequaled perhaps in its history, unless in periods of actual convulsion.'[56] Such was the state of alarm during the few days of ministerial interregnum,' wrote Coventry Union Corresponding Secretary William Hickling, 'that numbers [in the town] actually armed themselves to be prepared for the worst.'[57]

Political Unions saw the May Days as the final testing time of their support for Grey and the Whig Bill. It was also an opportunity for them to do what many had been founded to do: maintain control at a time of crisis. For reformers who had not thought it necessary to form or join a Political Union previously, this was the time to commit themselves. Throughout the country, Unionists new and old scrambled to do whatever they could to support the Whigs. They staged two dozen public rallies, all with speeches and protestations of support for Grey and loud denunciations of Wellington.

Dozens of English towns adopted resolutions, addresses and petitions voicing the same sentiments.[58]

Various Unions advanced, and began to implement, one or more of three broad strategies during the May Days. These included Unions arming themselves for a physical confrontation with the troops of the Iron Duke; a boycott of tax payments until the House of Lords passed the Reform Bill; and a run on the banks, to cause an economic crisis which would force the Tories' hand. These were the plans which the Political Unions devised to save the Reform Bill. They were never implemented, but threats to do so worked to great effect.

With news of the defeat spreading throughout the country, reformers and Unionists became more emotional and dramatic in desperate attempts to restore the Whigs to office. On 12 May, the BPU Council voted to hold daily sessions until the Bill became law and adopted the Solemn League and Covenant 'to stand, abide and hold-fast, the one by the other, in using and adopting all possible and lawful ways and means which God or Nature, Chance or Circumstances may furnish us, for the assertion and vindication of all our rights and liberties.'[59] The Council also urged members to 'wear on their breasts the ribbon of the Union Jack until the Bill of Reform is become law' as a show of support for Grey.[60]

In Coventry, the MP and Political Union ally Henry Lytton Bulwer tried to prevent overt violence. He lost no time in writing to Hickling to assure him that reform was not completely dead. 'The Party [Tories] *now* sees and admits the necessity of *some* [reform] . . . Forced by the overwhelming consent of public opinion to relinquish the ground on which they have so long contended against all Reform, they, sooner or later . . . adopt a new course.'[61] To make sure that the Union did not misunderstand him, Bulwer wrote again to Hickling on 11 May to report that he 'voted with Lord Ebrington on his motion considering under all circumstances that such was the best course to purse, as I sincerely [believe] that the vote to which we came last night will be the means of preserving the peace of the country and forwarding the views of the liberal and well-intentioned.'[62]

A public meeting was called by the Coventry Political Union for the 14th at Greyfriars Green. Before it began they staged a procession where the townspeople marched to the Green with a banner bearing the slogan 'Our patriot king and the people', the first three words covered with black crepe and the phrase 'A Cheap

Republic' written on the material.[63] Hickling called upon 'the intelligent citizens of Coventry [to use] their reason and not [rely on] their passions. He must be a wicked man who would encourage open force, as long as any other mode of redress was at hand or its success "incertain" [*sic*] and history teaches us that unsuccessful resistance always rivals more closely those claims it was intended to break.'[64]

Mr Merk, a member of the Union Council, condemned the actions of the Lords:

> The enemies of Reform say the present Bill is too extensive – too democratical – it will give the poor and ignorant their franchise, who will not know how to make good use of it. Now if it be acknowledged that this logic is correct, it goes to prove that a man who is without money must be without brains also . . . it is not the people's ignorance they are afraid of. No! It is their intellectual power. They know the people can see how they are oppressed, that they have their eyes upon their oppressor.[65]

Another speaker, Mr Raby, also of the Council, tried to make the audience both passionate and involved: 'These were not the times to be inactive, but that they impressively called upon every man to exert himself to stem that current of corruption which threatens in its course to overwhelm every thing that Britons hold dear to them . . . the people of England have asked for a restoration of their constitutional rights by having a voice in the choice of their representatives in the House of Commons,' he roared.[66] Sites of other large Union meetings included Leicester, Norwich, Newcastle, Brighton and Bristol.

It was also important that increasing numbers of people joined the Political Unions during the crisis and that new Unions formed. In Birmingham, 'upwards of 2000 persons have joined the Union since the resignation of the Ministry . . . The Bristol and other Unions were also daily increasing in number.'[67] Reports indicated that more religious leaders were joining the Union. On the 9th, the Union Council noted that within a few days, 'four Catholic priests enrolled themselves [in the Union] and we have heard about twenty Quakers became members.'[68] Parkes read a list of names and ceremoniously handed Attwood a number of five and ten pound notes, declaring: 'we . . . who have hitherto refrained from joining the Birmingham Political Union, deem it our duty at this awful crisis to come forward and join that body for the purpose of promoting the further union, order and determination of all classes in support of the common cause of parliamentary reform.'[69] The interest among respectable men might suggest that they saw the Union as a means to avoid bloody chaos in such tense circumstances. The Union Council believed this to be their role and promoted the idea within the town: 'the fact is, the people feel that it is by Union that the country can be saved from falling into a state of anarchy which is frightful to contemplate.'[70] At a Union meeting held the following week, the Reverend Hugh Hutton expressed sentiments similar to Parkes's: with Wellington forming a government, 'the enemies of Reform had gained a temporary triumph [that] he no longer hesitated to enroll himself a member of the Union.'[71]

John Bowes Wright, a member of the Northern Political Union Council, told thousands at a Union rally that,

> within the last few days, the NPU has enrolled a greater number of new names than it ever did during any six months of its previous existence. Hundreds of well educated converts have been made since the disastrous political changes in our government, men who have a stake in the country. They say 'we think at such a time you want help, and it is our duty, as the advocates of civil and religious liberty, to support you and to join you'.[72]

The Leicester Political Union called its own emergency meeting, at which 'the Political Union denounced the Duke, the objects of his first operations, [and] received every where a vast accession of numbers. The Union . . . we believe, trebled itself.'[73] The Nottingham Union reported: 'great accessions in the number of members have been made to the Council this past week.'[74] In Worcester, 'the Union received an increase of 470 new members within the last fortnight.'[75] The day of the Greyfriars Green meeting, 200 people joined the Coventry Political Union.[76] Approximately 700 people joined during the weeks of the May Days. An estimated 5,600 joined the NPU in London between 1 and 20 May 1832.[77]

Growing in numbers and confidence, provincial Political Unions criticized the Tories and the House of Lords, and resolved to take action at the public meetings held after Grey's resignation. Thomas Salt, a BPU Council member, remarked at a meeting of the Worcester Political Union that 'an individual and Peer of the realm, who lives on the confines of this county and with whom he had the honour to be acquainted . . . would have had no occasion to be afraid of the Unions if he had voted for the Reform Bill when first brought forward . . .'[78] The Union meeting in Coventry was largely an opportunity for Political Unionists to denounce the Duke of Wellington and prepare its members and fellow townspeople for an abrupt end to reform if the Duke formed a government. After burning the Duke in effigy, one speaker referred to him as a military and political despot and asked, 'What was to be expected from a minister who had declared all public meetings to be farces, and whose first act was to send back an address from the Birmingham Political Union, saying his Majesty acknowledged no such body?'[79]

Wellington was not the only Tory anti-reformer targeted by the Unions. The Northern Political Union branded the Marquis of Londonderry as 'the only one consistent to the last in opposing our bill'.[80] Unionists warned that 'your greatest enemies never could have done you so much mischief as your best friends have done . . . another little week, my lord, and the doom of you and your party is sealed forever.'[81] They, of course, received no response, though other addresses to other members of the Lords did. Their warnings might have been stronger had they known that the Marquis had earlier tried to scotch any thought of compromise with the Unions. 'Have the government separated themselves from the Radicals and the Unions?' he had asked Wellington in November.[82] 'If the separation has not taken place Lord Wharncliffe's negotiations will produce no effect excepting to withdraw from the cause of anti-reform the powerful support of himself, Lord Harrowby and others who will follow their example.'[83]

The Unionists clearly wanted to *do* something to bring Grey and the Whigs back into office with all the assurances from the King they would need to see the Bill through. In Newcastle, where the strategy of not paying taxes until the Reform Bill was enacted was first proposed, hundreds of new members were signed up in the days immediately following the cabinet's resignation.[84] Unions sent petitions to Westminster in vast quantities and the BPU delegation of Scholefield, Parkes and Joseph Green hand-delivered their its petition directly to Daniel O'Connell in London.[85]

The Northern Political Union again voiced their preference for a tax boycott. Severe criticism followed. A number of northern newspapers tried to discredit Fife and Larkin, claiming they were not really members of the Northern Union and that they thought nothing of 'talking treason'. One critic dismissed them: 'even supposing that mean what they say . . . [they] are a contemptible minority.'[86] Historian Michael Brock has pointed out that the plan was more a gesture of defiance than an important tactic in bringing the government to a halt, as only one-twelfth of tax revenue came from direct taxes.[87] But it was more than a gesture of defiance; it was a threat of things to come. It also provided an opportunity to make the authorities look foolish and ineffective. The plan's impact was dependent upon agreements that goods confiscated for non-payment of taxes would not be auctioned, nor bought by the public. Such agreements were made.[88] Enforcement of the law was difficult, since troops, as *The Times* put it, 'could make nothing of a charge against unbought feather beds in front of a broker's warehouse.'[89]

Other Political Unions picked up on the Northern Union's plan. In Birmingham, notices were posted in hundreds of windows in the city centre reading:

NO TAXES PAID HERE
UNTIL THE
REFORM BILL IS PASSED[90]

The Council was confident that there was 'one fixed and determined feeling [in the town] which it is impossible to suppress. We are morally certain, that if the Bill be not passed the people will not pay taxes. This they have determined.'[91] Council member George Muntz proudly proclaimed that he 'owed on half-year's taxes, and solemnly declared that he would never again pay another farthing until the Bill of Reform was carried into law. The tax-gatherer might come and take what he wanted, but (Mr. M.) would never voluntarily put his hand into his pocket and pay him money.'[92]

Though the BPU insisted that members should remain peaceful and act lawfully at all times, regardless of their frustration, the Council was not above hinting that things might get out of hand and that 'under these unexpected and extraordinary circumstances, the life and property of no man in England are safe, and that the only possible way of giving safety to all is to pass the Bill of Reform, unmutilated, into a law'.[93]

At the Worcester Political Union meeting, Mr Stevenson, a member of the Council, in giving his speech, also gave advice to Union members: 'Although it would be illegal for him to advise others to do so, he should exhibit in his window "No Taxes paid here until the Reform Bill is passed" and he would recommend those who had a penny to spare not to look for the sign over the door, but for the piece of paper in the window.'[94] The Worcester Union resolved that a petition of support and confidence be sent to Lord Grey, 'pledging themselves to the return of the Grey Ministry, to return reformers should there be a dissolution of Parliament . . . and discontinue money for supplies until the Bill became law.'[95]

The Norwich Political Union resolved:

> That having ineffectually tried every other constitutional means of accomplishing the object, in which it is our fixed and irrevocable determination to succeed, it is the decided opinion of this meeting that the only course now left for the people to pursue is to petition the House of Commons to withhold all further supplies until the House of Lords shall have assented to and passed the Reform Bill now before them, without any alterations detrimental to its leading principles, or calculated to impede its beneficial operation.[96]

The Leicester Political Union also resolved to end all tax payments.[97] J.W. Hall, a member of the Bristol Political Union and friend of Francis Place, advocated non-payment of taxes at the Union's 12 May meeting.[98] In Staffordshire, R.E. Heathcote, the Union organizer, urged members to follow his example, claiming he was 'prepared not only to resist the payment of taxes, but would even join his fellow countrymen in taking up arms . . .'[99]

The Manchester Political Union also adopted the strategy of a tax boycott and sent a petition to stop supplies to Westminster.[100] The *Manchester Guardian* reported that the Union Council ordered auctioneers withdraw from any enforces sales of confiscated property.[101] It appears they complied for the brief period of the crisis, though it is doubtful that the Union could have sustained their control over the auctioneers for a longer period of time.

Some of the Unions also discussed strategies for a general election if Wellington took office and called for one. In Coventry, Hickling wrote to Bulwer, assuring him that, 'in the event of a speedy election, the members of our Union have determined to return you and your worthy colleague, as far as they are concerned, free of expense, but I sincerely hope that an election will not be necessary . . .'[102] The Worcester Political Union was also concerned about the prospect of a general election under the Tories. At their public meeting in May, the Unionist Coates reminded the member of the Political Union and the freeholders of the city that 'it was their most imperious duty, in the event of a dissolution of Parliament, by every means they possessed, to unite for the purpose of sending such members only to the House of Commons as they could place the utmost reliance upon for ability and honesty not partial honesty.'[103]

The Leicester Political Union unanimously passed a resolution that prohibited the paying taxes or tithes should the bill fail again. The addition of tithes to the list was new, although many Unions discussed their abolition as a long-term goal following the Bill's enactment. This was the Dissenting influence talking – a reminder to the Tories that a significant number of people rejected their attachment to the Church as a sacred instrument within the English constitution along with their recalcitrance in expanding political representation. It was at this meeting that the framework-knitter and Union Council member Seal, claiming to speak for the working-class members of the Union, declared himself willing to take up arms if necessary, to assure that the Bill, and the electoral qualifications prescribed in it, not be altered to the disadvantage of artisans and working men.[104] The Sheffield Union also discussed, but never adopted, the no tax policy.[105]

Place and the NPU, though in full support of the provincial Unions' strategy, never encouraged it for the London reformers.[106] A more universal concern among Political Unions was how to maintain the peace locally and at the same time be prepared to defend themselves should the Duke order in troops to disband Union meetings. In Birmingham, at another meeting at Newhall Hill, Attwood lectured on tactics should the Unions be 'compelled ... in self-defence' to arm themselves, 'Englishmen could not hesitate to use [arms] for the putting down of their enemies.'[107] Colonel Macerone's pamphlet, *Defensive Instruction for the People*, had been well circulated in Birmingham, and Parkes reported that 'soldiers are enrolling themselves in our union ... and are all right!!!'[108] Alexander Somerville, a pro-reform leader of the 2nd Dragoons, stationed near Birmingham in May 1832 and BPU member, expressed his concerns when 'the Duke of Wellington ordered that barrack gates be locked on the 13th and ordered that swords were to be rough-sharpened.'[109] Somerville believed that the best way for the military to avoid any violence was not to prepare for action, but rather to let the public know they did not intend to obstruct Union meetings and rallies.[110] Informants twisted this information, and word reached London was that the soldiers, *en masse*, had joined the Union.[111] Somerville was ultimately arrested and charged with treason. The Brighton Political Unions raised a fund for his release.[112]

Some Unions were more restrained in their response to the crisis. At the Worcester meeting, Mr Charles Hanford, magistrate and Unionist, urged the crowd to remain peaceful. 'Recently, in this city, when it was thought that the prevailing excitement might endanger the public peace, the Union came forward and strongly urged upon their members and other inhabitants the necessity of preserving tranquility and good order; and when a trifling disturbance did occur, they were among the foremost to tender the authorities assistance . . .'[113]

The Norwich Political Union defended itself from accusations, variously of revolutionary republicanism or anarchism, when it passed a similar resolution. 'We are not "incendiaries", . . . we aim at Reform, not Anarchy!' proclaimed Union broadsides. 'To our calumniators we would say in the name and on the behalf of the united millions, that we will by all legal and constitutional means, continue to persevere in our humble efforts, till we procure a restoration of those civil rights which distinguish the freeman from the slave – by being admitted a share in the choice of representatives, and the framing of those laws by which we are to be governed . . . among those means will no future payment of taxes . . .'[114] The Norwich Political Union Council circulated handbills condemning the actions of the Lords and calling upon the citizens of Norwich 'to remain determined in their resolve concerning reform, but not be driven to violence'.[115] While some Coventry Unionists were prepared to take up arms if Wellington successfully formed a government, most hoped that the anti-reformers would recognize the people's will. But weaver and Council member Edward Goode was quick to remind the optimists, 'Never forget that an administration formed by the Duke of Wellington must be opposed to their dearest interests.'[116]

The prospect of violence increased each day it appeared that the Duke might take office. As Place told J.C. Hobhouse,

> If the Duke come[s] into power now, we shall be unable longer to 'hold to the laws'; break them we must, be the consequences whatever they may . . . towns will be barricaded, new municipal arrangements will be made by the inhabitants . . . Let the Duke take office as Premier, and we shall have a commotion in the nature of a civil war, with money at our command . . . in less than five days we shall have the soldiers with us.[117]

In an attempt to prevent violence, Place created another strategy to pressure Wellington and the Tories to yield up the King's commission. Place, some of the NPU Council and Joseph Parkes hatched a plan to stir financial anxiety among the politicians.[118] On the morning of 13 May, much of London was placarded with handbills bearing the famous slogan:

To Stop the Duke
Go for Gold[119]

Though Parkes was concerned that the placarding of the city would 'likely prove not only not beneficial with respect to the cause of reform, but seriously injurious in every way', the plan went forward.[120] Newspapers printed the slogan throughout the provinces and Political Unions applauded the notion. Withdrawals were made from Tory-owned banks, in the form of sovereigns. One man withdrew 20,000 pounds from his Bank and then continued to the Bank of England to demand sovereigns for the notes he received.[121] A former governor of the Bank told a Parliamentary Commission that he 'certainly never saw the hall of the Bank, for many years . . . so crowded with applicants tendering their notes.'[122] According to John Benjamin Smith, 620 depositors gave notice during the week of their intention to withdraw 16,700 pounds. 'This', he wrote, 'alarmed our Tory directors; I know not what they will say on Monday when they will be summoned to give notice to [the] Government for 20,000 . . .'[123] All told, the May Days saw some 1,600,000 pounds withdrawn from the Bank.[124]

Provincial Unions cheered the NPU's bold move, in part because it targeted the Bank of England and the Tories, not provincial banks, many of the owners of which were leading members of provincial Unions. Attwood revelled in the fact that 'political men . . . [were responsible for] all the mischief we can [exact] by the legal means in our power . . .'[125] The Union petitioned the House of Commons to 'instantly withhold all supplies' until new peers were created or His Majesty recalled the Whigs.[126] George Muntz also recommended an 'immediate withdrawal of supplies by every man at once abandoning the consumption of all exciseable goods'.[127] Someone suggested that a mass action 'might accomplish the end they had in view . . . by the workman keeping his money in his pocket instead of paying it into the Savings' Banks.'[128] But Attwood and a number of provincial bankers organized and sat on the Council of Unions. For all their concern for the Bill and their support of reform, they were not interested in encouraging disruption of the local economy might not have any immediate impact on the political situation.

THE MAY DAYS: A REPUBLIC?

Charles Larkin was one of those men whose frustration outweighed his patience. One of the leaders of the Northern Political Union, Larkin made one of the most famous republican speeches during the reform agitation during the May Days. In it, he denounced the King, insisting that

> A new, a greater, a more illustrious opponent of public liberty has appeared on the scene than any that has appeared before. No longer is out indignation scattered and dispersed upon many objects – it is fixed, it is collected, it is condensed. It rests and centres and burns upon a single personage. The king has refused to create peers . . . He has identified his cause with that of the enemies of the people . . . He has scorned the advise of His Commons. He has despised the affections of his people . . . We have a luxurious king, hostile to reform and incited to resist the wishes of his people . . .[129]

The Northern Union, which had expressed its loyal support for the King just a month earlier, now turned on the monarch, accusing him of abandoning his people for the familiarity of aristocratic privilege and unchallenged political domination. The newly formed Northampton Political Union expressed outrage with the King's failure to stand behind his ministers to the conclusion of the Reform Bill crisis, then went further still and adopted a resolution declaring 'the form of government best adapted for the happiness and welfare of a nation' was a republic.[130]

Most Unions did not go this far, but many grew disillusioned with the monarch's choice to rule for the privileged and powerful, not the faithful and oppressed. Robert Heathcote of the Staffordshire Union expressed what many Unionists felt: 'The King too . . . had apparently deserted them.'[131] Desperate to understand what the King was doing, Heathcote speculated:

> If it should, after all, turn that the King is a sincere Reformer, and has only wished to avoid, if possible, a step which, in future times and calmer moments, might be thought to as a shade on the great work of his reign; and, if it should appear that, under these circumstances, and with a mere view to place, the faction before averted to, had desperately resolved to bring their Sovereign into the dilemma of either doing violence to his own conscientious

scruples, which it is impossible not to respect, or accepting the resignation of his Ministers, and thereby of risking the love and duty of his people; ought not that odium, which some of us, in a moment of anger and disappointment may have been disposed to cast upon our Sovereign, to fall with ten-fold weight on those, who have at once outraged the feelings of their King and defied his people? I throw out this hint to those, who, like myself and other gentlemen who have addressed you, may believe the King to be sincere, and may be anxious to make some allowance for the difficulty in which he has been placed; and I do so the more willingly, because I was one of those who spoke, at our last meeting, with considerable warmth, of what I then feared had been his Majesty's conduct.[132]

A similar tone came from Union members in Brighton. One member denounced the King's decision to accept Grey's resignation. 'We have a King who is compelled against his own wishes to succumb to a conservative Club of Oligarchs! Can men boast of even a slight degree of Patriotism think of such a state of things without feeling a shudder of indignation creep over them! Shall we permit our King to be driven into a corner and kept in a state of thralldom? No! . . . the truth will prevail and prejudice must eventually vanish before treason.'[133]

Mr Salt of the BPU, attending a Worcester Political Union meeting during the crisis, also denounced the King, not simply for turning his back on Grey, but for his rejection of the hardship facing his subjects from the industrious classes. 'The palace is flourishing,' he told a cheering crowd, 'while the cottage is in ruins.'[134] But he also warned, 'Let the palace flourish – but only when peace and abundance are carried into the cottages of the poor . . . a patriotic King [must support] a righteous government and soothe the sorrows, and heal the wounds, and restore the liberties of the people.'[135]

In Warwick, P.F. Luard, MD, made an analogy between Adam and Eve and Wellington and William IV, urging the crowd to support the King in his efforts to resist temptation to sin.[136] The Hull Political Union resolved that 'the Head of State, by his recent refusals of the reasonable means for carrying the Reform Bill, has declared war against the interests of the nation . . .'[137] George Dewhurst of Blackburn denounced both the Parliament and King for ignoring the Unions' 'petitions and complaints and Radical reformers must attend them both.'[138] In Salisbury, the inaugural meeting of the local Political Union began with a loud denunciation of William IV for his part in the state of the Reform Bill. 'Whom have the people been betrayed?' fumed Edward Good, one of the Union's organizers. The crowd roared, 'The King, the King.' Good expressed his regrets that 'any diminution should have taken place in the affection of the people for their Sovereign, whose strange determination must have been occasioned by influence behind the throne.'[139] The crowd seemed to agree that that influence belonged to the Duke of Cumberland.[140]

In Bristol, where the Union drafted a petition of support for Grey and asked the Duke of Sussex to present it to the King, the Union strongly condemned the King's reaction to Sussex's 'liberal conduct'. Messrs Herapath and Pile claimed that Sussex had been 'banished from the presence of the throne', and he condemned the King for violating the right of petitioning.[141] 'What is the use of a right to present [a petition to the Crown], if the individual who presents it is to be visited with an infliction of royal displeasure his temerity?' Pile asked a perplexed and increasingly hostile crowd of Unionists from Bristol, Bath and the southeast of England.[142]

The May Days had brought tremendous disillusionment concerning the 'Patriotic King', not only because William seemed to abandon his ministers and the public's will for reform, but because he seemed to be abandoning English constitutional rights as well. The *Poor Man's Guardian* published a poem entitled 'Monarchy Unmasked' which seemed to reflect the tone of the people's betrayal:

When History's pen hereafter shall relate
The deeds that influence now a nation's fate;
When truly picturing those gaudy things,
Which nations feed, clothe, pay and christen kings;
When despots, dolts and debauchers arrayed,
Shall make Truth blush at what she has portrayed,
The meanest, vilest of this damned crew,
. . . will stand confessed to view!

Charles was a daring tyrant, and he kept
Some manliness about him; Pity wept
When Justice, and a nation's will, decreed
His death, lest other tyrants should succeed.
James we can almost name without a sneer,
And the third George – to doting humbug dear,
A foolish bigot – was at least *sincere*.

The *fourth* alone, and only in degree,
Thou regal hypocrite, approaches thee.
He lost in age the love he earned in youth,
Exchanged for ease and lust, desert and truth,
Dressed, dined, and lounged with peeresses and peers,
Dragged an unwieldy bulk through languid years,
And died without *one* claim on England's tears.

But *thou*, domestic, affable and kind,
Hast won with fairest show the general mind,
And masked, with seeming care for England's weal,
A heart too stupid or too cold to feel;
And from a height which ALFRED's self alone
Attained, – from something loftier than a throne,
Even from a kingdom's heart, – thou fall'st; and shame,
The scorn of millions, brands thy blighted name![143]

WAITING, RETURNING AND ENACTING THE REFORM BILL

Lord Grey patiently waited for the May Days drama to play itself out. He also received reports from Sir Francis Burdett concerning Union activities, including information from delegates from Birmingham, Manchester and Bristol Unions. Burdett was gravely concerned over their account 'of the feelings and determination and union of the hundreds and thousands of their districts is really enough to make the most reckless and thoughtless pause and think.'[144] Nonetheless, Burdett talked them out of any cooperation with the Duke of Wellington in forming a cabinet. 'They agreed to take no notice of the refusal to receive the Petition [from Unions in favour of the King's creation of peers willing to support the Bill], in short to leave all things to the management of those in whom they confide.'[145] Without doubt, the government was secretly directing the activities of the Political Unions on the public stage and letting them know in advance what the public face of the ministry would be, so as not to allow it to be interpreted at face value, thereby jeopardizing the cooperation between the two.

Grey immediately responded to Burdett's letter. 'What you have heard from the Birmingham delegates is indeed entitled to demand the most serious consideration; their conduct hitherto has been praiseworthy and I do hope, if we can bring this question to a satisfactory settlement, that they will see the necessity of doing all they can to put an end to further agitation . . . If things can only be kept quiet I have not the least doubt of being able in a very few days, to set everything right again.'[146] Grey hoped quiet would re-establish a working relationship with the King and secure reform. But some Political Unionists were beyond that.

By 15 May, the realities had become too great for even Wellington to disregard. He informed the King he was unable to form a government. The King then asked Grey to resume his ministerial duties and secure the Reform Bill 'with such modifications as may meet the view of those who may still entertain any difference of opinion upon the subject.'[147] Grey replied that the previous week had made modification impossible, but that he was willing to put the Bill to another vote without a creation of peers if he could get some type of guarantee from the Tory peers that they would cease to defeat the measure. He did, and the Whigs returned to office.

Once the Whigs returned to office, the Bill was once again on track, and Grey presented the Bill for a second reading. This time, it went through committee without amendment. Nearly all the opposition withdrew from the debate. On 4 June, the Whigs carried the third reading, 106 to 22, just seven days after its reintroduction. The royal assent was given by commission on 7 June 1832. The Reform Bill was finally law.

For Political Unions, the enactment of the Bill was a victory worth celebrating. Birmingham did so with new Union medals bearing Attwood's image, as well as commemorative pipes, beer mugs and blue garters inscribed with the words, 'Attwood Forever!'. The Unions held parades, rallies and dinners. Thanks and congratulations flowed freely. Even Attwood, always a showman, remarked in exhaustion that he was 'tired to death with honours and dinners.'[148] In Kenilworth, the Political Union organized a procession with banners and a band, marching through the centre of the village. The procession stopped 'at different houses inhabited by respectable gentlemen friendly to reform . . . the occupiers hailed with loud and continued cheers.'[149] In Frome, the Union placed paper tombstones on the houses of Tory supporters.[150] In Liverpool, the *Courier* and the *Chronicle* both reported that the Political Union was the only group that celebrated the passage of the Bill, the former remarking sourly, 'if a hole and corner meeting of the Political Union is to be considered [a celebration]'.[51]

Processions and dinners took place in Bath, Bristol, Bradford-on-Avon, Holt, Trowbridge, Hull, Yeovil, Taunton, Warwick and countless other towns and villages.[152] More than 12,000 Political Unionists led celebrations attended by an estimated 55,000 in Bath alone to celebrate the return of Lord Grey and the Whigs to office.[153] The Frome Political Union sent 2,000 members to participate in the parade and rally.[154] William Herapath of the Bristol Political Union spoke and James Crisp of Bath put the whole reform agitation and the Bill itself in context, summing up what, as a radical, the legislation meant to him: 'When I look back to the period of the French Revolution', he told the enormous crowd,

> and see the cruelties which were practiced on my fellow-subjects for advocating the cause of Reform, thousands doomed to banishment and every extreme of persecutions: when so recently as 1817, when so many were the objects of Government prosecutions, when I was obliged to leave Bath for a period, lest I should have the harpies of the Boroughmongers upon me; when shortly after occurred the vindictive and sanguinary attack on the defenseless people of Manchester; when I contemplate the hold that the Boroughmongering faction had upon the country; the thousands and tens of thousands of wealth which have been wrung from the country, I can never enough appreciate the victory we have gained.[155]

Crisp summed up the feelings of radicals throughout the country: victory was sweet.

The King was once again praised by Political Unionists, although with less flattery and greater scepticism about his concern for the common people. Mr Stone of the Leicester Political Unions expressed the sentiments of many when he claimed that 'the Reform Bill progress[ed] safely and satisfactorily to a speedy and successful termination, and that they should owe it, not to the King or the Lords, but to the invincible strength of the united people.'[156] Stone, nonetheless, thanked the King.

THE END OF POLITICAL UNIONS?

Grey insisted that the King need worry no further. Now that the Reform Bill was law, the Political Unions' objective met, they would disband, putting to rest all doubts as to their true objectives or their roles as constabularies. As proof that his speculation would be true, Grey sent Sir Herbert a copy of a resolution adopted by the Liverpool Political Union claiming it would disband when the Bill was law.[157] He certainly believed that those Unions that continued to meet would, in no way, feel compelled to arm themselves.

But most Political Unions did not disband. They chose to enter into the electoral process by seeking economic reform-minded candidates and preparing for the forthcoming general election. The Duke of Cumberland sent his brother printed 'proof' that the Political Unions had 'not the slightest intention of dissolving themselves, but, on the contrary, of setting themselves up over every one and every body, and of being the sole dictators.'[158]

Cumberland was right. New Unions formed in the months following the Bill's enactment.[159] The prospectus for a new publication *Political Unionist* appeared on 30 June. The Unions, rather than disappearing, seemed to be moving on to the next stage of their reform campaign:

> to create a medium or committee between the . . . unions of the kingdom, by reporting their most important proceedings, and publishing such of their documents as may be deemed of sufficient value to merit permanent record, and, secondly, to increase their numbers of friends, by giving extensive currency to their principles and operations . . . [160]

The King might well have agreed with his brother, but could do little against the Unions. The Proclamation had been issued, however useless it may have been. The rhetoric of loyalty had returned during the Union dinners and parades celebrating the Whigs' victory. Grey was not willing to do more, especially now that he believed the point was moot and that the Unions would disband, certainly after the general election. In fact, most would do just that. William IV, a tarnished, but none the less respected 'Patriot King', at least as far as Political Unionists were concerned, had no choice but to tolerate the Political Unions once again.

CONCLUSION

Political Unions faced a great challenge after the Whigs reintroduced the Reform Bill. Their existence inspired fear and criticism among many, and this only hurt the government. Still, the Unions represented the public will on reform, as evidenced by their increased numbers since October. The government wanted their assistance in stepping up the pressure on opponents, but did not want their activities to antagonize the King. Knowing this, most Political Unions kept a low profile during the third presentation of the Reform Bill. When, however, it appeared that the Tories in the House of Lords would repeat their opposition to reform by amending the measure in committee, Political Unions became very public in their denunciations of aristocratic obstructionism. More Unions formed. All staunchly supported the government and the Reform Bill.

The May Days were highly significant to the success of the Bill and were perhaps the high point of the Political Union campaign as well. During these few days when Wellington scrabbled to form a ministry, Political Unions used the power of public opinion to frustrate his attempts. Their threats to boycott payment of taxes and stage a run on the Tory Bank of England, as well as rumours of arming and other revolutionary activity among the Unions, all added credence to Grey's claim that the people would not tolerate a Tory government and the emasculation of the Reform Bill. Many Tories politicians agreed, refusing to join Wellington rather than risk setting off a revolution. The Tories could not successfully form a government because some of their party – notably Peel – believed that the public demanded an efficient reform, and unlike the Duke, would have no part in trying to carry one. Nothing was more important in creating this impression of public feeling than the activities of Political Unions.[161] The Unions certainly felt they played a significant role in bringing Grey back to office and, therefore, securing the support of the King to see the Bill through. Few understood how remarkable their achievement was in light of the strains developing in the relationship between Grey and the King as a result of their very presence in the political arena.

The Reform Bill agitation heightened a number of individual fears concerning political change. Certainly the aristocracy was unnerved as they saw their political oligarchy opening to new middle-class electors, and manufacturing and industrial economic interests challenged landed ones. The Tories feared that they would permanently suffer at the polls as they had blocked reform for so long in Parliament. Concerns about democracy and the mob flourished and there was great speculation about the impact of the October riots and their manifestations in future political challenges. The Duke of Wellington channelled that fear into concern over the Unions' place in undermining the constitution. He did his best to discredit the Whigs and Lord Grey by producing evidence that they were in league with the Political Unions and allowing them to arm themselves to serve as a National Guard, independent of the King, his military and his government.

But the accusations did not stick. The government received the undying support of the Political Unions, 'evidence' of the Unions' arming themselves, much to the relief of Grey, as well as the King, proved unfounded, and Grey kept abreast of Union activity through friends and informants discreetly, doing his best to avoid additional rumours which might undermine his efforts bring about reform peacefully. But William IV did not really have to fear revolution, or, for that matter, doubt the loyalty of English subjects. Only intense frustration during the May Days allowed for any republican sentiment to be voiced. Otherwise, loyalty to the person of William IV and the institution of the monarchy was part of the reform rhetoric and the objectives of the Political Unions created to secure the government's bill. Rather than instruments of revolution, Political Unions were monarchist organizations, seeking reform in order to maintain that which made the English constitution – the representation of the people.

Conclusion

> Until the British people had recovered their constitutional right to be really represented in the Commons House of Parliament, there was no hope that their sufferings would be relieved, or their wrongs obtain a remedy. Impressed with this truth, the men of Birmingham formed, in 1830, the Political Union, and, agreeably to the constitutional practice of their forefathers, claimed and demanded all those great birthrights, of which the people had, during a period of one hundred years been impiously defrauded. . . . Other towns and cities did the same until the union exhibited an aspect that could not be defined, strength that could not be defeated. The effect followed. In the spring of 1831, the Reform Bill was introduced into the House of Commons. This bill was regarded . . . as a mere compromise between wrong and right, yet, willing to secure the least extension of the franchise, and desire to move our country from civil strife . . . unions in general resolved to waive our convictions, and to postpone our full and equitable demands. We acceded to the bill and are glad of it.[1]

Political Unions appeared all over England between January 1830 and May 1832. Over 120 individual political associations were formed and chose to call themselves 'Unions' during the Reform Bill agitation. In doing so, their members adopted both a conception and a model of popular political organization. Thomas Attwood and the Birmingham currency reformers were perhaps the first, but far from the only reformers in England to appreciate the lessons of 'unity' and the forceful development of public opinion offered by Daniel O'Connell's Catholic Association in Ireland and its great victory in 1829. This study has examined, to the degree evidence allows, the nature and activities of most of those Political Unions.

But the fortunes of the Reform Bill itself, and the actions of Attwood, Grey, Wellington, the Bristol rioters and the King, all significantly affected the formation and dissolution of Political Unions. The promise of victory brought some reformers of uncertain commitment onto the Union bandwagon, just as the fear of failure prompted others into the Union movement in a last-ditch effort to save the Reform Bill from defeat. More personal and self-interested motives of profit or retribution doubtless drove other Union members away. It is, therefore, not surprising that a number of Political Unions appear to have been inconsistent in their devotion to the cause. Fluctuations in membership or financial support also prevented some Unions from being an active force throughout the campaign. When the Whig Reform Bill became law, some 60 Political Unions across England celebrated. This was more than half of all the Political Unions formed during the campaign and a significant number by any standard of extra-parliamentary political activity in the early nineteenth century.[2]

Critics will argue that if 50 per cent of all Political Unions had folded by the summer of 1832, members could not have very committed to a long-term reform campaign. I would argue that the opposite is true. It is remarkable that so many Political Unions, representing both communities that would benefit from the Reform Bill and those that would not, stayed the course and fought for Grey's ministry and its reform measure. Considering the inability of either the BPU or NPU to forge a recognizable position as national Union leader, the legal threat posed by the King's Proclamation and the utter frustration of the May Days, the fact that so many Unions still met after June 1832 shows a true determination to assert the authority of the people and help shape the future of the English electoral process. No previous popular political campaign had sustained itself so long on such a large scale. The Chartists and other nineteenth-century extra-parliamentary reformers learned much about popular political organization from the Political Unions.

The majority of Political Unions formed in the industrial north and midlands, mostly in towns which had no parliamentary representation. All told, more than half of all Political Unions were based in towns manufacturing cotton, worsted and woollen products. A fair number were also in towns concentrating in iron, metalworking and mining. Unions also represented the silk, carpet and shoe industries, in Coventry, Lichfield and Kidderminister, and Northampton, respectively. There was also a significant concentration of Unions in the southwest, generally in port or market towns dependent upon the textile trade (i.e. Barnstaple, Bridgwater, Frome, Taunton), or the West Indian trade in the case of Bristol. Some, such as Norwich, a declining textile town, conformed to existing patterns. Others – Brighton, for example – were more or less unique. Political Unions in southern communities were principally engaged in craft production (such as handloom weaving and spinning). Otherwise, they pretty much ran the gamut of Britain's major commercial interests – some in the ascendant, some in decline.

The parliamentary representation of growing industrial regions demanded a redistribution of parliamentary seats. For this, it would be necessary to sacrifice some of the boroughs in more rural areas. Aside from the obvious benefits in abolishing rotten and pocket boroughs, thus eliminating the aristocracy's hold on political power, a shift in parliamentary representation to the towns of the north also shifted policy-making towards urban and industrial concerns.

Of the 42 towns slated for representation on the first Reform Bill's schedules, 25 boasted Political Unions and London (receiving five seats) had three: the MPU, NUWC and NPU. About half of all Political Unions were based in towns that were already represented in Parliament and could be found in every type of parliamentary borough. Bridgwater, a scot and lot borough with fewer than 600 electors, founded one, as did Leicester, possessing a similar franchise, but with more than 5,000 electors.[3] Political Unions existed in the potwalloper boroughs of Preston (with over 5,000 electors) and Taunton (with fewer than 1,000 electors). The only burgage borough to have a Political Union was Horsham, and that an ephemeral Union.[4] Unions in existing parliamentary boroughs were frequently found in those boroughs whose electors were freemen and who faced tight-knit Corporations. Political Unionists were eager to abolish ancient abuses of political power at the town level. They supported the Reform Bill because it would eliminate arbitrary practices and establish a uniform property qualification for later generations. The Bill did not strip electors of their existing rights. It would have been a very different story had Union leaders urged the industrious classes to support a reform measure which would deny them their elector status. Like the unrepresented middle classes of the north and midlands, freemen joined the Unions. In short, what probably distinguishes towns with Political Unions is not the type of franchise they possessed, but rather the degree to which the franchise could be restructured.

There were times during the Reform Bill campaign when individual Political Unions formed to reflect strong local concerns about electoral inequities and corruption, and later a growing fear that the Reform campaign was failing. Of the Unions founded before the Bill's introduction in 1831, eight of the 12 were in towns unrepresented in the House of Commons. They were mostly large cities in the north – Manchester, Salford, Bolton, Stockport and Huddersfield, for example. They all demanded a redistribution of parliamentary representation. They all, regardless of the fact that many of those who founded these Unions (large manufacturers, for example) certainly met existing qualifications, sought universal manhood suffrage.

Between Wellington's resignation and the new Whig government's introduction of the Reform Bill, 11 Political Unions appeared in non-represented industrial towns including Leeds, Sheffield and Wolverhampton (as well as in existing boroughs such as Liverpool, Newark and Coventry). By the early months of 1831, however, twice as many Political Unions existed in towns already represented in Parliament as in non-represented towns. In most cases this probably suggested discontent with the existing franchise in the borough, but in some it may suggest that reformers were looking beyond the simple issue of their own town's representation and hoping to exert pressure on the new government to bring in the kind of broad reform, as we have seen, they had in mind. This was certainly the case in Newark and Liverpool, where the ballot and Corporation reform were very popular and in Leeds, Sheffield and Coventry where the larger reform agenda included the abolition of various taxes and tariffs, opening the door to free trade.

When the government introduced its Reform Bill on 1 March 1831, eight provincial Political Unions in unrepresented towns found them on the bill's schedule to receive two MPs (Birmingham, Bolton, Bradford, Leeds, Manchester, Stockport, Sheffield, Wolverhampton) and five were to receive one MP (Dudley, Walsall, Kidderminster, Salford, Huddersfield). Political Unions in these boroughs were naturally gratified by the success the Bill promised them both for their own electoral representation and the extension of the urban and commercial franchise in general. But Political Unions in towns not listed in the schedules also seem to reflect satisfaction by their actions. Radical demands such as universal suffrage, annual parliaments and the ballot, were dropped and Political Unions enthusiastically concentrated their efforts on supporting the Reform Bill.

With the Lords' rejection of the second Bill, by 199 to 158, in October 1831, the country erupted in indignation, and sometimes worse. Political Unions responded as well, posing as the alternative to the violence that broke out, most famously in Nottingham, where the castle was burned, and Bristol, where the Bishop's Palace, among other important buildings, suffered the same fate. Some observers feared that Political Unions were the cause of such behaviour. Few of the general public, however, seem really to have believed that the Unions were dangerous and arming themselves, as was rumoured by their detractors. Far more people appeared to believe that they were moderate in their designs and only patriotism and loyalty to the Crown prompted their heightened recruiting efforts and more frequent agitation following the riots. The Unions hoped their growing popularity and greater public participation in the political debate would demonstrate widespread support for the King and his government against the affront of the Lords rejecting the Bill.

The number of Political Unions more than doubled in November and December 1831. Clearly worried that the rejection of the Bill would mean an end to their hopes of acquiring parliamentary representation, Schedule C boroughs (slated for their first parliamentary representatives) Oldham, Wolverhampton, Stoke-on-Trent and Macclesfield formed Political Unions. Frome and Merthyr Tydfil from Schedule D also formed Unions. The remaining 31 Political Union creations (including Bath, Derby, Hull, Leicester and Norwich) all argued that their formation was intended to support the Bill while at the same time preventing riot and disorder. They saw themselves as the defenders of the King's peace, his government's authority and the public's will against an arrogant and stubborn aristocracy.

There was another small spurt of Political Union formation during the May Days crisis. Unions formed in Barnstaple, Lichfield, Northampton, Salisbury, Staffordshire and Trowbridge, giving public support to the government's claim that public opinion was solidly behind the Reform Bill. The post-riot Political Unions accounted for more than half of all Political Unions established during the Reform Bill agitation, indicating that rather than frightening people off, the Unions presented a vehicle of hope for attaining political power.

Political Unions were in theory and in fact independent of one another and not, in spite of arguments to the contrary, part of an organized national movement, in the sense of one main Union with satellites in urban centres and smaller towns throughout England. London, for example, never emerged as a centre of Political Union activity, let alone leadership, probably because it lacked the mixed class neighbourhoods which seems to have allowed tradesmen and artisans, manufacturers and labourers, to unite together with a real sense of community, as in Birmingham. As it was, the movement in London was jerky and spasmodic, like a steam engine without a proper governor.

Most Political Unions created an organizational structure modelled on the Birmingham Political Union. Yet, while Attwood's BPU was widely perceived to be the centre of the entire popular Reform Bill agitation, there was little communication between the BPU and any other Union outside its immediate vicinity. Unions differed in their reform objectives and the extent to which their leaders believed the organization should directly involve itself in electoral or economic actions during the reform campaign (and beyond) to pressure the King and government to hold firm against the Tory Lords. Political Unions were local organizations, founded and led by local reformers. Their unity as a political movement lay in their objective, not in their organization.

In general terms, Political Unions sought the passage of an 'effective reform' in parliamentary representation in order to restore 'the honour, integrity, and the purity of the electoral franchise'. Unions differed in their definitions of what was 'effective' and in what ways 'integrity' could be restored to the electoral process. With one significant exception, all Unions, however, agreed upon a three-plank programme of specific changes in the existing electoral arrangements: universal manhood suffrage, annual parliaments and vote by ballot. Sometimes these aims were simply agreed upon in resolutions and not always listed in the formal 'Objectives, Rules and Regulations' of the local Political Union. The objectives just mentioned were drawn directly from the 'Old Corruption' reform campaign and, in fact, were half of the specific goals detailed in Major John Cartwright's radical plan, *Take Your Choice* (1776). By adopting them, the Political Unions' goals were also, of course, identical to half the reform platform listed in *The People's Charter.* One Political Union alone did not share this set of goals – the Birmingham Political Union. At different times, Attwood endorsed universal manhood suffrage, household suffrage and the ten pound franchise. In fact, such matters were not as important to the leaders of the BPU as the economic reforms for which parliamentary reform was a means rather than an end.

Though currency reform was not the goal of any Union apart from Birmingham, all Political Unions made some type of economic or fiscal reform an objective. Most endorsed free trade and called for the abolition of the Corn Laws and the elimination, or at least significant reduction of, tariffs.[5] In addition, most Unions sought an end to monopolies generally, tithes and colonial slavery. Many called for a reduction in taxes – the malt and beer taxes, and taxes on knowledge all prominently mentioned – as well as a reduction of public expenditure, especially on the Civil List and poor relief. Political Unions also pledged themselves to return reformers to Parliament who would promote the interests of the industrious classes. The BPU was the initiator of the Political Union campaign, but it did not go as far as other Unions in the breadth of the reform called for, in its proposals to eliminate 'Old Corruption' and restore English liberties.

Political Unionists were reformers, not wild revolutionaries. The Unions reflected the concerns of those who took the initiative in founding them – an educated and urban middle class, active in the expansion of industrial manufacturing and the economic development of their communities. The BPU founder, Thomas Attwood, was a banker and Ultra-Tory, at least until he became disillusioned with Wellington's unwillingness to come around on parliamentary reform. (Other Ultras also adopted parliamentary reform for awhile, but none so completely and persistently as Attwood.)

Unions also had prominent political adherents. The mayor of Bridgwater, John Evered, was a member of its Union. E.D. Davenport, MP for Stafford, and Thomas Paget, MP for Leicestershire South, were members of the Stockport and Leicester Political Unions, respectively. Richard Edensor Heathcote, the former MP for Coventry (1826–30), founded the Hanley and Shelton Political Union in Staffordshire. In addition, the MPs from Bath, Bristol and Preston (the last being the Radical Henry Hunt, who was dubious about the Political Union, mainly because he did not organize it) were in regular communication with the Unions in their boroughs. In Coventry, the Political Union solicited and received a ten pound donation for its relief fund for the victims of the revolution in France from the town's MP, the government whip and Lord Grey's brother-in-law, Edward Ellice.

Iron, hosiery and lace manufacturers respectively dominated the Union Councils in Sheffield, Nottingham and Leicester. Bankers, lawyers, merchants and ministers, especially of the Dissenting variety, were Union Council members. A number of provincial newspaper publishers, also Dissenters, led Unions. Even some military men such as Thomas Bischoff, the cavalry captain from Leeds and

Major Norton Lift of Shepton Mallet, sat on their Political Union Councils. These overwhelmingly moderate types were the sort who founded Political Unions and led them by sitting on the Union Council, the small and select group of men who controlled the day-to-day operations of the Unions and set their policies. Council members were, as their professions suggest, in large part, their more affluent members who as a result of their local prominence in business, newspaper publishing or politics, were able to promote successfully the formation of a Union. Yet, while dominated, or at least guided, by middle-class men of wealth and standing, Unions were inclusive and boasted memberships drawn from the working as well as the middle classes.

Artisans and smaller shopkeepers formed the bulk of the general membership. Drapers, owners of bookshops, liquor and dry goods merchants are types common everywhere. Such people who joined Political Unions included Samuel Tucker, the Liverpool liquor dealer, William Capleman, the pawnbroker from Hull, and Joseph Seal, the Leicester newsagent. In Bath and Worcester, shoe and glove-makers joined the organizations by the hundreds, as did potters in Staffordshire. In Derby, there was Meakin the basketmaker; in Huddersfield, John Hill the cabinetmaker. John Beevor of Norwich was a joiner/carpenter and Richard Potter of Manchester, a blacksmith.

In Bath and Leeds, Union meetings took place at a publican member's establishment, and John Rogers' Cat and Wheel became home to the Bristol Political Union. The Huddersfield publican Thomas Vever was one of the Union's founders, along with John Heaton, grocer. In Norwich, Worcester and Newcastle local printers such as Dawson and Isaac Arrowsmith were responsible for providing the leaflets, handbills and broadsheets which kept members informed as to Political Union meetings and rallies, the directives of the Council, the status of the Bill, and the potential actions the Union might take to secure the measure. Ports such as Bristol, Liverpool and Hull included seafaring men (such as Robert Peck of Hull) as well as dockworkers. Dozens of individuals identified in town directories merely as 'retailers' appeared on Union dues lists or in newspaper accounts of Union meetings.

Political Unionists, particularly the founding members, were often radicals (in the contemporary sense) of long standing in the community. Creating a new reform organization such as a Political Union was a logical next step for many local reformers who had often been active in fomenting interest and activity in behalf of parliamentary reform since the 1790s (many Political Union towns had boasted Hampden Clubs earlier in the century). It is, therefore, no surprise that Dissenters played a significant role in the creation and operation of Political Unions. A nonconformist perception of freedom and individualism in the areas of conscience and political participation, though not necessarily exclusive to Dissenters, was at the heart of the reform philosophy.

As interesting as who Political Unionists were is who Political Unionists were not. There is no indication that Political Unions included agricultural labourers among their working-class members. Farmers were active in promoting reform through traditional local and county meetings, but the composition and objectives of the Unions indicate that urban and commercial interests were dominant among their memberships.

Women are also absent from Political Union rolls and in the few instances in which they played a role in Political Union activity, they formed their own 'auxiliary' Unions, but not until the campaign for reform was well underway. There is no evidence that women were deliberately excluded and there is nothing in the rules that would have done so. Yet, non-membership was not necessarily a sign of lack of interest, and one of the earliest accounts of a BPU general meeting notes that the meeting was 'so quiet and peaceable that ... women of all classes, in hundreds [attended], indeed the half of the crowd were women.'[6]

But unlike the later Chartist movement, in which it has been demonstrated that women, as well as men, were influential in the campaign for democratic reform, women were not part of the Political Union campaign for the Reform Bill.[7] Women were certainly present at the large Union parades and displays that the BPU was noted for. Women waved banners bearing reform slogans and cheered Attwood's speeches while they picnicked and watched their children play on Newhall Hill. Joseph Parkes remarked that during the May Days, 'our women [were] heroines' and the 'petticoats put up at Birmingham'.[8] But for the rest of the provincial Unions which did not attempt monster meetings, women were not recorded as present, much less active in the reform campaign.[9]

Some Political Unions changed course during the Reform Bill campaign, both in their desire to create and maintain unity between the middle and working classes, and in the nature of their reform objectives. While every Union but the BPU called for the same radical reform agenda drawn from Major Cartwright when the Tories held office, the introduction of the Whig Reform Bill changed the goals of most Political Unions. Believing themselves to be the Grey government's allies in the campaign for passing the bill, even though it fell short of their desired radical reform program, Political Unions generally now had but one immediate goal: passage of the Whig Reform Bill.

When the Lords rejected the measure, the unity between the middle and working classes within the Unions became even stronger, and Unions took a more active role. The Unions assumed the mantle of peacekeeper, partly to disarm the charges of their opponents, partly to show their power and determination. Only intense frustration during the May Days raised any hint of a violent response on the Unions' part and then only briefly. Political Union plans to boycott payment of taxes and stage a run on the Bank of England, as well as unsubstantiated rumours of arming and other revolutionary activity among them, added greater credence to the Whig claim that the people would not stand limitations on reform through drastic amending of the Bill.

Historians still differ about the seriousness of the Political Union threats during the May Days. But these things we do know. When the Whigs resigned, the King asked the Duke of Wellington to form a government, but with the stipulations that it must pledge itself to carrying extensive and efficient reform. Wellington was willing, but he could not convince others to join him. It was not because they believed that reform could or ought not to be revisited. As Peel wrote to J.W. Croker on 12 May: 'I foresee that a Bill for Reform, including everything that is really important and really dangerous in the present Bill must Pass.'[10] The 'tide', to use one of Peel's favourite metaphors in describing support for reform, could not be stemmed. He believed that it had been 'swollen' by the King, the government and the press. The tide, of course, was public opinion. But when did, Peel and the ruling class generally, get the impression that it could not be stemmed? As we have seen from this correspondence, it was primarily from the activities of the Political Unions.

In conclusion, Political Unions shared a belief in the power of public opinion and its importance in setting the political agenda. They saw proof in the Catholic Association of what a people could do when united against existing political powers and were not shy about flexing their newfound political muscle for Lord Grey, the

House of Lords, and the entire English political establishment to see. Unions created an atmosphere that brought about the introduction of a government-sponsored reform measure. While their initial demands for universal manhood suffrage, annual parliaments and the ballot were not adopted by the Whigs, they were, nonetheless, a major force in the shaping of such an extensive and Radical piece of legislation. The Whigs knew that only an extensive reform measure would gain public approval. The Unions kept up the pressure on both Grey and William IV to maintain their commitment to the measure as the organizations' popularity and authority grew dramatically among the English people during the ups and downs of the Reform Bill agitation. They convinced the ruling class in both political parties that public opinion and extra-parliamentary political agitation were a force which politicians could only ignore at their own risk. The Political Unions brokered their political power with care, ever mindful of crucial issues such as law and order and loyalty to the Crown, doing everything possible to maintain both while demonstrating the absolute necessity for both for peaceful reform. Through it all, Political Unions remained firm in their belief that they were simply demanding what was rightfully theirs as they understood the English constitution: parliamentary representation and the protection of citizens' political rights. Through their mass meetings, parliamentary petitions, plans for boycotts and runs on banks, the Political Unions played a critical role in organizing public opinion and steadily applying pressure to the government and the King, reminding them that reform was the only thing that would prevent widespread upheaval. The Political Unions' scrutiny and publicity of political action in Westminster helped secure the first of several parliamentary Reform Bills in English history. Together with the Whig ministry of Lord Grey, the English people – through the Political Unions' extra-parliamentary reform campaign – launched their country on the path of political democracy.

Epilogue

> I trust and believe that, if not irritated by an injurious interference, these Unions will die away; that many of them will be formally dissolved; that from others the most respectable persons, who had but lately been induced to join them, will withdraw themselves.
>
> Earl Grey[1]

> After the Reform Bill has been carried, the Political Unions will, in one shape or another, remain in existence. Under a reformed parliament there will be the same unaccountable leaning towards property in legislative measures, and the same neglect of the rights of industry...
>
> *Political Magazine*, 1831[2]

After the victory celebrations were over, the question of what the Reform Bill meant for the future of economic and political reform and the remaining radical agenda, still loomed large. With that, there was another question – namely, the issue of whether Political Unions were still necessary and what role they should take in the next stage of reform, the election of reformers to the new Parliament. Some argued that the Political Unions had achieved their goal and were no longer necessary in the political arena. Certainly this was a sentiment shared by William IV, Grey and the Tories who, for varying reasons, feared the Unions' continued presence as a threat.

But, much to the dismay of those who tolerated them in order to see the Bill secured, most reports indicated that the majority of Political Unions had decided to remain in operation pending a test of the success of the legislation. The *Sheffield Independent* warned its readers that the town's Political Union might 'be declared extinct' with the Bill's enactment, but immediately retracted when Council chair Thomas Asline Ward urged that the Union 'should see how the Reform Bill works before the Unions are dissolved. If all go right, they will be as dull as Pitt or Whig clubs.'[3] The Yeovil Union promised to fight for reform, 'as long as the Pitt and Conservative Clubs were in existence'.[4] The members of the Hanley and Shelton Union opted to 'continue to unite until a reform took place in the House of Lords' and 'to present a moral and physical power in protecting the people's rights'.[5] The Bristol Political Union was in the process of reforming itself as the Central Committee of Parochial Deputies whose main purpose was to compensate victims of the riots and institute a local police force.[6] Indeed, new Unions formed with this in mind.[7]

The main objectives for Political Unions after the Reform Bill's enactment was the selection and return of reformers to the new Parliament and the extension of reform policies. Some Political Unionists demanded that candidates demonstrate their commitment to reform by pledging themselves to promote additional reforms and the specific objectives of the Political Union. Others wanted to 'educate' the general electorate as to the candidates' voting records, in order to prevent a slick campaign from resulting in the return of an anti-reformers or a mouthpiece for the parties of the status quo. Still others, dissatisfied with their options, put up their own candidates for Parliament. At least a dozen members of Political Union Councils throughout England stood for Parliament in December. Thomas Attwood and Benjamin Heywood, were returned for Birmingham, as were John Fielden for Oldham, Daniel Gaskell for Wakefield, Mark Philips for Manchester and Joseph Brotherton for Salford, and John Brocklehurst, Jr, for Macclesfield. Others successful candidates such as George Faithfull of Brighton and Henry Lytton Bulwer of Coventry, were linked with local Political Unions but were not actually members. Political Unions were, to a degree, to gain representation in the new Parliament.

As a result, many Unionists who had demanded radical electoral reforms before the Whigs ever wrote their legislation, hoped this would be an opportunity for their original reform objectives – namely, universal manhood suffrage, annual parliaments and the ballot – to get a parliamentary hearing. If they could return candidates who would pledge themselves to produce additional legislation which would include these radical reforms, they could finally achieve their goal of attaining representation and protection of the rights and liberties of all Englishmen. Other Unionists, more moderate in their views and less willing to antagonize the very politicians who had produced and secured the Reform Act, sought out candidates who would pledge themselves to economic reform, namely reductions in tariffs, taxes, and other hindrances to free trade.[8] Whatever the objective, many Unionists shared the sentiments of J.T. Mayne of the Bath Political Union Council: 'If these Reform Bills are not followed up by others, then you will be deceived, and no good will arise from Reform.'[9]

But Mayne would have been disappointed with how few Unions failed to campaign for additional reform policies. Many Political Unions disbanded, including Mayne's own Bath Political Union, just as Grey had told the King they would, shortly after the general election of December 1832. Some waged small campaigns in the next few years – namely, through parliamentary petitions and newspaper reports of small public meetings – for the ballot and another extension of the franchise and against the Whigs' Irish Coercion Bill and the New Poor Law. But these paled in comparison to the Reform Bill agitation and were certainly not given the public attention that the Unions had been given before 1832.

Another phenomenon was also doing its bit to end the Political Union movement: class antagonism. A number of Political Unions found 'unity' between middle- and working-class reformers a difficult thing to maintain once the Reform Bill became law. Some members were enfranchised and others were still excluded from the vote. The tensions between the new electors who wanted to wait for a more political stable time before introducing and supporting another extension of the franchise and those who had tirelessly campaigned with their middle-class counterparts knowing full well they would not personally gain from the bill, turned into open hostility. Schisms in some Unions resulted in the creation of new working-class splinter unions named, appropriately, the Unions of the Working Classes.

What the Political Unions did or failed to do after 1832 is an important question in our understanding of the 'Decade of Reform' and the true impact of 1832. Whether the Unions had direct ties to the popular political campaign of Chartism at the end of the 1830s or were influential in persuading the governments of the 1830s to adopt various pieces of legislation, are important question which needs to be addressed. But that will need to wait for the next study of the people's campaigns and Political Unions.

Appendix Political Unions in England during Reform Bill Agitation

Political Union	*Creation Date*	*End of Union*
Alcester	5/1832	inactive
Alfreton	11/1831	inactive
Almondbury	8/1830	12/1832
Barnstaple	3/1832	12/1833
Bath	11/1831	6/1833
Bedworth		inactive
Belper	12/1831	inactive
Berkshire (county)	10/1830	12/1832
Birmingham	1/1830	through introduction of *The People's Charter*
Blackburn	8/1831	inactive
Bolton	4/1830	6/1832
Boston	12/1831	12/1832
Bradford	1/1831	inactive
Bradford-on-Avon	5/1832	inactive
Bridgwater	6/1831	6/1833
Briefcliffe	11/1831	inactive
Bristol	10/1831	6/1833
Burnley	10/1831	2/1833
Bury	11/1831	inactive
Carlisle	1/1831	displaced by UWC, 4/1831
Chadderton		1833
Chard	5/1832	inactive
Charlton-upon-lock	10/1831	inactive
Chorley	11/1830	5/1833
Congleton	11/1832	5/1834
Coventry	8/1830	6/1833
Cradley		inactive
Crameote	5/1832	inactive
Crompton	5/1832	12/1832
Derby	12/1831	12/1832

Political Union	Creation Date	End of Union
Dronfield	11/1831	5/1834
Dudley	4/1831	12/1832
Durham	8/1830	inactive
Edwinstowe	9/1832	inactive
Frome	10/1831	1833
Gloucester	12/1831	12/1832
Hales Owen	1/1831	4/1833
Halifax	4/1831	through Chartism
Hanley and Shelton	11/1831	6/1833
Hansworth		inactive
Harborne	branch of BPU	
Heanor	11/1831	6/1832
Hebden Bridge	12/1832	inactive
Heywood	12/1832	12/1832
Hilden Bridge	10/1832	inactive
Hinckley	11/1831	inactive
Holt (Wiltshire)	11/1831	inactive
Horsham	10/1832	2/1833
Huddersfield	11/1830	12/1832
Hull	10/1831	6/1833
Hyde and Newton	12/1830	inactive
Keighley	1/1831	12/1832
Kenliworth	8/1831	12/1832
Kidderminster	8/1830	inactive
Kirkheaton	10/1830	11/1833
Leamington	12/1832	4/1833
Leeds	11/1830	5/1833
Leicester	11/1831	4/1833
Lichfield	5/1832	inactive
Liverpool	1/1831	5/1832
Loughborough	branch of BPU	
Ludlow	11/1831	displaced by UWC, 4/1831
Macclesfield	10/1831	inactive
Manchester	11/1830	6/1833
Mansfield	11/1830	12/1832
Merthyr Tydfil	11/1831	6/1832
Metropolitan (London)	4/1830	8/1830
National (London)	11/1831	5/1833
Newark	8/1830	12/1832
Northampton	3/1832	6/1833
Northern (Newcastle upon Tyne)	8/1831	6/1834
Norwich	11/1831	12/1832

continued on page 176

Political Union	*Creation Date*	*End of Union*
Nottingham	4/1830	displaced by UWC, 4/1831
Oldham	6/1831	12/1832
Padiham	8/1831	4/1832
Potteries (Stoke-on-Trent)	11/1831	12/1832
Preston	10/1831	3/1834
Radford	6/1833	6/1833
Ramsgate	10/1831	inactive
Reading	11/1831	inactive
Redditch	5/1832	inactive
Rochdale	10/1831	6/1833
Royton	6/1833	6/1833
Salford	8/1830	inactive – probably merged with Manchester
Salisbury	5/1832	inactive
Sheffield	2/1831	12/1832
Shepton Mallet	11/1831	1833
Sittingbourne	11/1831	6/1832
Smethwick	branch of BPU	
Solihull	6/1832	6/1832
Somerton	10/1832	inactive
Southern (Surrey and Lambeth)	10/1832	10/1832
Stapleford	5/1832	inactive
Stockport	3/1831	12/1832
Stourbridge	5/1832	5/1832
Stratford-upon-Avon	5/1832	12/1832
Sunderland	5/1832	5/1832
Sutton-in-Ashfield	5/1832	inactive
Swanwick	11/1831	6/1832
Taunton	11/1831	4/1833
Tettenhall	1833	1833
Thanet	12/1831	6/1832
Tilbury	1/1833	1/1833
Todmorden	11/1830	displaced by UWC in 4/1831
Torrington	5/1832	inactive
Trowbridge	11/1831	12/1832
Wakefield	8/1831	3/1833

Political Union	Creation Date	End of Union
Walsall	8/1831	4/1833
Warminster	12/1832	inactive
Warwick	3/1832	12/1832
Wednesbury	11/1830	5/1833
West Bromwich	12/1831	inactive
Westminster		inactive
Winchester	6/1832	6/1833
Wolverhampton	11/1830	12/1832
Worcester	1/1830	5/1833
Wotton Underedge	6/1832	6/1832
Yeovil	11/1831	inactive

LIVERPOOL
JOHN MOORES UNIVERSITY
AVRIL ROBARTS LRC
TITHEBARN STREET
LIVERPOOL L2 2ER
TEL. 0151 231 4022

Notes

INTRODUCTION

1. HO 64:17, Prospectus for the new publication, *The Union.*
2. *Newcastle Courant*, 1 June 1833.
3. For what Grey thought constituted public opinion, see Richard W. Davis, 'The Whigs and the Idea of Electoral Deference', *Durham University Journal*, new series, 36, 1974.
4. Michael Brock, *The Great Reform Act*, London: 1973; Joseph Hamburger, *James Mill and the Art of Revolution* New Haven: 1963. Hamburger claimed that 'The [Political] Unions were feared because they claimed to represent the people, and they thus challenged the authority of Parliament', 267. For other acknowledgements of Political Unions during the Reform Bill agitation, see J.R.M. Butler, *The Passing of the Great Reform Bill*, London: 1914; G.M. Trevelyan, *Lord Grey of the Reform Bill*, London: 1920; Elie Halévy, *The Triumph of Reform 1830–41*, New York, 1961; John Cannon, *Parliamentary Reform: 1640–1832*, Cambridge: 1973; Peter Mandler, *Aristocratic Government in the Age of Reform Whigs and Liberals, 1830–52*, Oxford: 1990; E.A. Smith, *Lord Grey: 1764–1845*, Oxford: 1990; Asa Briggs, 'The Background of Parliamentary Reform in Three English Cities, 1830–32', *Cambridge Historical Journal*, 10, 1952; Henry Ferguson, 'The Birmingham Political Unions and the Government, 1831–32', *Victorian Studies*, 3, 1960; A.S. Turberville and F. Beckwith, 'Leeds and Parliamentary Reform 1820–32', *Thoresby Miscellany*, 12, 1954.
5. Derek Fraser, 'The Agitation for Parliamentary Reform', in J.T. Ward, ed., *Popular Movements*, London: 1970, 34.
6. L.G. Mitchell, 'Foxite Politics and the Great Reform Bill', *English Historical Review*, 108, 1993.
7. Norman Gash, *Politics in the Age of Peel*, London: 1953; and *Reaction and Reconstruction in English Politics, 1832–52*, Oxford: 1965; D.C. Moore, 'The Other Face of Reform', *Victorian Studies*, 4, 1961; 'Concession or Cure: The Sociological Premises of the First Reform Act', *Historical Journal*, 9, 1966; and *The Politics of Deference*, Hassocks: 1976.
8. For a refutation of this argument, see R.W. Davis, 'Toryism to Tamworth: The Triumph of Reform, 1827–35', *Albion*, 12, 1980; 'The Whigs and the Idea of Electoral Deference', *Durham University Journal*; and 'Deference and Aristocracy in the Time of the Great Reform Act', *American Historical Review*, 81, 1976; Ian Newbould, *Whiggery and Reform 1830–41: The Politics of Government*, Stanford: 1990; Frank O'Gorman, 'Whigs and Electoral Deference in Unreformed England, 1760–1832', *Journal of Modern History*, 56, 1984; Ellis Archer Wasson, 'The Great Whigs and Parliamentary Reform, 1809–30', *Journal of British*

Studies, 24, 1985; and *Whig Renaissance Lord Althorp and the Whig Party, 1782–1845*, New York: 1987.

9. Cannon, *Parliamentary Reform*; Peter Mandler, *Aristocratic Government in the Age of Reform*: 129.
10. Jonathan Parry, *The Rise and Fall of Liberal Government in Victorian Britain*, New Haven: 1993, 87.
11. E.A. Smith, 'Charles, Second Early Grey and the House of Lords', in R.W. Davis, ed., *Lords of Parliament Studies, 1714–1914*, Stanford: 1995, 79; *Lord Grey: 1765–1845.* Also see John W. Derry, *Charles, Earl Grey: Aristocratic Reformer*, Oxford: 1992.
12. John A. Phillips, *Electoral Behavior in Unreformed England,* Princeton: 1982; *The Great Reform Bill in the Boroughs, English Electoral Behaviour, 1818–41*, Oxford: 1992; 'The Structure of Electoral Politics in Unreformed England', *Journal of British Studies*, 1979; and 'Popular Politics in Unreformed England', *Journal of Modern History*, 52, 1982; John A. Phillips and Charles Wetherell, 'The Great Reform Act of 1832 and the Political Modernization of England', *American Historical Review*, 100, 1995; Frank O'Gorman, *Voters, Patrons, and Parties, The Unreformed Electoral System of Hanoverian England 1734–1832*, Oxford: 1989; *The Emergence of the British Two-Party System, 1760–1832*, London: 1982; 'Electoral Deference in 'Unreformed' England, 1760–1832', *Journal of Modern History*, 56, 1984; and 'Electoral Behaviour in England, 1800–72', in Peter Denley et al., *History and Computing II*, Manchester: 1989.
13. See nineteenth-century histories such as Jessie Buckley, *Joseph Parkes of Birmingham*, London: 1926; Asa Briggs, 'The Background of the Parliamentary Reform Movement in Three English Cities 1830–32'; and 'Press and Public in Early Nineteenth Century Birmingham', *Dugdale Society Occasional Papers*, 8, Oxford: 1949; Henry Ferguson, 'The Birmingham Political Union and the Government 1831–32'; Hamburger, *James Mill*; David J. Moss, *Thomas Attwood: The Biography of a Radical*, Montreal: 1990; Clive Behagg, *Politics and Production*, Manchester: 1990.
14. Flick lists these Unions as Leamington, Weillenhall, Nuneaton, Kenliworth, Warwick, Lye, Redditch, Hales Owen, Bromsgrove, Oldbury, Hinckley, Rowley Regis, Sedley, West Bromwich, Wolverhampton, Wednesbury, Studley, Stratford, Bridgnorth, Brierley Hill, Smethwick, Harborne, Stourbridge, Alcester, Shirley, Cradley, Bedworth, Hansworth, Solihull, Droitwich, and Tettenhall. Flick, 185–6.
15. Hamburger, *James Mill*, 90.
16. Briggs, in spite of his platitudes to Attwood, makes the same case in 'The Background of the Parliamentary Reform'.
17. The work of Briggs, Brock and Hamburger puts the number of Political Unions during the Reform Bill agitation at 30. Brock, *The Great Reform Act*, 78 and Hamburger, *James Mill*, 6; Hamburger, 90.
18. For an overview of popular politics in Britain, see D.G. Wright, *Popular Radicalism: The Working Class Experience, 1780–1880*, London: 1988. For a new interpretation of popular politics and popular radicalism, see Peter Spence, *The Birth of Romantic Radicalism: War, Popular Politics and English Radical Reformism, 1800–15*, Aldershot: 1996.

19. Dror Wahrman, *Imagining the Middle Class: The Political Representation of Class in Britain, c. 1780–1840*, Cambridge, 1996, 2–3, 17–18; E.P. Thompson, *The Making of the English Working Class*, London: 1963, 808.
20. James Vernon, *Politics and the People: A Study in English Political Culture, c. 1815–67*, 333; Dror Wahrman, *Imagining the 'Middle Class'*, 301.
21. See James E. Bradley, *Popular Politics and the American Revolution in England: Petitions, the Crown, and Public Opinion*, Macon, GA: 1986; E.C. Black, *The Association, British Extraparliamentary Political Organization 1769–93*; Colin Bonwick, *English Radicals and the American Revolution*, Chapel Hill, 1977; James Walvin, *English Radicals and Reformers, 1760–1848*, Lexington, KY: 1982; H.T. Dickinson, *The Politics of the People in Eighteenth Century Britain*, Houndsmills: 1995.
22. Ceri Crossley and Ian Smalls, eds, *The French Revolution and British Culture*, Oxford: 1991; Otto Dann and John Dinwiddy, eds, *Nationalism in the Age of the French Revolution*, London: 1988.
23. For more on this, see John Derry, *Charles James Fox*, 1972; L.J. Mitchell, *C.J. Fox and the Disintegration of the Whig Party, 1782–94*, Oxford: 1971; Frank O'Gorman, *The Whig Party and the French Revolution*; Albert Goodwin, *The Friends of Liberty: The English Democratic Movement in the Age of the French Revolution*; Cambridge, MA: 1979; J.E. Cookson, *The Friends of Peace: Anti-War Liberalism in England, 1793–1815*; E.A. Smith, *Lord Grey, 1764–1845*; M. Philip, ed., *The French Revolution and British Popular Politics*, Cambridge: 1991; G.A Williams, *Artisans and Sans-Culottes: Popular Movements in France and Britain during the French Revolution*, London: 1968; C.B. Cone, *The English Jacobins: Reformers in Late 18th Century England*, New York: 1968.
24. See Philip Harling, *The Waning of 'Old Corruption': The Politics of Economical Reform in Britain, 1779–1846*, Oxford, 1996; Ian Christie, 'Economical Reform and "The Influence of the Crown" 1780', *Cambridge Historical Journal*, 12, 1956; S.E. Finer, 'Patronage and Public Service: Jeffersonian Bureaucracy and the British Tradition', *Public Administration*, 30, 1952.
25. See Gregory Claeys, *Thomas Paine: Social and Political Thought*, London: 1989, 156–7.
26. This is the argument made by Philip Harling, in *The Waning of 'Old Corruption'*, 2.
27. Grey to Wyvill, 10 April 1817 as quoted in John Dinwiddy, *Christopher Wyvill*, 29.
28. For a new interpretation of this era of British Radicalism, see Peter Spence, *The Birth of Romantic Radicalism. War, Popular Politics, and English Radical Reformism*, Aldershot, 1996.
29. John Belchem, 'Henry Hunt and the Evolution of the Mass Platform', *English Historical Review*, 93, 1978; and 'Republicanism, Popular Constitutionalism and the Radical Platform in Early 19th Century England', *Social History*, 6, 1981.
30. *Birmingham Argus*, September 1830.
31. LRO, *Biggs Scrapbook*, 5 September 1830.
32. James Vernon, *Politics and the People: A Study in English Political Culture*, 6–7.

33. Charles Tilly, *Popular Contention in Great Britain: 1758–1834*, Cambridge, MA: 1995, 53.
34. Ibid., 339.
35. Jonathan Clark, *English Society, 1688–1832: Ideology, Social Structure and Political Practice*, Cambridge: 1985, 374–5.
36. BrCL, 'Requisition to the High Bailiff, William Chance', reprinted in *Aris's Gazette*, 18 January 1830.
37. Ibid.
38. The term industrious was a common one at the time, certainly not unique to the rhetoric of Political Unions. John Stuart Mill reflected the common usage in his *Autobiography* (1873) when he wrote, 'We yet looked forward to a time when society will no longer be divided into the idle and the industrious' (196).
39. HO 64:17, *Political Unionist*, prospectus, 30 June 1831.
40. Ibid.
41. *Poor Man's Guardian*, 22 September 1832.
42. Ibid.
43. *Speech of Thomas Attwood on the Distressed State of the Country*, 8 May 1929, 80.
44. *Report of the Proceedings of the Birmingham Political Union*, 25 January 1830.
45. HO 40:25, f. 444, A.C. to Peel, 10 November 1830; HO 40:26, f. 46, Lt. Col. I Shaw to Peel, 29 August 1830.
46. *Voice of the People*, 19 February 1831.
47. *Bath Journal*, 6 June 1831.
48. This calculation is based upon the numbers provided in provincial newspaper accounts or in the records of the Unions. The number is a best guess at the numbers and does not reflect changes in individual Union memberships as the reform bill campaign progressed.
49. This number, another composite of all estimates offered by all the Political Unions, includes only annual meetings, parades, rallies and demonstrations. It also reflects the famous May 1832 meeting of the BPU at Newhall Hill where an estimated 100,000 people turned up. The number does not include the numbers attending Union Council meetings, any overlap in membership or attendance of those attending a meeting of another neighboring Political Union, or the celebrations held following the enactment of the Reform Act itself.
50. I examine in detail both the question of Political Union membership and the inadequacy of sources in determining a more precise picture of overall Union composition later in this work.
51. This subject matter has been examined in J.T. Ward, ed., *Popular Movements c 1830–50*, London, 1970; D.J. Rowe, 'Class and Political Radicalism in London, 1831–32', *Historical Journal*, 13, 1970. Most recently, James Vernon's work *Politics and the People*, and Charles Tilly, *Popular Contention*, have considered this question.
52. William A. Mackinnon, *On the Rise, Progress, and Present State of Public Opinion in Great Britain, and Other Parts of the World*, London: 1828, 6.
53. This argument contradicts that offered by Joseph Hamburger in *James Mill*. For a critique of Hamburger's thesis, see G.B.A.M. Finlayson,

'Joseph Parkes of Birmingham, 1796–1865', *Bulletin for the Institute of Historical Research*, 46, 1973.

54. See Henry Earl Grey, ed., *The Correspondence of Earl Grey and William IV*, 2, London: 1867, for numerous examples of Grey's thought and fears on this matter. Also, see Ellis Archer Wasson, *Whig Renaissance Lord Althorp and the Whig Party 1782–1845*, New York: 1987, 204–8, for Althorp and other government members' feelings towards the necessity of enacting some kind of reform.
55. This reporting technique was popularized by provincial newspaper editors in the 1820s. For more, see Donald Read, *Press and the People, 1790–1850: Opinion in Three English Cities*, London: 1961; and 'John Harland: The Father of Provincial Reporting', *Manchester Review*, 8, 1958.
56. The Unions were located in Bath, Brighton, Bristol, Coventry, Dudley, Leeds, Leicester, Manchester, Newcastle upon Tyne, Norwich, Oldham and Worcester.
57. These include infrequent one-time meeting Unions at Belper, Alfreton, Hinckley, Holt (Wiltshire), Ludlow, Ramsgate, Swanwick, Thanet, Reading, Tilbury, Briercliffe, Burnley, Heanor, Lichfield, Redditch, Sunderland, Sittingbourne, Hales Owen, Torrington, Chard, Stapleford, Crameote, Sutton-in-Ashfield, Wootton Underedge, Congleton, Hebden Bridge, Leamington, Wincester, Horsham, and Surrey and Berkshire counties.

1 THE BIRMINGHAM POLITICAL UNION AND THE ORIGINS OF THE UNION CAMPAIGN

1. *The Political Union Register*, March 1832.
2. John Stuart Mill as found in Hugh Eliot, ed., *Letters of J.S. Mill*, vol. 1, 7, 20 October 1831.
3. See Carlos Flick, *The Birmingham Political Union and the Movements for Reform, 1830–39*, 93–4. Also see BRO, Isaac Arrowsmith Collection for a sample commemorative silk scarf.
4. BCL, *Report of the Proceedings of the Great Meeting of the Inhabitants of Birmingham and its Neighbourhood,* 20 May 1833.
5. Lord Durham to Joseph Parkes as related by the latter to George Grote, 18 May 1832, described by Harriet Grote in *The Personal Life of George Grote*, London: 1873, 79.
6. As quoted in C.M. Wakefield, *Life of Thomas Attwood*, London: 1885, 215.
7. Speech of Thomas Doubleday, Northern Political Union, *Newcastle Courant*, 18 August 1832.
8. Henry Grey, ed., *The Reform Act of 1832, The Correspondence of the late Earl Grey and His Majesty King William IV with Sir Herbert Taylor,* London: 1867, 1, 394–5; University College London, Parkes Papers; Scottish Record Office, Ellice Papers, MSS 15021, ff. 124–5.
9. See Grey, ed., *The Reform Act of 1832, The Correspondence of the late Earl Grey and His Majesty King William IV with Sir Herbert Taylor.*
10. See *Hansard*, 3rd series, vols 2 and 3.

11. Asa Briggs, 'Thomas Attwood and the Economic Background of the Birmingham Political Union' and 'The Background of the Parliamentary Reform Movement in Three English Cities, 1830–32'. For references to the BPU in Chartism, see 'The Background of the Parliamentary Reform Movement in Three English Cities, 1830–32', 181; James Epstein and Dorothy Thompson, eds, *The Chartist Experience: Studies in Working Class Radicalism and Culture, 1830–60*, London: 1982.
12. Briggs, 'The Parliamentary Reform Movement', 187.
13. Hamburger, *James Mill*, 90–1. For another interpretation of Joseph Parkes' role in the BPU, see W.E.S. Thomas, *The Philosophic Radicals Nine Studies in Theory and Practice 1817–41*, chapter 5.
14. Hamburger, *James Mill*, 90.
15. David J. Moss, *Thomas Attwood.*
16. Ibid.
17. Ibid.
18. Carlos Flick, *The Birmingham Political Union,* 12.
19. Ibid.
20. For the list of the smaller satellite Unions, see Hamburger, 90, fn 36 and Flick, 46, fn 15.
21. TWRO, Cowen MSS, *Northern Reform Record*, 1858.
22. See F.W. Fetter, ed., *Selected Economic Writings of Thomas Attwood,* London: 1964.
23. Attwood's brother Matthias was a London banker who become a Tory MP in 1819. While he and Thomas were united in their belief that currency was the solution to Britain's economic problems, Matthias remained a loyal Tory throughout the Reform Bill agitation and denounced the organization of Political Unions. Ironically, another brother, Charles, shared Thomas Attwood's quest for parliamentary reform, but did not embrace currency reform as part of the platform for his Newcastle-based Northern Political Union.
24. *Attwood on Distressed State of the Country*, 8 May 1829, 46.
25. Ibid., 78.
26. Ibid., 80.
27. For how this affected Attwood, see Moss, *Thomas Attwood*, 139–43.
28. *The Birmingham Argus and Public Censor,* October 1828.
29. Ibid.
30. BCL, Thomas Attwood, *The Distressed State of the Country*, 8 May 1829. Also see *A Collection of Circulars, Leaflets, Caricatures, etc. to the Birmingham Political Union*, 1829.
31. What Attwood really wanted was currency reform, namely the adoption of paper money. He recognized that the current political composition of Parliament rendered that impossible. For him, parliamentary reform and the BPU were means to an end: hard money.
32. BCL, Thomas Attwood, *The Distressed State of the Country*, 8 May 1829. Also see *A Collection of Circulars, Leaflets, Caricatures, etc. to the Birmingham Political Union*, 1829.
33. Ibid., 78.
34. Ibid., 74.
35. *Report of the Proceedings of the Great Meeting of the Inhabitants of*

Birmingham, 3 October 1831.

36. Attwood, *Distressed State of the Country*, 17.
37. Ibid.
38. Thomas Bailey, *A Letter to Early Grey, on the Necessity of Fixing a Principle of Representation in the Constitution*, London: 1831, 13. The term 'industrious classes' was not coined by Attwood but was part of the radicals' vocabulary in the early nineteenth century. There is evidence of such a concept in the 1815 publication of Patrick Calquhoun's *Treatise on Population, Wealth, Power and Resources of the British Empire*, London: 1815.
39. *Report of the Proceedings at the Meeting of the Inhabitants of Birmingham Report of the Proceedings . . .*, 25 January 1830.
40. The original organizing group included Charles Jones, a silversmith; Thomas C. Salt, a lamp manufacturer who began his agitation for currency reform in 1826 leading a protest again what he called a government programme of 'fiscal oppression'; Benjamin Hadley, a button manufacturer and Dissenter; and George Muntz, owner of a metal-rolling mill and greatly troubled by failing foreign trade as his business was dependent upon the export of a new metal alloy he had developed; and Joshua Scholefield, a successful merchant, banker and manufacturer.
41. For more on Edmonds, see E. Edwards, *Personal Recollections of Birmingham and Birmingham Men*, Birmingham: 1877.
42. HO/40/4D; HO 42/154.
43. *Report of the Proceedings . . .*, 25 January 1830.
44. They included John Betts, a metal refiner, James W. Evans, a japanner; Thomas Parsons, Jr, a metal dealer. All were Tory currency reformers. Radicals Felix and Urban Luckcock, lime and brick dealers and sons of a Unitarian minister, as well as Josiah Emes, a buttonshop owner and longtime radical reformer, also joined the organizers. Other late additions included Radicals John Pierce and Thomas Parking. Pierce, a thimble manufacturer, was a follower of John Cartwright and Parkin, an entrepreneur who had recently moved to Dudley after his latest venture, editing a Christian newspaper, failed in London, put his considerable speaking skills at the organization's disposal.
45. For more on Parkes, see Jessie Buckley, *Joseph Parkes of Birmingham*; W.E.S. Thomas, *The Philosophic Radicals*, chapter 5.
46. BCL, Thomas Attwood, *Leaflet with notation*, 10 December 1829.
47. Ibid.
48. Ibid.
49. BCL, *Authorized Copy of the Resolutions Passed at the Meeting at Birmingham, 15 January 1830, with the Declaration of their Political Council.*
50. Todmorden Political Union Rules and Regulations published in the *Voice of the People*, 19 February 1831.
51. BCL, *Report of the Proceedings at the Meeting of the Inhabitants of Birmingham*, 25 January 1830; *Birmingham Journal*, 13 February 1830 and 6 March 1830.
52. BCL, *Report of the Proceedings at the Meeting of the Inhabitants of Birmingham*, 25 January 1830.

53. See Cartwright's plans as discussed in F.D. Cartwright, *The Life and Correspondence of Major John Cartwright*; Naomi C. Miller, 'John Cartwright and Radical Parliamentary Reform, 1808–1819' *English Historical Review*, lxxxiii, 1968.
54. *Political Magazine*, September 1831.
55. BCL, *Authorized Copy of the Resolutions . . . 15 January 1830.*
56. Ibid.
57. For more on this, see chapter 5.
58. BCL, *Authorized Copy of the Resolutions . . . 15 January 1830.*
59. Ibid.
60. For a discussion of Parkes and 'steam', see Hamburger, *James Mill*, chapter 1.
61. Parkes MSS, Journal, 30 January 1830.
62. *Nottingham and Newark Mercury*, 4 March 1830.
63. BCL, *Authorized Copy of the Resolutions . . . 15 January 1830.* For a discussion of the impact of parliamentary petitioning in a popular political campaign, see James Bradley, *Popular Politics and the American Revolution in England*.
64. *Report of the Proceedings . . .*, 25 January 1830.
65. *Birmingham Journal*, 19 January 1830.
66. *Birmingham Journal*, 16 January 1830.
67. *Report of the Proceedings . . .*, 25 January 1830.
68. *Cobbett's Political Register*, LXIX, no. 5, 30 January 1830. William Redfern also criticized Attwood for included the currency question. He believed it would be divisive and defeat the purpose of creating a 'union' of classes.
69. Ibid.
70. BCL, *Report of the Proceedings . . .*, 25 January 1830 (bound volume, notes on inside cover by Joseph Parkes).
71. Ibid.
72. *Morning Journal*, 26 January 1830.
73. *Morning Advertiser*, 26 January 1830.
74. *Manchester Courier*, 27 January 1830.
75. *The Times*, 26 January 1830.
76. *Report of the Proceedings . . .*, 17 May 1830.
77. *Cobbett's Political Register*, 27 February 1830.
78. Ibid., 6 February 1830.
79. Cobbett apparently wrote to Attwood: 'The moment I hear of you having invited the sham king Burdett to Birmingham, I knew you to be a sham yourself.' Ibid., 7 August 1830.
80. *Manchester Lectures*, 1830.
81. Bromley-Davenport MSS, Attwood to Davenport, 25 February 1830 as quoted in Moss, 175.
82. *Coventry Observor*, 18 February 1830; ed. W.J. Fitzpatrick, *Correspondence of Daniel O'Connell, the Liberator*, London: 1888, O'Connell to Attwood, 16 February 1830.
83. Historians are not in agreement as to whether the Marquis fully understood the extent of his proposal. He made his opposition to universal manhood suffrage and the ballot clear in a letter written to the *Standard*

in July 1829, but clearly did not recognize that many Tories saw his proposal as almost equally as radical. See D.C. Moore, 'Concession or Cure?'.

84. Briggs, 'Thomas Attwood', in *Collected Essays*, 161.
85. *Birmingham Journal*, 20 March 1830.
86. *Corrected Report of the Proceedings of the First Meeting of the Birmingham Political Union Held at Beardsworth's Repository on Monday, May 27, 1830.*
87. Ibid.
88. *Report of the Proceedings . . ., 17 May 1830*. Bibb, who was sitting for the first time on the Council, later became the treasurer for the West Bromwich Political Union.
89. Edwards, *Personal Recollections*, 141–54.
90. *Birmingham Journal*, 31 July 1830.
91. Membership was still listed as 5,000, but Cobbett and Hunt had both recently condemned the BPU, probably prompting some to stay away. Cobbett had called Attwood an 'empty-gaping, shilly-shallying, shuffling fellow' and Hunt had urged workers to fight Attwood's efforts for moderate reform. 'Listen not to those who may tell you that . . . half a loaf is better than no bread. In this case half a loaf is no bread.' Together, Cobbett and Hunt urged the reformers of Birmingham not to sign a petition or give support to an organization which did not expressly call for universal manhood suffrage, annual parliaments, and the ballot. *Cobbett's Political Register*, 17 July 1830; *Morning Chronicle*, 9 July 1830.
92. *Report of Proceedings of the Birmingham Political Union Meeting and Dinner, Held at the Beardworth's Repository, October 11th 1830.*
93. *Birmingham Argus*, June 1831.
94. *Minutes of the Birmingham Political Union Council*, 13 December 1830; *The Examiner*, 9 October 1831. Also see Flick, *Birmingham Political Union*, 12–13.
95. *Birmingham Journal*, 29 January 1831.
96. BL, Add MSS 35, 148, f 67–70.
97. The creation of all these political unions will be discussed at length in chapter 2.
98. The estimated 50 different requests made by numerous provincial reformers for the BPU Rules and Regulations in the weeks following the October riots were unsolicited and often ignored. Flick, *The Birmingham Political Union*, 70; *Birmingham Journal*, 5 November 1831.
99. Galton MSS, University College, *Diary of S.T. Galton*, 4 April 1831, as quoted in Behagg, *Politics and Production*, 165.
100. Briggs, 'Thomas Attwood', 165.
101. Ibid., 140.
102. *Morning Chronicle*, 4 February 1831.

2 THE CREATION OF A MOVEMENT: POLITICAL UNIONS, MARCH 1830–FEBRUARY 1831

1. BL, Add MSS 27822, ff. 11–14.
2. *Weekly Free Press*, Hunt to members of the RRA, 1 February 1830. The open letters of 6, 20 and 27 February 1831 address the plans for the Metropolitan Political Union.
3. *Weekly Free Press*, 6 March 1830. John Belchem's account of the formation of the MPU describes Hunt's formation of a BPU-modelled extra-parliamentary organization as though he thoroughly approved of Attwood's objectives. In fact, Hunt was highly critical of the limited view of the BPU and certainly departed from Attwood significantly in promoting universal suffrage, annual parliaments, and the ballot, all of which were rejected by the BPU Council as too radical and unnecessary as a more moderate reform would still enable business interests to achieve currency reform. See Belchem, *'Orator' Hunt and English Working-Class Radicalism*, Oxford: 1985, 199–201.
4. Ibid.
5. BL, Add MSS 27822, ff. 11–14, *Authorized Copy of the Resolutions Adopted at the Great Meeting, consisting of 30,000 People . . . for Forming a Metropolitan Political Union, for the Recovery and Protection of Public Rights*, 13 March 1830.
6. Ibid.
7. An informant for the Home Office proclaimed the MPU dead in February 1831. HO 64:18, f. 382, 19 February 1831.
8. The new objectives included promises to 'raise the productive classes to their just and constitutional rank in the state, etc.', *Weekly Free Press*, 8–20, May 1830. Belchem claims that the Unions formed in Keighley, Morley and Almondbury near Huddersfield, all resulted from this campaign and were connected to the MPU. Belchem, *'Orator Hunt'*, 204.
9. *Nottingham Journal*, 6 February 1830; *Nottingham Review*, 1 March 1830.
10. *Nottingham Review*, 27 March 1830.
11. *Nottingham and Newark Mercury*, 27 March 1830.
12. Throughout March, April and May 1830, Sutton described the composition of those attending Political Union meetings, reading handbills posted on the streets, and stopping by the *Review* office to inquire about the organization.
13. *Nottingham and Newark Mercury*, 27 March 1830.
14. Ibid.
15. Ibid.
16. Ibid., 3 April 1830.
17. Another public demonstration of the Nottingham Union's commitment to the ballot came after the Reform Bill's presentation in the penny paper, *The Ballot*, 6 March 1831.
18. *Nottingham Review*, 3 April 1830.
19. Ibid.
20. *The Ballot*, 13 February 1831.

21. *Nottingham Journal*, 1 October 1830.
22. *Nottingham Review*, 9 July 1930.
23. Ibid., 4 October 1830.
24. *Nottingham Journal*, 1 October 1830.
25. *Nottingham Review*, 27 March 1831 and similar reports appeared throughout the spring and summer of 1831.
26. Ibid., 20 July 1830.
27. First mention of the Union is in the *Bolton Chronicle*, 13 April 1830; *Blackburn Gazette*, 27 October 1830. For a brief discussion of the Union in the context of Bolton's political evolution, see Peter Taylor, *Popular Politics in Early Industrial Britain: Bolton 1825–50*, Bodmin: 1995, chapter 2.
28. Ibid., 28 April 1830; *Liverpool Chronicle*, 24 April 1830.
29. *Bolton Chronicle*, 16 October 1830.
30. Ibid., 16 October 1830; *Blackburn Gazette*, 27 October 1830. Belchem contends that the MPU and Hunt's presence radicalized the Bolton Political Union in October, but there is no evidence to suggest that it was any more moderate in its position on reform back in April. Belchem, *'Orator' Hunt*, 211.
31. Ibid.
32. Ibid., 16 October 1830.
33. Ibid.
34. Ibid.
35. Despite the detailed research into both local politics and class relationships in cultivating political power at the local level in Bolton by John Garrard, *Leadership and Power in Victorian Industrial Towns, 1830–80*, Manchester: 1983, there is no mention of a Political Union in Bolton at all.
36. See Belchem, *'Orator Hunt'*, 211.
37. *Leeds Patriot*, 10 April 1830; 28 August 1830. This evidence contradicts Belchem's claim that it was a Huntite Union. Belchem, *'Orator' Hunt*, 204.
38. *Leeds Patriot*, 10 April 1830; Belchem, *'Orator' Hunt*, 204, 211. For Almondbury, see *Penny Papers for the People*, 18 June 1831.
39. See A.S. Turberville, *The House of Lords in the Age of Reform*, London: 1958.
40. Wellington MSS, WP1/1198/32, Anonymous letter to Wellington, 9 October 1830.
41. Ibid.
42. *Leeds Patriot*, 10 April 1830.
43. Ibid., 28 August 1830. This contradicts Belchem's claim that it was a Huntite Union. Belchem, *'Orator' Hunt*, 204.
44. *Hansard*, 3rd ser., 2, 18 February 1830, c. 706.
45. Grey MSS, Box 50B, File 6, Joshua Scholefield to Grey, 2 July 1830.
46. *Leeds Patriot*, 28 August 1830; *Penny Papers for the People*, 18 June 1831.
47. Though there is no mention of a Salford Political Union in the contemporary provincial press or in the Home Office papers, some useful background information concerning the city and local politics can be found in Garrard, *Leadership and Power*, 86.

48. *Bolton Chronicle*, 11 October 1830.
49. Ibid. Belchem briefly discusses the Chorley Union in *'Orator' Hunt*, 211.
50. *Blackburn Gazette*, 27 October 1830; *Manchester Courier*, 5 February 1831; *Penny Papers for the People*, 7 May 1831.
51. *Boston Gazette and Lincolnshire Advertiser*, 19 October 1830.
52. *Manchester Times*, 5 February 1831.
53. Cheetham worked with Edward Curran of the Manchester Political Union and John Knight of the Oldham Union to form the Union of the Working Classes in Manchester and Salford. *Penny Papers*, 29 April, 7 and 13 May 1831, reprinted in Manchester press reports. Belchem, *'Orator' Hunt*, 230.
54. Editorials of note concerning their view of reform and the Political Union appear in the *Mercury* on 3 December 1830 and 18 May 1832.
55. *Liverpool Chronicle*, 18 September 1830.
56. Ibid.
57. Ibid., 6 November 1830.
58. *Rules and Regulations of the Liverpool Political Union*, ibid.
59. Ibid.
60. Ibid., 2 December 1830.
61. Ibid.
62. Kevin Moore, '"This Whig and Tory Ridden Town": Popular Politics in Liverpool in the Chartist Era', in John Belchem, ed., *Popular Politics, Riot and Labour: Essays in Liverpool History 1790–1940*, Liverpool: 1992, 64.
63. *Liverpool Chronicle*, 1 January 1831.
64. *Lincoln and Newark Times*, 9 November 1831.
65. *Liverpool Mercury,* 29 April, 23 September, 14 October 1831; *Liverpool Courier*, 29 September 1831.
66. *Carlisle Journal*, 25 September 1831; HO 40:26, f. 136, 1 December 1830; Belchem places this meeting, directed by Hunt, in mid-September. Belchem, *'Orator Hunt'*, 210–11.
67. Ibid., 12 November 1830.
68. Wellington MSS, WP1/1144/3, Letter from Thomas Claney to Wellington, reporting an attack on the Duke by Henry Brougham, 1 October 1830.
69. HO 40:25, f. 444, AC to Peel, 10 November 1830.
70. HO 52:11; HO 52:12.
71. *Liverpool Chronicle*, 27 November 1830; *Lincoln and Newark Times*, 9 November 1831.
72. Grey, ed., *Grey Correspondence*, i, 68, Herbert Taylor to Grey, 16 January 1831.
73. Ibid., i, 182, William IV to Grey, 21 March 1831.
74. Grey to Maurice Fitzgerald, the Knight of Derry, winter 1830–1 as quoted in Trevelyan, *Lord Grey of the Reform Bill*, 237n.
75. *Hansard*, 3rd ser., col. 1141, 1327.
76. As quoted in Norman Gash, *Politics in the Age of Peel*, 16; H. Cockburn, *Letters on Affairs of Scotland*, as quoted in Gash, *Politics in the Age of Peel*, 15.

77. Grey, ed., *Grey Correspondence*, i, 180, William IV to Grey, 21 March 1831.
78. Ibid., ii, 125, Taylor to Grey, 16 January 1832.
79. Ibid.
80. Ibid., i, 376.
81. *Examiner*, 27 March 1831.
82. HO 64:11, f. 214, J. Stafford to Home Office, early 1831.
83. HO 40:28, f. 574, 6 February 1831, R.J. Ford to Lord Talbot.
84. HO 40:25, f. 444, AC to Peel, 10 November 1830; ibid.
85. *Nottingham Review*, 26 November 1830.
86. Ibid.
87. See Archibald Prentice, *Historical Sketches and Personal Recollection of Manchester*, Manchester: 1851; Absalom Watkin, *Extracts from his Journal, 1814–56*, London: 1920.
88. Nicholas Edsall, 'Attwood, Cobden and Municipal Reform', *Historical Journal*, 16, 1973, 105.
89. *Manchester Guardian*, 15 August 1830; *Manchester Times*, 4 August 1830; *Manchester Gazette*, 4 August 1830.
90. Ibid. While the Rules of the Metropolitan Political Union were essentially the same as those governing the BPU, it is interesting to note that Prentice did not contact Attwood for assistance. Perhaps the Manchester populace's connection to Henry Hunt was so strong that Prentice believed there would automatically be more support from the working classes from a Union connected to Hunt's organization. It is also possible that Prentice wished to distance his organization from one that was ready to accept a reform measure far more moderate than one seeking universal manhood suffrage.
91. *Manchester Chronicle*, 4 December 1830.
92. Ibid.
93. Ibid.
94. Ibid.
95. *Manchester Times*, 4 July 1831; HO 52:13.
96. *Manchester Chronicle*, 4 December 1830.
97. Ibid., 30 November 1830.
98. Ibid.
99. *Voice of the People*, January 1831.
100. J.M. Main, 'Working Class Politics in Manchester from Peterloo to the Reform Bill, 1819–32, *Historical Studies*, 6, 1955, 454.
101. Prospectus for a Political Union in Sheffield, Local Pamphlets, Sheffield City Central Library; *The Ballot*, 13 February 1831.
102. Although there are no details of the meeting, the event was recorded in the diary of Thomas Asline Ward, Sheffield City Central Library, SLPS, 153–7, Monday, 10 January 1831; Alexander Bell, ed., *Peeps into the Past Being Passage from the Diary of Thomas Asline Ward*, London: 1909.
103. *Sheffield Independent*, 29 January 1831.
104. Ibid.
105. Ibid.; *The Ballot*, 13 February 1831. Palfreyman is the only one specifically mentioned in Thomas Asline Ward's diary concerning the

Sheffield Union. SCCL, SLPS, 153–7, May 1832.

106. For more on Ironside, see Dennis Smith, *Conflict and Compromise Class Formation in English Society 1830–1914*, 75–80. Ironside was to become a devotee of radical David Urquhart and would work with him, as well as Charles Attwood of the Northern Political Union, in the 1850s on issues of concern for manufacturers during the Crimean conflict.
107. There is a very brief discussion of the Sheffield Political Union in Smith, *Conflict and Compromise*, 83.
108. *Nottingham Review*, 1 January 1831.
109. BL, Add. MS. 35,149, f. 188, J.A. Hunter to Thomas Asline Ward, 19 January 1831.
110. *Voice of the People*, 19 and 26 February 1831.
111. *Manchester Chronicle*, 4 December 1830.
112. *Voice of the People*, 19 and 26 February 1830.
113. Ibid.
104. Quoted in Stewart Weaver, *John Fielden and the Politics of Popular Radicalism*, London: 1987, 50. Though Weaver acknowledges the Union and Fielden's participation in it, not much detail is offered in this study of Political Unions generally or of Fielden's role in the creation of either the Todmorden or Manchester Political Unions.
105. 'Rules and Regulations of the Todmorden Political Union', in *Voice of the People*, 19 February 1831.
106. Ibid., *Voice of the People*, 26 February 1831.
117. This split and the creation of a Manchester Union of the Working Classes with a more radical reform agenda and tactics that included the use of physical force and a general strike, will be discussed later in the text.
118. BRO, 40145/Per/3d, *Declaration of the Worcester Political Union*, 8 December 1830; *The Ballot*, 6 February 1831; 'Rules and Regulations for the Worcester Political Union' in *Worcester Herald*, 18 December 1830.
119. Ibid. Arrowsmith was a printer and by 1838, the managing editor of the *Worcester Chronicle*. His obituary credited him with being 'a pioneer amongst Reformers . . . the leading spirit of the branch of the Political Union, founded in this city, and [he] made it a power by force of his intellect and will.' BRO, 40145/Per/7. He eventually left Worcester and started a printing and publishing business in Bristol. His business and Political Union correspondence and notes are housed in the Bristol Record Office. See also H.W. Gwilliam, *Old Worcester. People and Places*, Bromsgrove: 1985, 57–8; David Whitehead, *The Book of Worcester*, Buckingham: 1976, 359–60.
120. Ibid.
121. H.M. Gwilliam, *Old Worcester, People and Places*, 58.
122. Ibid.
123. WRO, *Report of the Proceedings of the Meeting of the Worcester Political Union at the Grand Stand, Pitchcroft, 14 May 1832*, BRO 40145/Per/3i; *Peace, Order and Concord, the Worcester Political Union* , BRO 40145/Per/3a; *To Mr. Dundas*, BRO 40145/Per/3e.

124. For Huddersfield, see *The Ballot*, 18 June 1831.
125. *Leeds Patriot*, 10 December 1830.
126. Ibid.
127. *Liverpool Chronicle*, 11 December 1830.
128. *Reports of the Staffordshire Reform Meetings*, 14 May 1832 as quoted in Asa Briggs, 'Thomas Attwood and the Economic Background of the Birmingham Political Union', *Collected Essays*, 143.
129. *Staffordshire Advertiser*, 11 December 1830.
130. See L. James, *A History of the Worsted Manufacture in England from the Earliest Times*. London: 1857; Derek Fraser, ed., *A History of Modern Leeds*, Manchester: 1980.
131. E. Baines, *Life of Edward Baines*, London: 1859, 133.
132. For more on the Leeds Association, see A.S. Turberville and F. Beckwith, 'Leeds and Parliamentary Reform, 1820–32', *Thoresby Society*, 12, 1954; Derek Fraser, 'The Fruits of Reform: Leeds Politics in the 1830s,' *Northern History*, 7, 1972.
133. HO 64:17 f. 23, November 1831.
134. See chapter 4 for more on this. Also see Donald Read, *Press and People 1790–1850, Opinion in Three English Cities*, 121–2; A.S. Turberville and F. Beckwith, 'Leeds and Parliamentary Reform'; Derek Fraser, 'The Fruits of Reform: Leeds Politics in the 1830s'.
135. A number of different local Political Unions formed in the region known collectively as the Potteries. The Stafford Political Union did not form until after the Bristol Riots and the same was true of the Hanley and Shelton Political Union. It is not clear where Ford got his information, or whether the deputies failed in persuading those in the Potteries to form their own Union. But the Potteries did not form Unions until the latter part of the Reform Bill campaign. In fact, one Union formed during the May Days.
136. HO 40:28, f. 574, R.J. Ford to Earl Talbot, 8 February 1831.
137. Ibid.
138. HO 40:28, f. 582, 12 February 1831.
139. Ibid.
140. HO 40:28 (4), f. 584, 13 February 1831.
141. HO 40:28 (4), f. 495, Earl Talbot to Melbourne, 15 January 1831.
142. *The Ballot*, 18 June 1831; D.G. Wright, *Popular Radicalism*, 137.
143. *Lincoln, Rutland and Stamford Mercury*, 21 January 1831.
144. Ibid.
145. Ibid.
146. Grey, ed., *Grey Correspondence*, i, 197–8, Grey to Taylor, 23 March 1831.
147. TWRO, 'Plan for the Objects of the Northern Political Union', Original Circular, Local Tracts, v. 8.
148. Grey, ed., *Grey Correspondence*, i, 268, William IV to Grey, 20 May 1831.
149. Thomas Asline Ward, *Sheffield Independent*, 29 January 1831.

3 POLITICAL UNIONS AND THE INTRODUCTION OF THAT REFORM BILL, MARCH–OCTOBER 1831

1. 'Manifesto of the Nottingham Political Union', *Nottingham Review*, 8 November 1833.
2. Grey, ed., *Grey Correspondence*, i, 105, Grey to William IV, 5 February 1831.
3. Ibid., i, 143–4, 4 March 1831.
4. Norman Gash shows that in selecting the new boroughs for enfranchisement the criterion was not mere population; and only partially the size of the new electorate. The motive that operated as powerfully as any was the desire to secure representation for 'interests'. 'In a sense the whole commercial and manufacturing community was an interest which the ministry felt should be more equitably represented in parliament.' Gash, *Politics in the Age of Peel*, 23.
5. For discussion of electoral ritual, see Frank O'Gorman, 'Campaign Rituals and Ceremonies: The Social Meaning of Elections in England 1780–1860', *Past and Present*, 135, 1992.
6. Brock, *The Great Reform Act*, 140.
7. Ibid., 138–9.
8. Those Unions were located in the towns of Birmingham, Bradford, Bolton, Salford, Kirkheaton, Manchester, Sheffield, Huddersfield, Wolverhampton, Leeds and Stockport.
9. *Annual Register*, III, 1831, 285.
10. Grey, ed., *Grey Correspondence*, i, 197–8, Grey to Taylor, 23 March 1831.
11. Unions and reformers throughout the country sent over 100 petitions to Parliament and dozens to the King, thanking them for the Reform Bill.
12. BCL, *Report of the Proceedings of the Birmingham Political Union*, 7 March 1831.
13. *Nottingham and Newark Mercury*, 10 March 1831; T.C. Turberville, *Worcestershire in the Nineteenth Century*, London: 1852, 70.
14. *Liverpool Chronicle*, 27 November 1830.
15. *Coventry Herald and Observor*, 12 March 1830; *Voice of the People*, 10 March 1831.
16. *Nottingham Review*, 4 March 1831.
17. *Voice of the People*, 17 March 1831.
18. *Manchester Times*, 7 May 1831.
19. Brock, *The Great Reform Act*, 166–71.
20. *Political Magazine*, 10 June 1831.
21. TWRO, 'Plan for the Objects of the Northern Political Union', Original Circular, Local Tracts, 8.
22. Grey, ed., *Grey Correspondence*, i, 268, William IV to Grey, 20 May 1831.
23. *Lincoln and Newark Times*, 2 March 1831.
24. Ibid.
25. Ibid.
26. Ibid.
27. Neighbouring Wolverhampton was on Schedule C and slated for two

MPs. Wolverhampton's Political Union formed the previous December and, no doubt, helped instigate, or at least give practical assistance to, Political Union organizers in Dudley and Walsall. For more on the Black Country's parliamentary and industrial relations in the nineteenth century, see Richard H. Trainor, *Black Country Elites The Exercise of Authority in an Industrialized Area, 1830–1900*, Oxford: 1993.

28. *Northampton Herald*, 26 May 1832.
29. George Barnsby, 'The Dudley Working Class Movement, 1815–67', unpublished MA Thesis, Birmingham University, 1965.
30. Cook was so active in radical political efforts that in April 1832, the Home Office had him arrested for seditious activities. Their case was thrown out of court for lack of evidence.
31. Dudley Central Library, Samuel Cook Correspondence, *The Rules and Regulations of the Dudley Political Union*, 1831.
32. *Bath Chronicle*, 10 November 1831.
33. Brock, *The Great Reform Act*, 171.
34. Ibid., 183.
35. Ibid., 183–8.
36. UNMD, Nec 4, 560, Rotherton to Newcastle, 28 April 1831.
37. UNMD, Nec 4, 527/1–2, Talbot to Newcastle, 24 April 1831.
38. Ibid., 186–92. For the planning of the amendment, see Broughton, *Recollections*, iv, 99.
39. Even though Sheffield was not yet a parliamentary borough, Thomas Asline Ward, secretary of the Political Union, recorded in his diary that the Council began to prepare for recruiting and supporting a Radical candidate to be returned to Parliament. Evidently, this election would be treated by the Sheffield Unionists as a practice run for when the Bill was law. SCCL, Thomas Asline Ward Diaries, SLPS 153–7, 26–29 April 1831.
40. Brock, *The Great Reform Act*, 196–201.
41. *Blackwoods*, December 1831, as quoted in Brock, *The Great Reform Act*, 210.
42. UNMD, Nec 4, 526/1–2, Tallert to Newcastle, 22 April 1831; Nec 4, 531, Harrowby to Newcastle, 25 April 1831; Nec 4, 532, Mossely to Newcastle, 25 April 1831; Nec 4, 533, Middleton to Newcastle, 26 April 1831; Nec 4, 528, Tallert to Newcastle, 26 April 1831; Nec 4, 536, D. Gilborne Deale to Newcastle, 26 April 1831; Nec 4.529, Tallert to Newcastle, 27 April 1831.
43. *Coventry Herald*, 22 April 1831.
44. Ibid.
45. Ibid., 29 April 1831.
46. Ibid.
47. Ibid.
48. It had been rumoured that Joshua Scholefield, Vice President of the BPU, was prepared to challenge Fyler if Bulwer had not stepped in and offered to stand for the town. See *Coventry Herald*, 3 June 1831.
49. For a discussion of Bulwer's reform sentiments and his role in the crucial vote on the second reading, see Brock, *The Great Reform Act*, 177–8.

50. BL, Add. MSS 36,466 f. 410, Bulwer to Hobhouse, April 1831.
51. Ibid.
52. *Bristol Mercury*, 14 and 21 June 1831; Keene's *Bath Journal*, 6 June 1831; John Eagles, *The Bristol Riots, Their Causes, Progress, and Consequences*, Bristol: 1832.
53. The election numbers were as follows: R.H. Davis – 5,012; Baillie – 3,377; Prothero – 2,840; James Acland, editor of the *Bristolian*, 25.
54. BrCL, Jeffries Collection, Bristol Elections, 1831–32, ACL 73969, Broadsides, ff. 1–10; *Bristol Liberal*, 5 June 1831; *Bristol Mercury*, 7 June 1831; *Felix Farley's Bristol Journal*, 19 June 1831.
55. *Bristol Liberal*, 5 June 1831; *Bristol Mercury* 7 June 1831.
56. Some accounts also refer to it as the Bristol General Union. BrCL, Jeffries Collection, B4782/7426, Collection of Newspaper Extracts, Reports, Placards, Etc. Relating to the Riots of 1831; BrCL, B24930, MS Materials Relating to the Bristol Riots, 1831, *Rules and Orders of the Bristol General Union, Established 7 June 1831*, Bristol: 1832.
57. University of Bristol Special Collections, R-5, Charles Pinney on the Bristol Riots to Lord Melbourne, nd.
58. John Eagles, *The Bristol Riots*, 43.
59. *Bristol Mercury*, 21 June 1831; HO 40:28, f. 120; BrCL, B4782/7426, Jeffries Collection, Newspaper Extracts, Reports, Placards, Etc. Relating to the Riots of 1831; BrCL, B24930, Materials Relating to the Bristol Riots, 1831. For information on Herapath, see 'Reminiscences by 'L', *Bristol Times and Mirror*, 9 April 1888, 5.
60. Graham Bush, *Bristol and its Municipal Government 1820–51*, Gateshead: 1976.
61. BL, Add. MSS, 27,790, f. 106, 'Record of Public meeting at White Bear, Earl Street, Bristol, Monday, 30 May 1831'; HO 40: 28. ff. 120–1; *Keene's Bath Journal*, 6 June 1831.
62. HO 40:28, ff. 121–2.
63. Ibid.
64. Ibid.
65. During the summer of 1831, Union membership was said to be around 1,000. At the time of the Bristol Riots according to the testimony at the trials which followed in the early months of 1832, membership was nearly double what it had been in the previous summer.
66. BrCL, Jeffries Collection, Election Papers, B20877.
67. *Bristol Gazette*, 11 August 1831; *Bristol Mirror*, 5 October 1831.
68. *Bath Chronicle*, 26 May 1831; *Bristol Mercury*, 31 May 1831.
69. Tynte stood again in 1832, but W. Tayleur ran unopposed for the second seat. Both labelled themselves Liberals.
70. *Keene's Bath Journal*, 6 June 1831.
71. Ridley's hostility to the Political Union and its middle-class leaders does not square with the pro-reform, pro-respectable middle-class image of the MP in the 1820 as described by Dror Wahrman, *Imagining the Middle Class*, 253.
72. TWRO, Local Tracts, Original Circulars, 8, Plan for a Northern Political Union, June 1831; *Newcastle Courant*, 2 July 1831.
73. Ibid.

74. For more on Losh, see his diary in the *Camden Society*. Also see Edward Meachen, 'James Losh' in Joseph O. Baylen and Norbert J. Gossman, eds., *Biographical Dictionary of Modern British Radicals,* 1, 1770–1830, Atlantic Highlands: 1979, 299–302.
75. The reference to Hepburn being among the Union organizers came from an informant. HO 40:28 (4) f. 495, Lord Talbot to Melbourne, 15 January 1831.
76. TWRO, Local Tracts, 73, 'The objects and rules of the Northern Political Union passed at a meeting held in the Music Hall, Newcastle upon Tyne on Monday, 27 June 1831 with the Declaration of the Council of the Union'.
77. TWRO, 634C/6.
78. To join the Northern Political Union, all that was required was that members conform to its rules and follow the guidance of the Union Council. There was no set number of Council members, but it would be led by a treasurer and two secretaries, to be chosen annually by ballot at a general meeting of the Union. The Council was to meet weekly during sittings of Parliament, fortnightly when not in session. Members were also asked to pay a subscription of no less than one shilling per quarter. See TWRO, Local Tracts, 73, 'The Rules and Regulations . . .'
79. Appleby in Westmorland was shifted in committee by the opposition from Schedule A to B on 19 July, initiating a strong assault on the Reform Bill and resulting the government's lowest majority – 74. Brock goes so far as to argue that some Whig MPs voted against the government in the case of Appleby (and others) as a result of Political Union pressure. There is no proof that Alderman Thompson for the City of London voted against the government because of the influence of the NUWC, as he suggests. See Brock, *The Great Reform Act*, 214, 220.
80. NoRO, ZR1 25/62, Handbill, 'Reform Question', July 1831.
81. Ibid.
82. Ibid.
83. Ibid.
84. *The Times*, 21 May 1831. Peel believed that the BPU had sent the reporter 'or was connected with that society'. BL, Peel MSS, 40,333, f. 115–16, Peel to Golburn, 24 May 1831.
85. Brock, *The Great Reform Act*, 222–30.
86. SRO, Hatherton MSS, Littleton Diary, 4 August 1831.
87. Brock, *The Great Reform Act*, 228–30.
88. West Yorkshire, Leeds District Archives, Har\Lieutenancy, Box 2, John L.L. Hayes to Lord Harewood, 18 July 1831.
89. *Preston Chronicle*, 27 August 1831; *Penny Papers for the People*, 21 May 1831.
90. For a discussion of Hunt's role in the post 1831 election in both Parliament and in the north of England and Political Unions generally, see Belchem, *'Orator' Hunt*, 230–41.
91. *Preston Chronicle*, 27 August 1831.
92. HO 40:30, f. 239, Broadsheet, 'The Rules, Regulations and Objec-

tives of the Padiham Political Union, 15 October 1832', *Penny Papers for the People*, 21 May 1831.
93. *Brighton Gazette*, 1 September 1831.
94. *Brighton Herald*, 8 May 1830.
95. Ibid.
96. *Manchester Times*, 19 November 1831; For some discussion of the Oldham Political Union, see Vernon, *Visions of the People*; Michael Winstanley, 'Oldham Radicalism and the Origins of Popular Liberalism, 1830–52', *Historical Journal*, 36, 1993'; D.S. Gadian, 'Class Formation and Class Action in North-west Industrial Towns, 1830–50', in R.J. Morris, ed., *Class, Power and Social Structure in British Nineteenth Century Towns* Leicester: 1986.
97. For more on Knight, see W. Calvin Dickinson, 'John Knight', in Baylen and Gossman, *Biographical Dictionary of Modern Radicals,* l, 279–80.
98. H. McLachlan, *The Methodist Unitarian Movement*, 1919, 1–18.
99. *Manchester Times*, 19 November 1831.
100. *Coventry Herald*, 29 July 1831.
101. Ibid.
102. Derby MSS, Grey to Lord Stanley, 18 May 1831.
103. Wellington MSS WP1/1195/9, Thomas Bruce, seventh Earl of Elgin, to Wellington, 10 September 1831.
104. WP1/ 1207/15, Draft of Memorandum by the Duke of Wellington. 22 September 1831.
105. BCL, *Report of the Proceedings*..., 3 October 1831; *Aris's Birmingham Gazette,* 10 October 1831; *Representative*, 8 October 1831.
106. This is the argument made by Richard W. Davis in 'The Duke of Wellington and Resurgence of the House of Lords', in Davis, ed., *Lords of Parliament Studies, 1714–1914*.
107. *Leicester Chronicle*, 15 October 1831.
108. *Coventry Herald*, 14 October 1831.
109. Ibid.
110. 'Full Report of the Reform Meeting in Bath, 13 October 1831', 18.

4 THE REFORM RIOTS AND POLITICAL UNIONS AS PEACEKEEPERS: OCTOBER–DECEMBER 1831

1. Cited as a quotation from *The Times* by the Duke of Wellington. For his reaction to Hume's statement, see Wellington MSS WP1/ 1203/12, 22 November 1831.
2. Colonel Jones, MP for Bath, speaking to the Bath, Bristol, Frome, Trowbridge, Bradford-on-Avon and Holt Political Unions, printed in *Bath Herald*, 2 June 1832.
3. Yale University, Beinecke Library, 1977–97, 'An Address to all Classes and Conditions of Englishmen by the Duke of Newcastle', London: 1832, 17.
4. Abraham Kriegel, ed., *The Holland House Diaries 1831–40*, London: 1977, 75, entry dated 12 November 1831.
5. For the London riots, see Hamburger, *James Mill*, 147–54. For all,

see Home Office papers HO 52:14 and Metro 1:49 and 1:50.

6. For example, see George Rudé, 'English Rural and Urban Disturbances, on the Eve of the First Reform Bill, 1830–31', *Past and Present* 37, 1967; Hamburger, *James Mill and the Art of Revolution*; Malcolm I. Thomis and Peter Holt, *Threats of Revolution in Britain 1789–1848*, London 1977.
7. For an account of the Nottingham riots, see Malcolm Thomis, Politics and Society in Nottingham, 1785–1835; R.A. Preston, 'Nottingham and the Reform Bill Riots of 1831'; and John Wigley, 'Nottingham and the Reform Bill Riots of 1831'. For the Bristol riots, see Jeremy Caple, *The Bristol Riots of 1831 and Social Reform in Britain*. Susan Thomas argues in *The Bristol Riots*, Bristol: 1974, that the riots, three weeks after the Bill's rejection and targeting more than anti-reformers, was not a reform riot. Also see Mark Harrison, *Crowds and History Mass Phenomena in English Towns, 1790–1835*, Cambridge: 1988.
8. BL, Add. Papers, Add MSS 27790, f. 51.
9. Abraham D. Kriegel, *The Holland House Diaries*, 75, entry dated 12 November 1831.
10. Hugh Eliot, ed., *The Letters of John Stuart Mill*, 1, 7, J.S. Mill to J. Sterling.
11. Tilly, *Popular Contention in Great Britain, 1785–1834*, 338.
12. Jonathan Clark, *English Society, 1688–1832*, 374–5.
13. The accounts of the Nottingham riots can be found in the NtRO, NC/Q 420, *Account of the Nottingham Riots narrated by John Armitage*; NtRO, DDE 69/9, *Manuscript Account by Mr. Thomas Moore of Ruddington, High Sheriff for Nottinghamshire in 1831, Of the Reform Riots in Nottingham in 1831*. Also refer to HO 41/10, Melbourne to the Duke of Newcastle, 6 and 30 November, 3 December 1831; H.C. Wylly, *The Military Memoirs of Lt. General Sir Joseph Thackwell*, 1908. There are also numerous Home Office accounts in HO reports and papers. See 40:5, HO 40:28, HO 49:1 and HO 50:1 and in the *Annual Register of 1832* in Nottingham and the *Records of the Borough of Nottingham*, 8, Nottingham: 1952, 403–5.
14. *Records of Nottingham*; UNMD, Newcastle Papers 5001, 5010, Lt. Colonel Joseph Thackwell to the Duke of Newcastle, 1 November 1831; HO 52:15, Thackwell to Melbourne, 14 October 1831; for paperwork on the troops, see WO 3:83; Nottingham and Newark Mercury, 15 October 1831. For the arrest writs and assize records dealing with the Nottingham riots, refer to the collection in the NtRO, DB FS 1/334–361.
15. Butler, *The Reform Bill*, 298; John Martineau, *The Life of Henry Pelham, Fifth Duke of Newcastle*, London: 1908, 28; T.C. Hine, *Nottingham, Its Castle*, Nottingham: 1876.
16. HO 41:10, f 228, S.M. Phillips to Gen. Bouverie, 13 October 1831; Bouverie to Philips, HO 40:29, 15; HO 52:15, 13 October 1831 to Melbourne; LRO DG24/983/5, W. Dunelm, Atchland Castle to Henry Halford, 18 October 1831.
17. HO 40:5 f. 101.
18. HO 41:10 f. 443–5; Melbourne to Newcastle, 30 November 1831.

19. HO 52:12, Town Clerk at Derby to Melbourne, 2 and 23 December 1831.
20. *Nottingham Review*, 12 November 1831.
21. Ibid., 28 November 1831.
22. For the best historical account of these riots, see Hamburger, *James Mill and the Art of Revolution*, 158–61. Also see Thomis and Holt, *Threats of Revolution*, 87–8.
23. Wylley, *Thackwell*, 95; HO 52:12: Major Buckley to Melbourne, 10 October 1831; undersheriff at Derby to Melbourne, 11 October 1831; C.H. Colville, Sheriff, to Melbourne, 14 October 1831; 'Statement of the Circumstances and Time of the Attack on the County Gaol' enclosed along with another statement by J. Roberts, Keeper of Borough Gaol, 26 October 1831.
24. *The Times*, 15 October 1831.
25. *Morning Chronicle*, 12 October 1831.
26. *The Times*, 15 October 1831.
27. Ibid.
28. *Derby Riots, The Trial of Eleven Persons Charged with Breaking Open the Gaol of the Borough of Derby*, Derby: 1832, 21.
29. BL, Add MSS, 27,790, f. 8. Clearly, Place was unaware of the Nottingham Union and the size and authority of the Bristol Union. It was this authority that helped put down the riots and redefine Political Unions and their campaign across the country.
30. John Eagles, *The Bristol Riots, Their Causes, Progress and Consequences*; BrCL, B8692, W.H. Somerton, *A Narrative of the Bristol Riots*, Bristol: 1832; Anon., *Particulars of the Dreadful Riots in Bristol on Saturday and Sunday, October 29 and 30, 1831*, Bristol: 1831; T.J. Manchee, *The Origin of the Riots of Bristol and the Causes of Subsequent Outrages, Bristol*: 1832; BrCL, B21218, *A Plain Account of the Riots at Bristol in the Bristol Job Nott, 15 December 1831; The Trial of Charles Pinney, Esq. on an Information Charging him with Neglect of Duty in his Office as Mayor of Bristol during the Riots, Bristol: 1833; Report of the Commissioners Appointed under the Bristol Damages Compensation Act*, Bristol: 1835; *The Courts-Martial upon Imputed Neglect of Duty During the Bristol Riots*, Bristol: 1832; Francis Place, 'Account of the Bristol Riots', BL, Add MSS 27,790, f. 145; BrCL Jefferies Collection, VII; BRO/PB, Bristol Riots Collection; Dr. L. Carpenter, 'On the Bristol Riots', *Monthly Repository*, 5, 1831; John Latimer, *The Annals of Bristol in the Nineteenth Century*, Bristol: 1887; Latham Browen, *The Burning of Bristol: A Reminiscence of the First Reform Bill*, reprinted in the *National Review*, September 1884. See also Graham Bush, *Bristol and its Municipal Government, 1820–51*; Geoffrey Amey, *City Under Fire: The Bristol Riots and Aftermath*, London: 1979.
31. BL, Add MSS 27,790 f. 183.
32. See BrCL 4782, Collection of Newspaper Extracts, Reports, Placards, Etc., Relating to the Riots of 1831; HO 40:28 f. 8, Correspondence between Christopher Claxton and Lord Melbourne, 17 October 1831; BRO, Bristol Riot Box, Mr. Claxton's Statement during the trials of Mayor Charles Pinney.

33. BrCL, B10112, *Notice of Resolutions in 'Troubles in Bristol, by Politicks, Fire, and Pestilence; Bristol Gazette*, 20 October 1831; *Bristol Mirror*, 22 October 1831.
34. BL, Add MSS 27,790, f 151.
35. HO 20:28 f. 8, 17 October 1831.
36. Eagles, *The Bristol Riots*, 44–5.
37. BL, Add MSS 27,790, f 151.
38. BrCL, B2436-CL, Ham to Place, 10 August 1835; Caple, 10.
39. BrCL, B24936-CL, Reynolds to Herapath, 20 October 1831; BrCL, B24936, papers of Mr. J.P. Ven, Secretary of the Bristol Political Union sent to Francis Place at the request of John Ham, Esq., 1 September 1835, HO 40:5 f. 132–3. This copy of Ham's account of the riots was found at Bishopsgate Institute, London, apparently left in an old cupboard.
40. According to Susan Thomas, Herapath had frequently boasted of the Political Union's ability, if needed, to secure the peace in Bristol. See her *The Bristol Riots*, 8.
41. Ibid.
42. BrCL, B24936, Herapath to Daniel, 21 October 1831. Also see account of this record in HO 40:5 f. 132–3.
43. BrCL, B24936, Herapath to Daniel, 26 October 1831; HO 40:5 f. 134.
44. BrCL, B8692; HO 40:5 f.132–3; J.P. Ven, 25 October 1831 as in W.H. Somerton, *Narrative of the Bristol Riots*.
45. Ibid.
46. Somerton, *The Riots*, 10.
47. HO 40:5, f. 148.
48. HO 40:5, f. 148–54.
49. Ibid.
50. Ibid.
51. HO 40:5 f. 132–3; BL Add MSS 27,790 f. 183.
52. *Report of the Commissioners Appointed under the Bristol Damages Compensations Act*, Bristol: 1835.
53. HO 40:28, f 21–2, Brereton to Somerset, 30 October 1831; *The Courts-Martial upon Imputed Neglect of Duty During the Bristol Riots*, 31–2.
54. HO 40:28, f. 27, 128, 192.
55. BRO, Bristol Riot Box.
56. See Hamburger's analysis of these descriptions in *James Mill and the Art of Revolution*, 174–8. He shows that contemporaries described the rioters as predominantly among the lower classes, poor, Irish, and 'mean' and 'lower grades', rather than the more respectable working classes and lower middle classes who joined the Union.
57. BRO, Bristol Riot Box, Evidence of William Gregory of Bristol, re. Charlotte Street, 29 October 1831, 29.
58. BrCL, *General Oral Proof as Applying to the Cases of the Magistrates*, 27.
59. *United Services Journal*, November 1831.
60. This figure comes from Hamburger's work, *James Mill and the Art of Revolution*, 169.
61. BrCL, B24936-CL, Ham to Place, 10 August 1835.

62. H.W. Gwilliam, *Old Worcester*, 57–8; David Whitehead, *The Book of Worcester*.
63. *Worcester Herald*, 12 November 1831.
64. Ibid.
65. Ibid.
66. WRO, Churchill MSS, 4221.32, Mr. Beale Cooper to Lord Northwick, 18 November 1831.
67. 'Addresses from Henry Hunt, Esq., MP (hereafter AHH) to the Radical Reformers of England, Ireland and Scotland, on the Measures of the Whig Ministers Since They have Been in Place and Power', 20 and 27 October and 4–12 November 1831.
68. AHH, 4–12 November 1831, *Bolton Chronicle*, 5 and 12 November 1831.
69. AHH (4) and (5), 3–12, November 1831; *Preston Chronicle*, 5 November 1831.
70. HO 52:13, ff. 292–7, Magistrates of Blackburn to Melbourne, 9 November 1831; HO 52:13, ff. 276–9, 283–7, 310–11, letters from the mayor and town clerk of Preston to Melbourne, 7–10 November 1831; HO 41:10, ff. 385–6, 422–5, Melbourne to Derby, 12 and 22 November 1831.
71. Lord Althorp to Earl Spencer, 10 October 1831, as in Sir Denis LeMarchant, *Memoir of John Charles, Viscount Althorp*, 355.
72. BL, Add MSS. 27,790, f. 99.
73. For a detailed discussion on this, see later in chapter.
74. HO 61:5, Captain Bowles, 'Suggestions for the organization of special constables', 9 November 1831.
75. Grey, ed., *The Correspondence of Earl Grey and William IV*, i, 401, Taylor to Grey, 4 November 1831.
76. HO 40:5, f. 97–9.
77. SRO, D260/m/5/26/77, Talbot to Littleton, 9 November 1831.
78. *Political Magazine*, November 1831.
79. Ibid.
80. ScRo, Ellice MSS, 61, f. 22. Edward Ellice to Edward Ellice, Jr, 7 November 1831.
81. Address printed in the *Birmingham Journal*, 30 November 1831.
82. Grey, ed., *The Correspondence of Earl Grey and William IV*, i, 410, Grey to Taylor, 8 November 1831.
83. Ibid., i, 401, Taylor to Grey, 4 November 1831.
84. Ibid., i, 395, Grey to William IV, Grey to Taylor, 1 November 1831.
85. Wellington MSS, WP1/1201/6, Lord Fitzroy Somerset to Wellington, 2 November 1831; WP/1201/7, Lord Granville Somerset to Wellington, 3 November 1831.
86. WP1/1199/12, Lord Bradford to Wellington, 17 October 1831.
87. *Leicester Chronicle*, 15 October 1831.
88. *Coventry Herald*, 14 October 1831.
89. Ibid.
90. Belper is cited in the *Derby and Chesterfield Reporter*, 24 November 1831; Heywood is mentioned in the *Bolton Chronicle*, 10 December 1830; Holt is mentioned *in Brighton Herald*, 18 June 1832 as well as

R.S. Neale, *Bath 1680–1850 A Social History*, London: 1981, 343; Hales Owen cited in *Bath Chronicle*, 10 November 1831; Hulme cited in *Bath Herald*, 5 November 1831; Ramsgate and Thanet cited in *East Anglian*, 1 November 181; Alfreton, Ludlow and Swanwick cited in the *Durham Advertiser*, 9 November 1831; Macclesfield cited in *Macclesfield Courier and Herald*, 2 December 1831; Reading and Hinckley cited in *Bath Journal*, 7 November 1831 and *Nottingham and Newark Mercury*, 10 November 1831; Merthyr Tydfil cited in *Alfred-Bridgwater and Somersetshire Advertiser*, 23 January 1832; HO 52:16. Torrington cited in *Western Luminary* (Exeter), 18 October 1832.

91. *Derby and Chesterfield Reporter*, 29 December 1831.
92. Ibid., *Derby and Chesterfield Reporter* 5 January 1832.
93. Ibid., 29 December 1832.
94. *Bristol Liberal*, 7 December 1832.
95. Ibid.
96. Ibid.
97. *Staffordshire Gazette*, 7 December 1831.
98. Ibid.; SRO, D/4216/F/18, Talbot to King's troops in Manchester, 20 May 1831. Other accounts to the Home Office suggest that the Potteries had 'abandoned their Political Unions in deference to the government', but this was, if at all true, probably a temporary situation to appease local officials. During the May Days, Staffordshire and Potteries reformers organized into active Unions again. SRO, D260/m/f/5/26/7, Littleton Diary, 1 December 1831; SRO, D260/M/7/5/27/53, Correspondence of the Reverend W. Leigh, 40–3, 11 November 1831 and 159, 11 January 1832.
99. *Lincoln, Rutland and Stamford Mercury*, 11 November 1831; *Lincoln Herald*, 26 November 1831.
100. Ibid.; *Boston Gazette*, 30 November 1831.
101. Ibid.
102. *Bath Herald*, 18 November 1831 discusses the creation of the Union, but the objectives of the Union were reprinted in the *Bath Herald*, 25 August 1832.
103. *Derby and Chesterfield Reporter*, 3 November 1831. In addition to Dronfield, this edition of the newspaper reported the creation of another Political Union at Alfreton, although no details were offered.
104. *Derbyshire Courier, Chesterfield Gazette*, 24 December 1831.
105. *The Ballot*, 20 November 1831.
106. HO 40:29 f. 476, November 1831.
107. HO 40:30 f. 296, 21 November 1831.
108. *Boston Gazette*, 15 November 1831; *Bath and Cheltenham Gazette*, 14 July 1832.
109. *Western Luminary* (Exeter), 18 October 1831.
110. *Derby and Chesterfield Reporter*, 24 November 1831.
111. *Bath Herald*, 22 November 1831; *Brighton Herald*, 18 June 1832.
112. *Bristol Liberal*, 12 November 1831; *Bath Chronicle*, 16 November 1831.
113. *Bath Chronicle*, 16 November 1831.
114. *Taunton Courier*, 23 November 1831.
115. Ibid.

116. *Western Luminary* (Exeter), 18 October 1831.
117. HO 40:29, ff. 437 and 439, 1 November 1831; *Brighton Herald*, 18 June 1832. The Frome Union is also mentioned in R.S. Neale, *Bath, 1680–1850*, 343.
118. For Yeovil, see *The Ballot*, 21 May 1831; HO 40:30, f. 239. For Blackburn, see HO 40:30, assorted documents from October and November 1831, particularly HO 40:30 f. 34, Dixon Robinson to Melbourne, 21 November 1831. For Briercliffe and Burnely, see HO 40:30, assorted documents, October–November 1831.
119. For more on the Leicester Reform Association, see R.W. Greaves, *The Corporation of Leicester 1689–1836* London, 1939, and A. Temple Patterson, *Radical Leicester*; LRO, *A History of Leicester Railroad People, etc.*, nd.
120. See R.G. Kirby and A.E. Musson, *The Voice of the People*; LRO, 5 D6i/2 (u16) William Biggs Scrapbook.
121. Ibid., 15 October 1831. LRO, DE 667/189, 1 November 1831.
122. *Leicester Chronicle*, 7 November 1831.
123. LRO, 5 D6i/2 (u16), William Biggs Scrapbook.
124. LRO, 5 D6i/2 (u16), William Biggs Scrapbook, Broadside address of council of Leicester and Leicestershire Political Union, Tuesday, 7 November 1831.
125. *Leicester Chronicle*, 7 November 1831.
126. Broadside address of Council of Leicester and Leicestershire Political Union, Tuesday, 7 November 1831.
127. Ibid.
128. Ibid.
129. Ibid.
130. Ibid.
131. Ibid.
132. *Leicester Herald*, 23 November 1831.
133. LRO, 5 D61/2(u16) Biggs Scrapbook.
134. BaRL, B942.38, *Full Report of the Reform Meeting in Front of the Sydney Hotel, Bath, 13 October 1831*, Bath: H.E. Carrington, 1831. For more on the Bath Political Union, see the broadsides in the Thomas Falconer Collection, Bath Library.
135. BaRL, Local Collections, Falconer Collection, 1832.
136. *Full Report of the Meeting*..., 13 October 1831, 6–7.
137. Ibid., 7.
138. Ibid., 10.
139. Ibid.
140. Ibid., 15.
141. *Bath Herald*, 15 November 1831.
142. *Full Report of the Meeting*..., 9–10.
143. BaRL, Local Studies, *Letter to the Inhabitants of Bath on Political Unions*, Bath: B. Higman Printers, November 1831.
144. HO 40:29 f. 400, Joseph Page to Lord Melbourne, 9 November 1831.
145. The secretary of the Union was John Noble, Jr, the son of the printer and correspondent for the *Stamford Mercury*.
146. *Hull Portfolio*, 12 November 1831.

147. Ibid., 12 October 1831.
148. Ibid., 12 November 1831.
149. Ibid., 12 October 1831.
150. Ibid., 12 November 1831.
151. Ibid., 31 December 1831.
152. Ibid., 29 November 1831.
153. Ibid., 15 May 1832.
154. NCL, Local Studies, Broadside, 'Union is Strength', 27 October 1831.
155. Ibid.
156. Ibid.; NCL, Broadside, 'Norwich Political Union', 8 May 1832.
157. NCL, 'Objects of the Norwich Political Union', 11 June 1832.
158. *East Anglian*, 8 November 1831.
159. Accounts of the National Political Union have been offered by Graham Wallas, Hamburger, *James Mill and the Art of Revolution*; Dudley Miles, *Francis Place, The Life of a Remarkable Radical 1771–1854*, Brighton: 1988. For analysis of the NPU's formation in regard to rioting and potential revolution, the best account is still Hamburger's, *James Mill and the Art of Revolution*, 77–90.
160. HO 64:12, f. 7; HO 64:17, *Report of the Council to the First Annual General Meeting of the National Political Union, 2 February 1832*; HO 64:18, f. 382.
161. BL, Add MSS, 27791, f. 20, 92, 272. Add MSS. 27792, ff. 7–12; *Poor Man's Guardian*, 1 December 1831; *The Ballot*, December 1831.
162. *Hansard,* vi, 30 August 1831, 871–2.
163. BL, Add MSS 27792, f.12.
164. BL, Add MSS 27790, f. 22–3.
165. BL, Add MSS 27,791, f. 92.
166. BL, Add MSS, 27791, f. 153.
167. BL, Add MSS, 27791, f. 13f. Placard for National Political Union, 16 November 1831.
168. Ibid.
169. BL, Add MSS 27791, 49–50.
170. BL, Add MSS 27791, ff. 89–90
171. William Lovett, *The Life and Struggles . . .*, London: 1876, 75; *Poor Man's Guardian*, 5 November 1831.
172. BL, Place Newspaper Cuttings Collection, Set 63, 1, ff. 87–97, Minutes for 7 February 1832.
173. BL, Add MSS 27791, 'Resolutions Passed at a Public Meeting, 31 October 1831', distributed on a placard, 2 November 1831.
174. BL, Add MSS 27,791, f. 90.
175. *Newcastle Courant*, 15 October 1831.
176. Ibid.
177. *Worcester Herald*, 17 November 1831.
178. Ibid., 9.
179. *Voice of the People*, 26 November 1831
180. HO 40:29 f. 476, November 1831.
181. *Boston Gazette*, 15 November 1831; *Bath and Cheltenham Gazette*, 14 July 1832.
182. *Bristol Liberal*, 12 November 1831; *Bath Chronicle*, 16 November 1831.

183. Peter Jupp, *British and Irish Elections 1784–1831*, New York: 1973, 199.
184. Ibid., 200.
185. Alexander Bell, ed., *Peeps Into the Past, The Diaries of Thomas Asline Ward*, 297.
186. Ibid.
187. George J. Barnsby, *The Dudley Working Class Movement 1750–1832.*
188. LRO, Biggs Scrapbook, Broadside, *Leicester and Leicestershire Political Union*, 7 November 1831.
189. Ibid.
190. Ibid.
191. Although the number seems unlikely, 100,000 was the figure reported in all provincial and metropolitan newspapers, as well as Home Office reports. Historians have generally accepted the number, assuming that it included Unionists throughout the midlands and possible visiting delegations from towns further away.
192. *Morning Chronicle*, 1 November 1831.
193. Ibid.
194. Ibid., 12 November 1831.
195. Ibid., 19 November 1831.
196. HO 40/29; anonymous letter to Lord Melbourne signed 'Truth'.
197. Wellington MSS WP1/1199/8, Francis Lloyd to Wellington, 19 October 1831.
198. Grey, ed., Grey Correspondence, Ibid., i, 411, Grey to Taylor, 8 November 1831.
199. Ibid.
200. Ibid.
201. WP 1/1201/20, William IV to Wellington, 9 November 1831; Grey MSS, Box 47, File 9, 5, copy of letter, William IV to Wellington, 9 November 1831.
202. Letters from Captain John Debenham of Chelsea to Wellington included copies of *The Republican,* which he no doubt associated, however incorrectly, with the Political Unions. See WP1/1201/21, Captain Debenham to Wellington, 9 November 1831.
203. WP1/1199/20, Duke of Gloucester to Wellington, 29 October 1831.
204. BL, Add. MSS 27,790, ff. 248–9, Duke of Buckingham, 6 December 1831.
205. WP1/1201/24, Grey to Wellington, 10 November 1831; Grey MSS, Box 47, File 9, 14, Remarks to Wellington from Grey, nd.
206. Grey MSS, Box 8, File 11, 12, Burdett to Grey, 24 October 1831.
207. Grey, ed., *Grey Correspondence*, i, 394, Grey to Taylor, 1 November 1831, including addendum, Attwood to Grey, 31 October 1831.
208. Parkes MSS, Althorp to Parkes, 3 November 1831.
209. BL, Althorp MSS, H14, Parkes to Althorp, 13 November 1831.
210. Ibid.
211. Ibid.
212. Ibid.
213. Ibid.
214. Ibid.
215. WP1/1201/26, Sir James Scarlett to Wellington, enclosure of a letter

from Birmingham to Scarlett, 11 November 1831; Alhorp MSS, H14, Parkes to Althorp, 13 November 1831.

216. Grey MSS, Box 47, File 9, 11, Grey to William IV, 11 November 1831.
217. NCL, Local Studies Pamphlets, Guernsey, 'Remarks on the Danger of Political Associations', 20 November 1831.
218. 'Letter to the Inhabitants of Bath on Political Unions, November 1831', Bath: B. Higman, 1831, 1, 3–4.
219. Wellington MSS WP1/1205/24, Lord Stuart de Rothesay to Wellington, 31 December 1831, enclosure.
220. For fuller details of the threat of Political Union arming the reactions of the King, his government and the opposition, see chapter 5.
221. Mention of the financial situation of the BPU was made in a letter to Wellington from Melbourne, cited in WP1/1201/23, 10 November 1831.
222. For the same financial reasons, Joseph Hamburger dismissed the whole 'plan' as a ruse of some of the Birmingham leaders who were interested in heightening the anxieties of the government; The selection of John Portlock, a gunmaker, to the Union Council in late November was very likely part of the same ruse. Historian Henry Ferguson simply dismissed this rumor of arming in Birmingham as nothing more than, 'merely a feint in the political warfare.' Ferguson, 'Political Unions and the Government', 268–69.
223. Grey MSS, Box 47, File 9, 11, Grey to William IV, 11 November 1831.
224. Ibid.
225. Ibid.
226. Abraham D. Kriegel, *The Holland House Diaries*, 83, entry dated 19 November 1831.
227. Grey MSS, Box 47, File 9, 16, 39 Geo. III 79 and notes.
228. 39 George III c. 79 and 57 George III c. 19. These statutes, enacted in 1799 and 1817 respectively, and established strict definitions for sedition, and illegal political associations and societies.
229. 39 George III, c. 79, 1799, 71.
230. Ibid.
231. 57 George III, c 19, 1817, 34.
232. Wellington MSS WP1/1203/16, Wellington to Lord Westmorland, 23 November 1831.
233. WP1/1203/17, Wellington to Lord Grey, 24 November 1831.
234. Grey, ed., *Grey Correspondence*, ii, 473, Grey to William IV, 19 June 1832.
235. Moss, *Thomas Attwood*, 205–8.
236. See Joseph Hamburger, *James Mill and the Art of Revolution*, 95–6, 243–5.
237. BL, Add, MSS 27791, f. 20; 35,149, f. 188, 7 July 1832.
238. *The Ballot*, 13 November 1831.
239. Ibid., 20 November 1831.
240. TWRO, Wilson Collection, no. 750, Broadsheet, 'The Northern Political Union and the Royal Proclamation'.

241. Ibid.
242. *Bath Herald*, 19 November 1831.
243. See *Bath Herald, Leicester Chronicle, Leeds Mercury*, and *Hull Portfolio* during the last week in November and the first few weeks in December 1831.
244. *Derby and Chesterfield Reporter*, 29 December 1831.
245. HO 40:28, ff. 117–19, Herapath to Melbourne, 23 November 1831.

5 POLITICAL UNIONS AND THE FINAL CAMPAIGN: AGITATION, THE MAY DAYS AND VICTORY, JANUARY–JUNE 1832

1. *Bath Herald*, 2 June 1832.
2. John Eagles, *The Riots in Bristol*, 26.
3. 'Monthly Retrospects, Addressed Particularly to Political Unions', *Political Union Register*, 1 March 1832, 3.
4. Grey, ed., *Grey Correspondence*, ii, 224–5, 15 January 1832, William IV to Grey.
5. Brock, *The Great Reform Act*, 268–79.
6. Grey, ed., *Grey Correspondence*, ii, 137, Grey to Taylor, 18 January 1832.
7. Wellington MSS WP1/1213/9, T. Rowbotham, Bristol to Wellington, 14 January 1832; WP1/1213/22, Marquis of Salisbury to Wellington, 16 January 1832; WP1/1203/21, Wellington to Lord Eldon, 27 November 1831.
8. Grey MSS, Box 46, no. 20, 17 January 1832.
9. See chapter 4 for details of these days in the Reform Bill campaign.
10. Grey, ed., *Grey Correspondence,* ii, 126, Taylor to Grey, 16 January 1832.
11. Ibid.
12. BL, Add MSS, 27,792, f. 21.
13. BL Add MSS, 27, 790, f. 295.
14. Ibid.
15. Grey, ed., *Grey Correspondence*, ii, 152, Taylor to Grey, 26 January 1832.
16. West Yorkshire, Leeds District Archives, Harewood Lieutenancy, Box 2: John Coates to Harewood, 25 January 1832.
17. Brougham, *Recollections*, iv, 174; Durham MSS, J. Scholefield to Lord Durham, 10 March 1832.
18. Richard Welford, *Men of the Mark Twixt Tyne and Tweed*, vol. III, 8 as quoted in Peter Cadogan, *Early Radical Newcastle*, Consett, 1975, 89.
19. *Northern Tribune*, 336.
20. The plan, without ever being implemented, warranted an entry in the diary of Mrs Sharples in Bristol who wrote: 'Political Unions [are] assembling all over England [as are] numerous meetings of various classes, [all of whom] . . . threaten not to pay taxes unless the Bill passes . . .' BrCL, 19720, Mrs Sharples' Diary, 11 May 1832.
21. Grey MSS, Box 5, File 2, Charles Attwood to Lord Grey, 18 April 1832.

22. Ibid.
23. Ibid., Grey to Charles Attwood, April 1832.
24. For a discussion of the breakdown in relations between the ministry and the King, see Brock, *The Great Reform Act*, 280–92.
25. *Bristol Liberal*, 3 March 1832.
26. *Northampton Herald*, 24 March 1832.
27. *Hansard*, xii, 447.
28. J.E. Thorold Rogers, ed., *John Bright, Public Addresses*, 1879, 415.
29. ScRO, Ellice MSS, E. 41, f. 5, Ellice to Parkes, undated; J.K. Buckley, *Joseph Parkes*, 91–4.
30. *Tyne Mercury*, 24 April 1832.
31. For Thomas Attwood's reaction to the proposal, see G. J. Holyoake, *Sixty Years of an Agitator's Life*, I, London: 1892, 26. For Baines' reaction, see *Leeds Mercury*, 21 April 1832. For Parkes' sense of the importance of the ten pound qualification, see *The Times,* 9 May 1832.
32. *Leicester Chronicle*, 14 April 1832.
33. *Morning Chronicle*, 30 April 1832; *The Times*, 9 May 1832 (for the speeches of Parkes and McDonnell at the BPU meeting on 7 May).
34. For a good account of the event, as analysed by Joseph Parkes, see Jessie Buckley, *Joseph Parkes*, 99–115.
35. *Report of the Proceedings at the Grand Meeting of the Birmingham Political Union at Newhall Hill, 7 May 1832.*
36. *Newcastle Courant*, 18 August 1832.
37. *North Devon Journal and General Advertiser*, 23 May 1832.
38. Ibid.
39. Ibid.
40. *Warwick General Advertiser*, 19 May 1832.
41. *Salisbury and Winchester Journal*, 21 May 1832.
42. Ibid.
43. Ibid.
44. Ibid.
45. BL, Add MSS 35,150, f. 110–11, 15 May 1832.
46. *Boston Gazette*, 15 May 1832; BL, Add MSS 35,150, f. 110–11. There is also mention of the Union in R.S. Neale, *Bath 1680–1850*, 343.
47. *Lichfield Mercury*, 18 May 1832.
48. *Sherbourne, Dorchester and Taunton Journal*, 20 July 1832; *Brighton Herald*, 18 June 1832; *Huntington, Bedford and Peterborough Gazette and Cambridge and Hereford Independent Press*, 2 June 1832; *Bath Gazette*, 22 September 1832.
49. *Staffordshire Mercury*, 26 May 1832.
50. SRO, D4216/F/18, Published circular from Committee convened by High Constables of Burslem, Hanley, Shelton, Longton and Lane End, 8 January 1824.
51. Ibid.
52. *Staffordshire Gazette*, 7 June 1832.
53. Thomis and Holt, *Threats of Revolution*, 86; Cole and Postgate, *The Common People, 1746–1938*, 248; Hamburger, *James Mill*, 195–9. Only Derek Fraser has argued that the May Days was a period when 'what people thought was happening was of more importance than what

was actually happening.' Fraser, 'The Agitation of Parliamentary Reform', in J.T. Ward, *Popular Movements*, 46.

54. Broughton, *Recollections*, 4, 234; Grote, *Life of George Grote*, Parkes to Grote, 18 May 1832, 79–80.
55. *Hansard*, 3rd ser., xii, 971–2, 1832.
56. Ibid.
57. NRO, Bul 1/5/60 (561x5), Hickling to Bulwer, 14 May 1832.
58. *Bath Journal*, 14 May 1832; *Bristol Liberal*, 15 May 1832; *Warwick General Advertiser*, 19 May and 2 June 1832.
59. BL, Add MSS 27, 793, f. 86–150.
60. BCL, 467725, Proceedings of the Public Meeting of the Inhabitants of Birmingham at Newhall Hill, 10 May 1832, convened by the Political Union for the Purpose of Determining what measures were Necessary to be Taken on the Resignation of the Ministers *Report of the* Proceedings *of the Birmingham Political Union . . .*, 10 May 1832, 4.
61. CRO, 323/25, Percy Fitzpatrick (for Bulwer) to William Hickling, 8 May 1832.
62. CRO, 323/8, Coventry Reform Meeting on Monday, 14 May 1832 with a note on the back of the minutes from Bulwer to Hickling, dated 11 May 1832.
63. Ibid.
64. CRO, 323/8, Coventry Reform Meeting, 14 May 1832.
65. Ibid.
66. Ibid.
67. *Birmingham Journal*, 11 May 1832.
68. BCL, 467725, *Proceedings of the Public Meeting of the Inhabitants of Birmingham at Newhall Hill, 10 May 1832, convened by the Political Union for the Purpose of Determining what measures were Necessary to be Taken on the Resignation of the Ministers.*
69. BL, Add MSS 27,793, f. 92.
70. BCL, 467726, *Report of the Proceedings of the Public Meeting of the Inhabitants of Birmingham held at Newhall Hill, 16 May 1832, convened by the Council of the Political Union for the Purpose of Presenting An Address to Earl Grey.*
71. Ibid.
72. As quoted in Cadogan, *Early Radical Newcastle*, 91.
73. William Biggs in the *Leicester Chronicle*, 19 May 1832.
74. *Huntingdon, Bedford and Peterborough Gazette, Cambridge and Hertford Independent Press*, 2 June 1832.
75. *Worcester Herald*, 19 May 1832.
76. *Coventry Herald*, 25 May 1832.
77. Hamburger, *James Mill*, 130.
78. BRO, 40145/Per/3i, *Proceedings of the Meeting of the Worcester Political Union at Pitchcroft Hill, 14 May 1832*; *Worcester Herald*, 19 May 1832.
79. *Coventry Herald*, 18 May 1832.
80. Address sent by Jon Wilson of the NPU to the Marquess of Londonderry, 26 May 1832 reprinted in *Dorset County Chronicle and Somersetshire Gazette*, 7 June 1832.

81. Ibid.
82. Wellington MSS, WP1/1202/16, Marquis of Londonderry to Wellington, 23 November 1831.
83. Ibid.
84. For more on the threats to stop tax payments, see *Hansard*, 12, 876, 879–80, 12 May 1832; 1034, 17 May 1832.
85. BCL, *Report of the Proceedings*, 10 May 1832, 5.
86. *Salopian Journal*, 2 May 1832.
87. *Morning Post*, 12 May 1832 as quoted in Brock, *The Great Reform Act*, 297.
88. *Morning Chronicle*, 11 May 1832.
89. *The Times*, 12 May 1832.
90. BCL, *Report of the Proceedings*, 10 May 1832, 1.
91. Ibid., 1.
92. Ibid., 6.
93. Ibid., 4.
94. BRO, 40145/Per/3i, *Proceedings of the Meeting of the Worcester Political Union at Pitchcroft Hill, 14 May 1832; Worcester Herald, 19 May 1832.*
95. Ibid.
96. NCL, Local Studies, Broadsides, 'Resolutions passed at a most numerous and respectable meeting of the inhabitants and electors of the city of Norwich', Norwich Political Union, 14 May 1832.
97. *Leicester Chronicle*, 19 May 1832.
98. *Bristol Mercury*, 12 May 1832; *Bristol Gazette*, 16 May 1832; *Felix Farley's Bristol Journal*, 16 May 1832.
99. *Staffordshire Advertiser*, 16 June 1832; *Staffordshire Gazette*, 16 June 1832.
100. Manchester Public Library, Smith MSS, John Benjamin Smith to Mr. James Shuttleworth, 12 May 1832.
101. *Manchester Guardian*, 12 May 1832.
102. NRO, Bul/1/5/60, Hickling to Bulwer, 13 May 1832.
103. *Worcester Herald*, 19 May 1832; BRO. 40145/Per/7.
104. Ibid.
105. SCCL, Thomas Asline Ward Diaries, SLPS, 153–57, Tuesday, 10 May and Thursday, 19 May 1832.
106. BL, Add MSS 27,792, f. 40.
107. Wakefield, C.M., *Life of Thomas Attwood*, 195.
108. BL, Add MSS 27,794, f. 10, Parkes to Grote, 14 May 1832.
109. *Poor Man's Guardian*, 11 April 1832; *Cosmopolite*, 14 and 28 April 1832. In addition, see Macerone's own account in *Memoirs*, 1838, ii, 458–68.
110. Alexander Somerville, *Autobiography of a Working Man*; 'Report of Court Inquiry on the Case of Alexander Somerville', *Parliamentary Papers*, 1831–32 (714), xxvii, 24; *Scotsman*, 19 May 1832.
111. Quoted in Trevelyan, Lord Grey to Lord Hill, 340; 14 May 1832; *Weekly Dispatch*, 14 May 1832; *Standard*, 18 May 1832.
112. *Political Unionist*, 30 June 1832.
113. *Worcester Herald*, 19 May 1832; David Whitehead, *The Book of Worcester*; BRO 40145/Per/7.

114. NCL, Local Studies, Broadsides, 'Norwich Political Union', 8 May 1832.
115. NCL, Local Studies, Broadsides, 'Fellow Citizens, Read, Mark, Learn and inwardly Digest', 10 May 1832; 'Resolutions passed at a most numerous and respectable meeting of the inhabitants and electors of the city of Norwich', Norwich Political Union, 14 May 1832.
116. *Coventry Herald*, 18 May 1832.
117. Wallas, *Life of Francis Place*, 315–16.
118. BL, Add MSS 27,793, f. 86–150 give an account of these crucial days.
119. *Morning Chronicle*, 14 May 1832.
120. BL, Add MSS, 35,149, f.141, Parkes to Place, 14 May 1832.
121. *Parliamentary Papers*, 1831–32 (722), vi. 398 (Q.4984) as quoted in Brock, *The Great Reform Act*, 298–9.
122. 'Report from the Committee of Secrecy on the Bank of England Charter with the Minutes of Evidence, 11 August 1832', *Hansard*, 12, 14 May 1832.
123. Smith MSS, John Benjamin Smith to Mr. Tollock, 12 May 1832.
124. 'Report . . . on the Bank of England Charter', 1832.
125. Hamburger, *James Mill and the Art of Revolution*, 104.
126. BCL, *Report of the Proceedings . . .*, 10 May 1832, 5.
127. Ibid., 6.
128. Ibid.
129. TWRO, Local Tracts, 'Charles Larkin's Speech at St. Nicholas Square, Newcastle upon Tyne', 15 May 1832.
130. *Northampton Herald*, 24 May 1832.
131. *Staffordshire Gazette*, 13 June 1832.
132. *Staffordshire Mercury and Pottery Gazette*, 26 May 1832.
133. *Brighton Gazette*, 16 May 1832.
134. *Worcester Herald*, 19 May 1832.
135. Ibid.
136. *Coventry Herald*, 15 May 1832.
137. *Hull Portfolio*, 15 May 1832.
138. *Manchester Times*, 7 May 1832.
139. *Salisbury and Winchester Journal*, 21 May 1832.
140. Ibid.
141. *Bath Herald*, 2 June 1832.
142. Ibid.
143. Anonymous, dated 11 May 1832, published in *Poor Man's Guardian*, 17 November 1832.
144. Grey MSS, Box 8, File 11, no. 25, Sir Francis Burdett to Grey, 22 May 1832.
145. Ibid.
146. Ibid., Box 8, File 11, no. 26, Grey to Burdett, 22 May 1832.
147. Grey, ed., *Grey Correspondence*, ii, 412 , William IV to Grey, 15 May 1832.
148. Wakefield MSS, Attwood to Mrs. Attwood, 26 May 1832 as quoted in Flick, *The Birmingham Political Union*, 89.
149. *Coventry Herald*, 15 June 1832.
150. *Bath Journal*, 4 June 1832.

151. *Liverpool Courier*, 19 June 1832.
152. *Bath Herald*, 2 June 1832; *Bath Chronicle*, 31 May 1832; *Keene's Bath Journal*, 4 June 1832; *Derby and Chesterfield Reporter*, 9 June 1832; *Sherborne, Dorchester and Taunton Journal*, 21 June 1832; *Taunton Chronicle*, 23 May 1832; *Coventry Herald*, 13 July 1832.
153. *Bath Herald*, 2 June 1832.
154. Ibid.
155. Ibid.
156. *Leicester Chronicle*, 2 June 1832.
157. Grey, ed., *Grey Correspondence*, ii, 445, Grey to Taylor, 24 May 1832.
158. Ibid., ii, 469–70, enclosure, Duke of Cumberland to William IV, 16 June 1832.
159. The Crompton Political Union formed in June protect English liberties and fight oppression. In its Rules and Objectives, it stated that 'when a government violates the rights of the people, resistance becomes the most sacred and the most justifiable duties.' Giles Shaw MSS, MS942.72S14, 82, 98–101. This, no doubt, was interpreted as proof of Cumberland's fears. In October, the Torrington Union was established, *Western Luminary* (Exeter), 18 October 1832.
160. *Political Unionist*, 30 June 1832.
161. Derek Fraser, 'The Agitation for Parliamentary Reform', in J.T. Ward, ed., *Popular Movements c. 1830–1850*, 46; Belchem, *'Orator' Hunt*, 260.

CONCLUSION

1. *Nottingham Review*, 8 November 1833.
2. This number does not reflect all the extra-parliamentary organizations formed during the two and a half years of the Reform Bill agitation, but only those choosing to include 'Political Union' in their name. It does not include inactive or 'ephemeral' organizations which met briefly and ceased to exist. Still, of the nearly 120 Political Unions that formed during the Reform Bill agitation, approximately 60 were still active in June 1832.
3. The following examination of pre-1832 boroughs is based on information from J. Holiday Philbin, *Parliamentary Representation, 1832, England and Wales*, New Haven: 1965; Edward Porritt, *The Unreformed House of Commons: Representation before 1832*, Cambridge, 1903; J. Addy, *Parliamentary Elections and Reform, 1807–32*; William Wardell Bean, *Parliamentary Representation*, Hull: 1890.
4. Scot and lot boroughs allowed a man who paid poor rates to vote. The potwalloper allowed every male resident in the borough to vote, while the burgage borough required the ownership of ancient property from which the vote derived.
5. These included Bath, Brighton, Bristol, Coventry, Dudley, Hanley and Shelton, Hull, Leeds, Leicester, Liverpool, Manchester, Newark, Northern (Newcastle upon Tyne), Norwich, Nottingham, Oldham, Potteries, Sheffield, Stafford, Todmorden, Warwick and Worcester.

6. Wellington MSS, WP1/1198/32, Anonymous letter to the Duke of Wellington, 9 October 1830.
7. Jonathan Fulcher, 'Gender, Politics and Class in the Early Nineteenth Century Reform Movement', *Historical Research*, 67, February 1994; Jutta Schwarzkopf, *Women in the Chartist Movement*, London: 1991; Dorothy Thompson, *The Chartists: Popular Politics in the Industrial Revolution*, Aldershot: 1986; and 'Women in Radical Politics: The Lost Dimension', in Juliet Mitchell and Ann Oakelly, eds., *The Rights and Wrongs of Women,* Harmondsworth: 1976; Anna Clark, *The Struggle for the Breeches, Gender and the Making of the British Working Class*, Berkeley, 1996.
8. BL, Add MSS, 27,794, f. 10, Parkes to Grote, 14 May 1832.
9. The women's auxiliaries appeared in the flurry of other Union activities following the October riots. Notices were published in newspapers announcing the creation of a Manchester Free Women's Political Union in January 1832. (*Hull Advertiser*, 13 January 1832). Women were also forming their own Political Union in Brighton in October of that year. *Bath Chronicle*, 12 January 1832; 25 October 1832 and *Lichfield Mercury*, 27 October 1832.
10. C.S. Parker, *Sir Robert Peel*, 3 vols, London: 1899, ii, 205–6; R.W. Davis, 'Toryism to Tamworth: The Triumph of Reform', 142–3.

EPILOGUE

1. Charles Grey, ed., *Grey Correspondence* ii, 470, 19 June 1832.
2. *Political Magazine*, September 1831.
3. *Sheffield Independent*, 22 May 1832; Alexander Bell. ed., *Peeps Into the Past,* 299.
4. *Sherborne, Dorcheser and Taunton Journal*, 21 June 1832.
5. *Staffordshire Advertiser,* 16 June 1832; *Staffordshire Gazette*, 16 June 1832.
6. BrCL, Jeffries Collection, Election papers, 1832.
7. These included Unions in Congleton, Hebden Bridge, Horsham, Leamington, Radford and Winchester. *Poor Man's Guardian,* 18 December 1832; 17 November 1832; 27 October 1832; 12 December 1832, respectively.
8. The majority of Unions seemed to incorporate both political and economic issues in their election platform.
9. *Bath Herald*, 2 June 1832.

LIVERPOOL
JOHN MOORES UNIVERSITY
AVRIL ROBARTS LRC
TITHEBARN STREET
LIVERPOOL L2 2ER
TEL. 0151 231 4022

Bibliography

SELECT MANUSCRIPTS COLLECTIONS

Bath Reference Library
Thomas Falconer Collection: A Collection of Posters, Broadsides, Pamphlets, etc., 1832.

Birmingham Central Reference Library
Birmingham Political Union printed reports

Bristol Record Office
Isaac Arrowsmith Papers
Bristol Riot Collection

Bristol Reference Library
Jeffries Collection

British Library
Francis Place Papers
Broughton Papers
J.C. Hobhouse Papers

Coventry Record Office
William Hickling Papers

Durham University
Grey Papers

Leicestershire Record Office
William Biggs Papers and Scrapbook

Norfolk Record Office
William Henry Lytton Earle Bulwer Papers

Southampton University
Wellington Papers

Tyne and Wear Record Office
Cowen Papers

University College, London
Joseph Parkes Papers

Worcester Record Office
Churchill Papers

SELECT SECONDARY SOURCES: BOOKS

Amey, G., *City under Fire: The Bristol Riots and Aftermath*, London: 1979.

Bateson, Mary, ed., *Records of the Borough of Leicester, V–VII 1689–1835*, London: 1899–1974.

Barnsby, George J., *The Dudley Working Class Movement 1750–1832*, Dudley: 1966.

——— *A History of Wolverhampton*: Wolverhampton: 1977.

——— *Birmingham Working People: A History of the Labour Movement in Birmingham 1650–1914*, Wolverhampton: 1989.

Baylen, Joseph O. and Gossman, Norbert J., ed., *Biographical Dictionary of Modern British Radicals,* 1: *1770–1830*, Hassocks: 1979.

Behagg, Clive, *Politics and Production in the Early Nineteenth Century*, London: 1990.

Belchem, John, *Industrialization and the Working Class: The English Experience, 1750–1900*, Aldershot: 1990.

——— *'Orator' Hunt: Henry Hunt and English Working-Class Radicalism*, Oxford: 1985.

——— ed., *Popular Politics, Riot and Labour, Essays in Liverpool History 1790–1940*, Liverpool: 1992.

Bell, Alexander, ed., *Peeps into the Past Being Passages from the Diary of Thomas Asline Ward*, London: 1909.

Black, Eugene C., *The Association: British Extraparliamentary Political Organization 1769–93*, Cambridge, MA: 1963.

Bradley, James E., *Popular Politics and the American Revolution in England, Petitions, the Crown and Public Opinion*, Macon, GA: 1986.

——— *Religion, Revolution, and English Radicalism, Nonconformity in Eighteenth Century Politics and Society*, Cambridge: 1990.

Brent, Richard, *Liberal Anglican Politics. Whiggery, Religion, and Reform 1830–41*, Oxford: 1987.

Briggs, Asa, *The Age of Improvement, 1783–1867*, London: 1959.

Brock, Michael, *The Great Reform Act*, London: 1973.

Buckley, Jessie, K., *Joseph Parkes of Birmingham*, London: 1926.

Bush, Graham, *Bristol and its Muncipal Government 1820–51*, Gateshead: 1976.

Butcher, E., ed., *Bristol Corporation of the Poor, 1696–1834*, III, Bristol: 1932.

Butler, J.R., *The Passing of the Great Reform Act*, London: 1914.

Bythell, Duncan, *Handloom Weavers*, Cambridge: 1969.

Butler, J.R.M., *The Passing of the Great Reform Bill,* London: 1914.

Cadogan, Peter, *Early Radical Newcastle*, Consett: 1975.

Cannon, John A., *Parliamentary Reform 1640–1832*, Cambridge: 1973.

——— and McGrath, Patrick, eds., *Essays in Bristol and Gloucestershire History*, Bristol: 1976.

Caple, Jeremy, *The Bristol Riots of 1832*, Lewiston: 1992.

Clark, J.C.D., *English Society 1688–1832, Ideology, Social Structure and Political Practice during the Ancien Regime*, Cambridge: 1985.

Clarke, Peter, *Lancashire and the New Liberalism*, Cambridge: 1971.

Clifford, J., ed., *Man vs. Society in the Eighteenth Century*, Cambridge: 1968.

Cole, G.D.H., *Attempts at a General Union*, London: 1953.
——— and Postgate, Raymond, *The Common People, 1746– 1938*, London: 1938.
Culiffe, Barry, *City of Bath*, Bath: 1987.
Davidoff, Leonore, and Hall, Catherine, *Family Fortunes: Men and Women of the English Middle Class 1780–1850*, London: 1987.
Davies, V.L. and Hyde, H., *Dudley and the Black Country, 1760–1860*, Dudley: 1970.
Davis, H.W.C., *The Age of Grey and Peel*, Oxford: 1967.
Davis, Richard W., *Dissent in Politics 1770–1830: The Political Life of William Smith MP*, London: 1971.
——— *Political Change and Continuity, 1760–1885: A Buckinghamshire Study*, London: 1972.
——— ed., *Lords of Parliament. Studies, 1714–1914*, Stanford, CA: 1995.
Derry, John W., *Charles, Earl Grey, Aristocratic Reformer*, Oxford: 1992.
Dickinson, H.T., *Radical Politics in the North–East of England in the Later Eighteenth Century*, Durham: 1979.
——— *The Politics of the People in the Eighteenth Century*, New York: 1995.
Dinwiddy, John, *Christopher Wyvill and Reform 1790– 1820*, York: 1971.
Dunbabin, J.P.D., ed., *Rural Discontent in Nineteenth Century Britain*, New York: 1974.
Dyck, Ian, *William Cobbett and Rural Popular Culture*, Cambridge: 1992.
Elliot, Hugh, ed., *The Letters of John Stuart Mill*, London: 1910.
Emsley, Clive, and Walvin, James, eds., *Artisans, Peasants and Proletarians: 1760–1860, Essays Presented to Gwyn Williams*, London: 1985.
Epstein, James, *Radical Expression. Political Language, Ritual and Symbol in England, 1790–1850*, Oxford: 1994.
——— and Thompson, Dorothy, eds., *The Chartist Experience: Studies in Working Class Radicalism and Culture, 1830–60*, New York: 1982.
Evans, Eric Jr, *The Great Reform Act of 1832*, London: 1983.
Evans, R.H., *The Biggs Family of Leicester*, Thoroton Society of Nottingham, Transactions 48, 1945.
Fetter, Frank W., *Development of British Monetary Orthodoxy 1797–1875*, Cambridge: 1965.
——— *Selected Economic Writings of Thomas Attwood*, London: 1964.
Finlayson, G.B.A.M., *England in the 1830s: Decade of Reform*, New York: 1969.
Fitzpatrick, W.J., ed., *Correspondence of Daniel O'Connell, the Liberator*, London: 1888.
Flick, Carlos, *The Birmingham Political Unions and the Movements for Reform in Britian, 1830–39*, Hamden, CT: 1979.
Fraser, Derek, ed., *A History of Modern Leeds*, Manchester: 1980.
——— ed., *Municipal Reform and the Industrial City*, Leicester: 1982.
——— *Urban Politics in Victorian England: The Structure of Politics in Victorian Cities*, Leicester: 1976.
——— ed., *Cities, Class and Communication*, NY: 1990.
——— and Sutcliffe, Anthony, ed., *Pursuit of Urban History*, London: 1983.
Garrard, John, *Leadership and Power in Victorian Industrial Towns, 1830–80*, Manchester: 1983.

Gash, Norman, *Politics in the Age of Peel, A Study in the Technique of Parliamentary Representation, 1830–50,* London: 1953.

——— *Reaction and Reconstruction in English Politics, 1832–52*, Oxford: 1965.

——— *Pillars of Government and other Essays on State and Society c. 1770–1880*, London: 1986.

——— ed., *Wellington. Studies in the Military and Political Career of the First Duke of Wellington*, Manchester: 1990.

Goodwin, Albert, *The Friends of Liberty: The English Democratic Movement in the Age of the French Revolution*, Cambridge, MA: 1979.

Greaves, Robert, *The Corporation of Leicester 1689– 1836*, London: 1939.

Grego, Joseph, *A History of Parliamentary Elections and Electioneering from the Stuarts to Queen Victorian*, London: 1892.

Grey, Charles, ed., *Some Account of the Life and Opinions of Charles, Second Earl Grey*, 1861.

——— ed., *The Reform Act of 1832, The Correspondence of Earl Grey and King William IV, with Henry Taylor*, London: 1867.

Gwilliam, H.W., *Old Worcester, People and Places*, Bromsgrove: 1983.

Halévy, Elie, *The Growth of Philosophical Radicalism*, London: 1972.

——— *The Triumph of Reform 1830–41*, New York: 1961.

Hall, P.W., *British Radicalism, 1791–97*, New York: 1912.

Hamburger, Joseph, *James Mill and the Art of Revolution*, New Haven: 1963.

——— *Intellectuals in Politics: John Stuart Mill and Philosophic Radicals*, New Haven: 1965.

Hanham, H.J., ed., *Charles R. Dodd's Electoral Facts, 1832–58*, London: 1972.

Harling, Philip, *The Waning of 'Old Corruption'. The Politics of Economical Reform in Britain, 1779–1846*, Oxford: 1996.

Harrison, Brian, *Peaceable Kingdom. Stability and Change in Modern Britain*, Oxford: 1982.

Harrison, Mark, *Crowds and History, Mass Phenomena in English Towns, 1790–1835*, Cambridge: 1988.

Harvey, A.D., *Britain in the Early Nineteenth Century*, London: 1978.

Harvey, Charles, and Press, John, eds., *Studies in the Business History of Bristol*, Bristol: 1988.

Hempton, D., *Methodism and Politics in British Society 1750–1850*, London: 1984.

Hill, B.W., *British Parliamentary Parties 1743–1832*, London: 1985.

Hill, R.L., *Toryism and the People, 1832–46*, London: 1929.

Hilton, Boyd, *Corn, Cash, Commerce: The Economic Policies of the Tory Governments, 1815–30*, Oxford: 1977.

Hine, T.C., Nottingham, *Its Castle, Nottingham*: Nottingham: 1876.

Hobsbawm, Eric, *Primitive Rebels. Studies in Archaic Forms of Social Movement in the 19th and 20th Centuries*, Manchester: 1963.

Hollis, Patricia, ed., *Pressure from Without in Early Victorian England*, London: 1974.

——— *The Pauper Press: A Study in Working-Class Radicalism of the 1830s*, Oxford: 1979.

——— *Class and Conflict in Nineteenth Century England, 1815–50*, London: 1973.

Hone, J. Ann, *For the Cause of Truth. Radicalism in London 1796–1821*, Oxford: 1982.

Horn, Pamela, *The Rural World, 1780–1850: Social Change in the English Countryside*, New York: 1979.

Huish, Robert, *The History of the Private and Political Life of Henry Hunt*, London: 1835.

Jessop, Bob, *Social Order, Reform and Revolution: A Power Exchange and Institutionalization Perspective*, London: 1972.

Jones, William, *Biographical Sketches of the Reform Ministers*, London: 1832.

Joyce, Michael, *My Friend H: John Cam Hobhouse, Baron Broughton of Broughton de Gyfford*, London: 1948.

Judd, Geritt, P., IV, *Members of Parliament 1734–1832*, New Haven: 1955.

Jupp, Peter, *British and Irish Elections 1784–1831*, New York: 1973.

Kidd, Alan J., and Roberts, K.W., ed., *City, Class and Culture Studies of Social Policy and Cultural Production in Victorian Manchester*, Manchester: 1985.

Kinzer, Bruce, *The Ballot Question in Nineteenth Century Politics*, New York: 1982.

Kirby, R.G. and Musson, A.E., *The Voice of the People: John Doherty, 1798–1854*, Manchester: 1975.

Kirk, Neville, *The Growth of Working Class Reformism in Mid-Victorian England*, London: 1985.

Koditschek, Theodore, *Class Formation in Urban Industrial Society, Bradford, 1800–50*, Cambridge: 1990.

Koss, Stephen, *The Rise and Fall of the Political Press in Britain: The Nineteenth Century*, Chapel Hill, N.C.: 1981.

Kriegel, Abraham, ed., *The Holland House Diaries, 1831–40*, London: 1977.

Langford, Paul, *A Polite and Commercial People: England, 1727–83*, Oxford: 1989.

Latimer, John, *The Annals of Bristol in the Nineteenth Century*, Bristol: George's, 1970.

Linton, W.J., *James Watson, A Memoir*, Manchester: 1880.

Llewellyn, Alexander, *The Decade of Reform: The 1830s*, New York: 1972.

McCord, Norman, *The Anti-Corn Law League*, London: 1968.

McLachlan, H., *The Unitarian Movement in the Religious Life of England*, London: 1934.

——— *The Methodist Unitarian Movement*, London: 1919.

Machin, G.T., *Catholic Question in English Politics, 1820–30*, Oxford: 1964.

——— *Politics and the Churches in Great Britain, 1832– 68*, Oxford: 1977.

Maehl, W.H., *The Reform Bill of 1832: Why Not Revolution?*, London: 1967.

Mandler, Peter, *Aristocratic Government in the Age of Reform: Whigs, Liberals, 1830–53*, Oxford: 1990.

Marshall, L.S., *The Development of Public Opinion in Manchester, 1780–1820*, Syracuse, N.Y.: 1946.

Marshall, P., *Bristol and the Abolition of Slavery*, Bristol: 1975.

Martineau, John, *The Life of Henry Pelham, Fifth Duke of Newcastle 1811–64*, London: 1908.

Mathieson, W.L., *England in Transition, 1789–1832: A Study of Movements*, London: 1920.
Mellor, Robert, *Men of Nottingham and Nottinghamshire*, Notthingham: 1924.
Messinger, Gary, *Manchester in the Victorian Age*, Manchester: 1985.
Midwinter, E.C., *Law and Order in Early Victorian Lancashire*, York: 1986.
Miles, Dudley, *Francis Place, 1771–1854,* Brighton: 1988.
Mitchell, Austin, *The Whigs in Opposition 1815–30*, Oxford: 1967.
Moleworth, W.H., *The History of the Reform Bill of 1832*, London: 1865.
Money, John, *Experience and Identity: Birmingham and the West Midlands, 1760–1800*, Manchester: 1990.
Moore, D.C., *The Politics of Deference*, London: 1976.
Morris, R.J., *Class, Sect and Party, The Making of the British Middle Class, Leeds, 1820–50*, Manchester: 1990.
——— *Class and Class Consciousness in the Industrial Revolution, 1780–1850*, London: 1979.
Moss, David, *Thomas Attwood: The Biography of a Radical*, Montreal: 1990.
Neale, R.S., *Class and Ideology in the Nineteenth Century*, London, 1972.
——— *Class in English History, 1680–1850*, Oxford: 1981.
——— *Bath 1680–1850, A Social History, or A Valley of Pleasure, Yet a Sink of Iniquity*, London: 1981.
Newbould, Ian, *Whiggery and Reform 1830–41: The Politics of Government*, Stanford: 1990.
Nossiter, T.J., *Influence and Political Idioms in Reformed England*, London: 1975.
O'Gorman, Frank, *Voters, Patron, and Parties, The Unreformed Electoral System of Hanoverian England, 1734–1832*, Oxford: 1989.
——— *The Emergence of the British Two-Party System, 1760–1832*, London: 1982.
Osborne, John, *John Cartwright*, Cambridge: 1972.
Parry, Jonathan, *The Rise and Fall of Liberal Government in Victorian Britain*, New Haven: 1993.
Patterson, A. Temple, *Radical Leicester, A History of Leicester, 1780–1850*, Leicester: 1954.
Patterson, M.W., *Sir Francis Burdett and His Times 1770–1844*, 2, London: 1931.
Philbin, J. Holladay, *Parliamentary Representation, 1832, England and Wales*, New Haven: 1965.
Philip, M. ed., *The French Revolution and British Popular Politics*, Cambridge: 1991.
Phillips, John A., *Electoral Behavior in Unreformed England, Princeton*: Princeton, N.J.: 1982.
——— *The Great Reform Act in the Boroughs, English Electoral Behaviour, 1818–41*, Oxford: 1992.
Plamentz, John, *The English Utilitarians*, Oxford: 1958.
Porritt, Edward, *The Unreformed House of Commons: Representation before 1832,* Cambridge: 1903.
Prothero, Iorwerth, *Artisans and Politics in Early Nineteenth Century London: John Gast and His Times*, Baton Rouge: 1979.

Raybould, T.J., *The Economic Emergence of the Black Country*, Devon: 1973.

Read, Donald, *The Press and the People 1790–1850: Public Opinion in Three English Cities*, London: 1961.

Reader, W.J., *Professional Men. The Rise of the Professional Classes in Nineteenth Century in England*, London: 1966.

Reed, Mick and Wells, Roger, eds, *Class, Conflict and Protest in the English Countryside, 1700–1880*, London: 1990.

Rimmer, W.G., *Marshalls of Leeds, Flax Spinners 1788–1886*, Cambridge: 1960.

Roberts, K.W., ed., *City, Class and Cultural Studies of Industrial Production and Social Policy in Victorian Manchester*, Manchester: 1985.

Roebuck, J.A., *History of the Whig Ministry of 1830*, London: 1852.

Royle, Edward, *Radical Politics 1790–1900: Religion and Unbelief*, London: 1971.

——— and James Walvin, *English Radicals and Reformers 1760–1848*, Brighton: 1982.

Rudé, George, *The Crowd in History 1730–1848: A Study of Popular Disturbances in France and England*, New York: 1964.

Sack, James, *From Jacobite to Conservative. Reaction and Orthodoxy in Britain, c. 1760–1832*, Cambridge: 1993.

Sadlier, M., *Bulwer: A Panorama*, London: 1931.

Salter, F.R., *Dissenters and Public Affairs in Mid-Victorian England*, London: 1967.

Scarlett, P.S., *A Memoir of James, First Lord Abinger*, London: 1877.

Smith, Dennis, *Conflict and Compromise: Class Formation in English Society, 1830–1914*, London: 1982.

Smith, E.A., *Lord Grey 1765–1845*, Oxford: 1990.

——— *The House of Lords, In British Politics and Society, 1815–1911*, New York: 1992.

——— *Whig Principles and Party Politics, Earl Fitzwilliam and the Whig Party 1748–1833*, Manchester: 1975.

Smith, Edward, *A Biography of William Cobbett*, London: 1878.

Smith, Mark, *Religion in Industrial Society. Oldham and Saddleworth, 1740–1865*, Oxford: 1994.

Somerset, Anne, *The Life and Times of William IV*, London: 1980.

Southgate, D., *Passing of the Whigs*, London: 1962.

Spater, George, *William Cobbett: The Poor Man's Friend*, Cambridge: 1982.

Spence, Peter, *The Birth of Romantic Radicalism. War, Popular Politics and English Radical Reformism, 1780– 1815*, Aldershot: 1996.

Stainton, H., *The Making of Sheffield 1865–1914*, Sheffield: 1924.

Stedman Jones, Gareth, *Languages of Class, Studies in English Working Class History, 1832–1982*, Cambridge: 1983.

Stevenson, J., *London in the Age of Reform*, Oxford: 1977.

Taylor, Peter, *Popular Politics in Early Industrial Britain: Bolton 1825–50*, Bodmin: 1995.

Taylor, R.W., *Leeds Worthies*, Leeds: 1865.

Thickett, B., *Radical Activity in Sheffield, 1830–48*, Sheffield: 1951.

Tholfsen, Trygve R., *Working Class Radicalism in Mid-Victorian England*, New York: 1977.

Thomas, Susan, *The Bristol Riots*, Bristol: 1974.
Thomas, W.E.S., *Philosophical Radicals: Nine Studies in Theory and Practice 1817–41*, Oxford: 1979.
M. Thomis, *Politics and Society in Nottingham, 1875– 35*, Oxford: 1969.
——— and Peter Holt, *Threats of Revolution in Britain 1789–1848*, London: 1977
Thompson, Dorothy, *The Chartists, Popular Politics in the Industrial Revolution*, New York: 1984.
——— *Early Chartists*, Columbia: 1971.
——— and Epstein, James, eds, *The Chartist Experience: Studies in Working Class Radicalism and Culture, 1830–60*, London: 1982.
Thompson, E.P., *The Making of the English Working Class*, London: 1963.
Tilly, Charles, *Popular Contention in Great Britain 1758–1834*, Cambridge, MA: 1995.
Trevelyan, G.M., *British History in the Nineteenth Century and After 1782–1919*, London: 1922.
——— *Lord Grey of the Reform Bill*, London: 1920.
Trainor, Richard H., *Black Country Elites, The Exercise of Authority in an Industrialized Area, 1830–1900*, Oxford: 1994.
Turberville, A.S., *The House of Lords in the Age of Reform 1814–37*, London: 1958.
Veitch, G.S., *The Genesis of Parliamentary Reform*, London: 1920.
Vernon, James, *Politics and the People. A Study in English Political Culture, c. 1815–67*, Cambridge: 1993.
Vigier, François, *Change and Apathy: Liverpool and Manchester during the Industrial Revolution,* Cambridge, MA: 1970.
Vogler, Richard, *Reading the Riot Act, The Magistracy, the Police and the Army in Civil Disorder*, Milton Keynes: 1991.
Wahrman, Dror, *Imagining the 'Middle Class'. The Political Representation of Class in Britain, c. 1780– 1840,* Cambridge: 1995.
Wakefield, C.M., *Life of Thomas Attwood*, London: 1885.
Wallas, Graham, *The Life of Francis Place, 1771–1854*, London: 1925.
Walton, John K., *Lancashire: A Social History, 1558– 1939*, Manchester: 1987.
Walvin, James, *English Radicals and Reformers, 1760–1848*, Lexington: 1982.
Ward, J.T., *Popular Movements c. 1830–50*, London: 1970.
Wasson, Ellis Archer, *Whig Renaissance. Lord Althorp and the Whig Party 1782–1845*, New York: 1987.
Watts, Michael R., *The Dissenters, Volume II: The Evolution of Evangelical Nonconformity, 1791–1859*, Oxford: 1995.
Weaver, Stewart Angus, *John Fielden and the Politics of Popular Radicalism 1832–47*, Oxford: 1987.
White B.D., *A History of the Corporation of Liverpool, 1835–1914*, Liverpool: 1951.
Whitehead, David, *Book of Worcester: The Story of the City's Past*, Buckingham: 1976.
Wiener, Joel H., *The War of the Unstamped: The Movement to Repeal the British Newspaper Tax 1830–36*, Ithaca: 1969.
Wright, D.G., *Chartist Risings in Bradford,* Bradford: 1986.

——— *Popular Radicalism, The Working Class Experience, 1780–1830*, New York: 1988.

Wylly, H.C., *The Military Memoirs of Lt. General Sir Joseph Thackwell*, London: 1908.

Ziegler, Peter, *Melbourne*, London: 1976.

——— *King William IV*, London: 1971.

SELECTED SECONDARY SOURCES, ARTICLES

Alford, W.B.E., 'The Economic Development of Bristol in the Nineteenth Century: An Enigma?', in Patrick McGrath and John Cannon, eds., *Essays in Bristol and Gloucestershire History*, Bristol: 1976.

Asquith, Ivon, 'The Whigs and the Press in the Early Nineteenth Century', *Bulletin of the Institute of Historical Research*, 49, 1976.

Baxter, J.L. and Donnelly, F.K., 'The Revolutionary "Underground" in the West Riding: Myth or Reality?', *Past and Present*, 64, 1974.

Beard, Lilian, 'Unitarianism in the Potteries from 1812', *Transactions of the United Historical Society*, 6, 1935–8.

Beckett, J.V. 'Aristocrats and Electoral Control in the East Midlands, 1660–1914', *Midland History*, 18, 1993.

Behagg, Clive, 'Custom, Class and Change: The Trade Societies of Birmingham', *Social History*, 93, 1978.

Belchem, John, 'Henry Hunt and the Evolution of the Mass Platform', *English Historical Review*, 93, 1978.

——— 'Republicanism, Popular Constitutionalism and the Radical Platform in Early Nineteenth Century England', *Social History*, 6, 1981.

——— '1848: Feargus O'Connor and the Collapse of the Mass Platform' in James Epstein and Dorothy Thompson, eds, *The Chartist Experience: Studies in Working-Class Radicalism and Culture 1830–60*, London: 1982.

——— 'Orator' Hunt, 1773–1835', *History Today*, 35, 1985.

——— 'Radical Language and Ideology in Early Nineteenth Century England: The Challenge of the Platform', *Albion*, 20, 1988.

Bradley, James E., 'Whigs and Nonconformists: "Slumbering Radicalism" in English Politics 1739–89', *Eighteenth Century Studies*, 9, 1975.

Brett, P.D., 'The Newcastle Election of 1830', *Past and Present*, 74, 1988.

Breuilly, John, 'Artisan Economy, Artisan Politics, Artisan Ideology: The Artisan Contribution to the 19th Century Labour Movement', in Clive Emsley and James Walvins, eds., *Artisans, Peasants and Proletarians, 1760–1840*, London: 1985.

Briggs, Asa, 'Thomas Attwood and the Economic Background of the Birmingham Political Union', 1948, reprinted in *The Collected Essays of Asa Briggs, I: Words, Numbers, Places, People*, Urbana: 1985.

——— 'Press and Public in Early Nineteenth Century, Birmingham: *Dugdale Society Occasional Papers*, 8, 1949.

——— 'The Background of Parliamentary Reform in Three English Cities', *The Collected Essays of Asa Briggs, I: Words, Numbers, Places, People* Urbana: 1985.

'Middle-class Consciousness in English Politics 1780– 1846', *Past and Present*, 9, 1956.

——— 'The Language of "Class" in Early Nineteenth Century England', in Asa Briggs and John Saville, eds, *Essays in Labour History*, London: Papermac, 1967 revised edition.

——— 'The Language of "Mass" and "Masses" in Nineteenth-Century England', in David Martin and David Rubinstein, eds, *Ideology and the Labour Movement: Essays Presented to John Saville*, London: 1979.

Brooks, Steven, 'Bath and the Great Reform Bill', in John Wroughton, ed., *Bath in the Age of Reform*, Bath: 1974.

Cannon, John, 'Bristol Chartism', in John Cannon, ed., *The Chartists in Bristol, Bristol Branch of the Historical Association*, 1964.

Checkland, S.G., 'The Birmingham Economists', *Economic History Review*, Series 2, 1, 1949.

Davis, Richard W., 'The Whigs and the Idea of Electoral Deference', *Durham University Journal*, New series, 36, 1974.

——— 'Deference and Aristocracy in the Time of the Great Reform Act', *American Historical Review*, 81, 1976.

——— 'The Duke of Wellington and Resurgence of the House of Lords' in R.W. Davis, ed., *Lords of Parliament. Studies, 1714–1914*, Stanford: 1995.

——— 'Toryism to Tamworth: The Triumph of Reform, 1827–35', *Albion*, 12, 1980.

Davis, Sally, 'All That's Left is a Toast!', *Bath and West Evening Chronicle*, 27 December 1984.

Davison, Graeme, 'Explanations of Urban Radicalism: Old Theories and New Histories', *Historical Studies*, 18, 1978–9.

Dickinson, W. Calvin, 'John Knight', in Baylen, Joseph O. and Gossman, Norbert J., eds., *Biographical Dictionary of Modern British Radicals,* 1: *1770–1830*, Hassocks: 1979.

Dinwiddy, John, 'Sir Francis Burdett and Burdettite Radicalism', *History*, 5, 1980.

——— and Baxter, J.L., 'Sheffield and English Revolutionary Tradition, 1791–1820', *International Review of Social History*, 20, 1975.

Driver, F. 'Tory Radicalism? Ideology, Strategy and Locality in Popular Politics During the 1830s', *Northern History*, 27, 1991.

Dyck, Ian, 'William Cobbett and the Rural Radical Platform', *Social History*, 18, 1993.

Eastwood, David, 'Toryism, Reform, and Political Culture in Oxfordshire, 1826–37', *Parliamentary History*, 7, 1988.

Edwards, J.K., 'The Decline of the Norwich Textile Industry', *Yorkshire Bulletin of Economic and Social Research*, 16, 1964.

——— 'Chartism in Norwich', *Yorkshire Bulletin of Economic and Social Research*, 19, 1967.

——— 'Developments in Local Government in Norwich, 1780–1900', in Christopher Barringer, ed., *Norwich in the Nineteenth Century*, Norwich: 1984.

——— 'Industrial Development of the City, 1780–1900', in Christopher Barringer, ed., *Norwich in the Nineteenth Century*, Norwich: 1984.

Ellis, Harold, 'The Whig Model of Parliamentary Reform 1792–1832', *Journal of Modern History*, supplement, 1979.

Epstein, James, 'Understanding the Cap of Liberty: Symbolic Practice and Social Conflict in Early Nineteenth Century England', *Past and Present*, 122, 1989.

——— 'The Constitutional Idiom: Radical Reasoning, Rhetoric and Action in Early Nineteenth Century England', *Journal of Social History*, 23, 1990.

Falconer, David, 'People's Champion Beat Purse and Power', *Bath and West Evening Chronicle*, 29 December 1982.

Ferguson, Henry, 'The Birmingham Political Union and the Government, 1830–32', *Victorian Studies*, 3, 1959–60.

Finlayson, G.B.A.M., 'Joseph Parkes of Birmingham, 1796–1865', *Bulletin for the Institute of Historical Research*, 46, 1973.

——— 'Wellington, the Constitution, and the March of Reform', in Norman Gash, ed., *Wellington, Studies in the Military and Political Career of the First Duke of Wellington*, Manchester: 1990.

Flick, Carlos, 'The Fall of Wellington's Government', *Journal of Modern History*, 37, 1975.

Fraser, Derek, 'The Press in Leicester, c. 1790–1840', *Transactions of the Leicestershire Archaeological and Historical Society*, 42, 1966–7.

——— 'Mid-Victorian Leicester', *Transactions of the Thoroton Society*, 41, 1965–6.

——— 'The Nottingham Press, 1800–50', *Transactions of the Thoroton Society*, 67, 1963.

——— 'The Fruits of Reform: Leeds Politics in the 1830s', *Northern History*, vii, 1972.

——— 'The Agitation for Parliamentary Reform', in J. T. Ward, ed., *Popular Movement c. 1830–50*, London: 1970.

Fraser, Peter, 'Public Petitioning and Parliament before 1832', *History*, 46, 1961.

Gadian, D.S., 'Class Consciousness in Oldham and Other North-West Industrial Towns, 1830–50', *Historical Journal*, 21, 1978.

——— 'Class Formation and Class Action in North-West Industrial Towns, 1830–50', in R.J. Morris, ed., *Class, Power and Social Structure in British Nineteenth Century Towns*, Leicester: 1986.

Gash, Norman, 'English Reform and French Revolution in the General Election of 1830', in R. Pares and A.J.P. Taylor, eds, *Essays Presented to Sir Lewis Namier*, London: 1956.

——— 'The Duke of Wellington and the Prime Ministership, 1824–30', in his *Wellington, Studies in the Military and Political Career of the First Duke of Wellington*, Manchester: 1990.

Gatrell, V.A.C., 'Incorporation and the Pursuit of Liberal Hegemony in Manchester, 1790–1939', in Derek Fraser, ed., *Municipal Reform and the Industrial City*, Leicester: 1982.

Harling, Philip, 'Rethinking "Old Corruption"', *Past and Present*, 147, 1995.

——— and Mandler, Peter, 'From "Fiscal-Military" State to Laissez-Faire State', *Journal of British Studies*, 32, 1993.

Hawkins, Angus, '"Parliamentary Government" and Victorian Political Parties, c. 1830–80', *English Historical Review*, 104, 1989.

Hennock, E.P., 'Sociological Premises of the First Reform Act', *Victorian Studies*, 14, 1971.

Hobsbawm, Eric, 'Methodism and the Threat of Revolution in Britain', *History Today*, 7, 1957.

Hollis, Patricia, 'Anti-Slavery and British Working Class Radicalism in the Years of Reform', in Christine Bolt and Seymour Drescher, eds, *Anti-Slavery, Religion and Reform*, Folkestone: 1980.

Innes, Joanna, 'Representative Histories: Recent Studies of Popular Politics and Political Culture in Eighteenth and Early Nineteenth Century England', *Journal of Historical Sociology*, 4, 1991.

Jaggard, Edwin, 'Cornwall Politics, 1826–32: Another Face of Reform?', *Journal of British Studies*, 22, 1983.

——— 'The Parliamentary Reform Movement in Cornwall, 1805–26', *Parliamentary History*, 2, 1983.

James, E.P., 'The Political Reform Movement in Sheffield', *Transactions of the Hunter Archeological Society*, 4, 1937.

Knox, Thomas R., 'Popular Politics and Provincial Radicalism: Newcastle upon Tyne, 1769–85', *Albion*, 1975.

Kriegel, A.D., 'Liberty and Whiggery in Early Nineteenth Century England', *Journal of Modern History*, 52, 1980.

——— 'Biography and the Politics of the Early Nineteenth Century', *Journal of British Studies*, 29, 1990.

LoPatin, Nancy, 'Political Unions and the Great Reform Act of 1832', *Parliamentary History*, 11, 1991.

——— 'The Coventry Political Union and the Great Reform Act', *Midland History*, 20, 1995.

Main, J.M., 'Radical Westminster, 1807–20, *Historical Studies (Austrialia and New Zealand)*, 12, 1966.

——— 'Working Class Politics in Manchester from Peterloo to the Reform Bill, 1819–32', *Historical Studies (Australia and New Zealand)*, 6, 1955.

Marshall, L.S., 'The First Parliamentary Election in Manchester', *American Historical Review*, 47, 1942.

Mather, F.C., 'Achilles or Nestor? The Duke of Wellington in British Politics, 1832–46', in Norman Gash, *Wellington, Studies in the Military and Political Career of the First Duke of Wellington,* Manchester: 1990.

Meachen, Edward, 'James Losh', in Joseph O. Baylen and Norbert J. Gossman, *Biographical Dictionary of Modern Radicals, Baylen and Gossman, Biographical Dictionary of Modern Radicals*, I, Hassocks: 1979.

Miller, Naomi Churgin, 'John Cartwright and Radical Parliamentary Reform, 1808–1819', *English Historical Review*, lxxxiii, 1968.

——— 'Major John Cartwright and the Founding of the Hampden Club', *Historical Journal*, 17, 1974.

Milton-Smith, John, 'Earl Grey's Cabinet and the Objects of Parliamentary Reform', *Historical Journal*, 15, 1972.

——— 'Whigs and Parliamentary Reform Before 1830', *Historical Studies (Australia and New Zealand)*, 1965.

Mitchell, L.G., 'Foxite Politics in the Great Reform Bill', *English Historical Review*, 108, 1993.

Money, John, 'Birmingham and the West Midlands, 1760–93: Politics and Regional Identity in the English Provinces in the Later Eighteenth Century', *Midland History*, 1, 1971.

Moore, D.C., 'The Other Face of Reform', *Victorian Studies*, 4, 1961.

——— 'Concession or Cure: The Sociological Premises of the First Reform Act', *Historical Journal*, 9, 1966.

Moore, K.C., 'Liverpool in the "Heroic Age" of Popular Radicalism, 1815–20', *Transactions of the Historic Society of Lancashire and Cheshire*, 138, 1989.

——— '"This Whig and Tory Ridden Town": Popular Politics in Liverpool in Chartist Era', John Belchem, ed., *Popular Politics, Riot and Labour, Essays in Liverpool History 1790–1940*, Liverpool: 1992.

Morris, R.J., 'Voluntary Societies and British Urban Elites, 1780– 1850', *Historical Journal*, 26, 1983.

——— 'The Leeds Middle Class, 1820–50', *Report to the Committee of Economic Affairs*, SSRC, 1983.

——— 'The Middle Class and British Towns and Cities of the Industrial Revolution 1780–1870', in Derek Fraser and Anthony Sutcliffe, *Pursuit of Urban History*, London: 1983.

Neale, R.S., 'Class and Class Consciousness in Early Nineteenth Century England: Three Classes or Five?', *Victorian Studies*, 12, 1968.

Newbould, Ian, 'Whiggery and the Dilemma of Reform: Liberals, Radicals, and the Melbourne Administrations 1835–9', *Bulletin of the Institute of Historical Research*, 53, 1980.

——— 'The Emergence of a Two-Party System in England from 1830–41', *Parliaments, Estates, and Representations*, 5, 1985.

Nicholls, David, 'Radicalism as Middle Class Ideology', *Journal of British Studies*, 5, 1980.

——— 'The English Middle Class and the Ideological Significance of Radicalism, 1760–1886', *Journal of British Studies*, 24, 1985.

Noyce, Karen A., 'The Duke of Wellington and the Catholic Question', in Norman Gash, ed., *Wellington, Studies in the Military and Political Career of the First Duke of Wellington*, Manchester: 1990.

O'Gorman, Frank, 'Electoral Deference in Unreformed England, 1760–1832', *Journal of Modern History*, 56, 1984.

——— 'Party Politics in the Early Nineteenth Century, 1812–32', *English Historical Review*, 102, 1987.

——— 'Electoral Behaviour in England, 1700–1872', in Peter Denley et al., eds, *History and Computing II*, Manchester: 1989.

——— 'Campaign Rituals and Ceremonies: The Social Meaning of Elections in England 1780–1860', *Past and Present*, 135, 1992.

O'Neil, Mark and Martin, Ged, 'A Backbencher on Parliamentary Reform, 1831–32', *Historical Journal*, 23, 1980.

Osborne, J.W. 'Henry Hunt, 1815–30: The Politically Formative Years of the Radical MP', *Red River Valley Historical Journal of World History*, 1981.

——— 'Henry Hunt's Career in Parliament', *Historian*, 39, 1976.

Parssinen, T.M., 'Association, Convention and Anti-Parliament in British Radical Politics, 1771–1848', *English Historical Review*, 88, 1973.

Peacock, A.J., 'Village Radicalism in East Anglian 1800–50', in J.P.D. Dunabin, *Rural Discontent in Nineteenth Century Britain*, London: 1974.

Phillips, John A., 'Popular Politics in Unreformed England', *Journal of Modern History*, 52, 1982.

——— 'The Many Faces of Reform: The Reform Bill and the Electorate', *Parliamentary History*, 1, 1982.
——— 'From Municipal Matters to Parliamentary Principles', *Journal of British Studies*, 27, 1988.
——— 'The Social Calculus: Deference and Defiance in Later Georgian England', *Albion*, 21, 1989.
——— 'The Structure of Electoral Politics in Unreformed England', *Journal of British Studies*, 19, 1979.
——— and Charles Wetherell, 'The Great Reform Act of 1832 and the Political Modernization of England', *American Historical Review*, 100, 1995.
Plumb, J.H., 'Political Man', in J. Clifford, ed., *Man vs. Society in the Eighteenth Century*, Cambridge: 1968.
Preston, R.A., 'Nottingham and the Reform Bill Riots of 1831', *Transactions of the Thoroton Society of Nottinghamshire*, 77, 1973.
Procter, W., 'Orator Hunt, MP for Preston, 1830–32', *Transactions of the Historic Society of Lancashire and Chesire*, 114, 1962.
Prothero, Iorwerth, 'William Benbow and the Concept of the General Strike', *Past and Present*, 63, 1974.
Quinault, R., 'The Warwickshire County Magistracy and Public Order 1830–70', in J. Stevenson and R. Quinault, eds, *Popular Protest and Public Order: Six Studies in British History 1790–1820*, London: 1974.
Read, Donald, 'John Harland "The Father of Provincial Reporting"', *Manchester Review*, 8, 1958.
Rimmer, W.G., 'John Marshall, Flaxspinner', *Leeds Journal*, v. 31, 2, 1960.
Roberts, A.W., 'Leeds Liberalism and Late Victorian Politics', *Northern History*, 1972.
Rose, J.H., 'The Unstamped Press, 1815–36', *English Historical Review*, 12, 1897.
Rowe, D.J., 'Class and Political Radicalism in London, 1831–32', *Historical Journal*, 12, 1970.
——— 'London Radicalism in the Era of the Great Reform Bill', in J. Stevenson, ed., *London in the Age of Reform*, Oxford: 1977.
Rubinstein, W.D., 'The End of "Old Corruption" of Britain, 1780–1860', *Past and Present*, 101, 1983.
——— 'Wealth, Elites and the Class Structure of Modern Britain', *Past and Present*, 76, 1977.
——— 'The Victorian Middle Classes: Wealth, Occupation and Geography', *Economic History Review*, 30, 1977.
Rudé, George, 'English Rural and Urban Disturbances on the Eve of the First Reform Bill, 1830–31', *Past and Present*, 37, 1967.
——— 'Why Was There No Revolution in England in 1830 or 1848?', in Manfred Kossok, ed., *Studien über die Revolution*, Berlin: 1969.
Sack, James. 'Wellington and the Tory Press, 1828–30', in Norman Gash, ed., *Wellington, Studies in the Military and Political career of the First Duke of Wellington*, Manchester: 1990.
——— 'The House of Lords and Parliamentary Patronage in Great Britain, 1802–32', *Historical Journal*, 23, 1980.
Salter, F.R., 'Political Nonconformity in the Eighteen-Thirties', *Transactions of the Royal Historical Society*, 5th series, 3, 1953.

Searby, Peter, 'Paternalism, Disturbance and Parliamentary Reform: Society and Politics in Coventry, 1819–32', *International Review of Social History*, 22, 1977.

——— 'Coventry in the Age of the Chartists', *Coventry and North Warwickshire History Pamphlets*, Coventry: 1964.

Seed, John, 'Unitarianism, Political Economy and the Antinomies of Liberal Culture in Manchester, 1830–50', *Social History*, 7, 1982.

Shaw, Giles, 'James Butterworth of Oldham', *Transactions of the Lancashire and Cheshire Antiquarian Society*, 26, 1908.

Smith, E.A., 'Charles, Second Earl Grey and the House of Lords', in R.W. Davis, ed., *Lords of Parliament. Studies, 1714–1914*, Stanford: 1995.

Sykes, R.A. 'Some Aspects of Working-Class Consciousness in Oldham, 1830–42', *Historical Journal*, 23, 1980.

——— 'Early Chartism and Trade Unionism in South-East Lancashire' in James Epstein and Dorothy Thompson, eds., *The Chartist Experience*, New York: 1982.

Tholfsen, Trygve, 'The Artisan and the Culture of Early Victorian Birmingham', *University of Birmingham Historical Journal*, 1954.

——— 'The Chartist Crisis in Birmingham', *International Review of Social History*, 1958.

Thomas, W.E.S., 'Francis Place and Working Class History', *Historical Journal*, 5, 1952.

——— 'The Philosophical Radicals', in Patricia Hollis, ed., *Pressure from Without*, London: 1974.

Thompson, Dorothy, 'Women and Nineteenth Century Radical Politics', in Juliet Mitchell and Ann Oakely, eds., *The Rights and Wrongs of Women*, London: 1976.

Thompson, F.M.L., 'Whigs and Liberals in the West Riding 1830–40', *English Historical Review*, 84, 1959.

Turberville, A.S. and Beckwith, F., 'Leeds and Parliamentary Reform, 1820–32', *Thoresby Society*, 12, 1954.

Wahrman, Dror, 'Virtual Representation: Parliamentary Reporting and the Languages of Class in the 1790s', *Past and Present*, 136, 1992.

Wasson, Ellis A., 'The Great Whigs and Parliamentary Reform, 1809–30', *Journal of British Studies*, 24, 1985.

Wells, Roger, 'Rural Rebels in Southern England in the 1830s', in Clive Emsley and James Walvin, eds., *Artisans, Peasants, and Proletarians*, London: 1985.

Wigley, John, 'Nottingham and the Reform Bill Riots of 1831, Part II', *Transactions of the Thoroton Society of Nottinghamshire*, 77, 1973.

Wilson, Richard George, 'Records for a Study of the Leeds Woolen Merchants 1700–1830', *Archives,* 8, 37, 1907.

Winstanley, Michael, 'News from Oldham: Edwin Buttersworth and the Manchester Press, 1829–48', *Manchester Regional History Review*, 4, 1990.

——— 'Oldham Radicalism and the Origins of Popular Liberalism, 1830–52', *Historical Journal*, 36, 1993.

Woolley, S.F., 'The Personnel of the Parliament of 1833', *English Historical Review*, 53, 1938.

Wright, D.G., 'A Radical Borough: Parliamentary Politics, Bradford, 1832–41', *Northern History*, 4, 1969.
Young, R., 'The Norwich Chartists', in A.F.J. Brown, *Chartism in East Anglia*, Norwich: 1951.

UNPUBLISHED THESES

Bush, G.W.A., 'The Old and the New: The Corporation of Bristol, 1820–51', Bristol University, PhD, 1965.
Clark, J.C., 'From Business to Politics: The Ellice Family 1760–1860', Oxford University, DPhil, 1972.
Corfield, Penelope, 'The Social and Economic History of Norwich, 1650–1850: A Study in Urban Growth', University of London, PhD, 1976.
Fearn, E., 'Reform Movements in Derby and Derbshire 1790–1832', Manchester University, MA, 1964.
Hayes, B.D., 'Politics in Norfolk 1750–1832', Corpus Christi College, Cambridge University, PhD, 1957.
Manton, C.H., 'Reform, Radicalism and Reaction: Brighton Politics, 1830–37', Southampton University, BA Dissertation, 1976.
O'Sullivan, D.S., 'Politics in Norwich, 1705–1805', University of East Anglia, MPhil, 1975.
Searby, Peter, 'Weavers and Freemen in Coventry, 1820–61', Warwick University, PhD, 1972.
Simes, D.G.S., 'Ultra Tories in British Politics, 1824–34', Oxford University, DPhil, 1974.

Index